Landowners in Colonial Peru

Latin American Monographs, No. 61
Institute of Latin American Studies
The University of Texas at Austin

Landowners in Colonial Peru

By Keith A. Davies

 University of Texas Press, Austin

Library of Congress Cataloging in Publication Data

Davies, Keith A.
  Landowners in colonial Peru

  (Latin American monographs/Institute of Latin American
Studies, the University of Texas at Austin; no. 61)
    Includes bibliographical references and index.
    1.Land tenure—Peru—Arequipa (Dept.)—History.
I. Title. II. Series: Latin American monographs (University of
Texas at Austin. Institute of Latin American Studies); no. 61.
HD559.A73D38 1984   333.3'0985132 83-16749
ISBN 0-292-74639-3

First Edition, 1984
Requests for permission to reproduce material from
this work should be sent to:
  Permissions
  University of Texas Press
  P.O. Box 7819
  Austin, Texas 78713

To my mother and father

Contents

Maps

Plates

Figures

Tables

Preface

As I approached Arequipa by bus at daybreak, through the stark hills and plains that lie along the coast, it seemed strange that I planned to spend several years investigating Spanish agriculture in such a setting. Southwestern Peru is beautiful but can be forbidding. Our descent into a coastal valley shortly afterward and later, my first view of the magnificent Arequipa Valley relieved some anxiety. During the months that followed all doubts about the wisdom of my choice faded as I worked through the voluminous documentation wonderfully preserved by the ideal climate. My stay in Arequipa was made all the more pleasant by the interest and generosity of the people there: historians, students, archivists, officials, landowners, and so many others. I would particularly like to thank Dr. Eduardo L. Ugarte y Ugarte, former director of the old Archivo Histórico de Arequipa; Dr. Guillermo Galdos Rodríguez, head of the Archivo Departamental de Arequipa; and Professor Alejandro Málaga Medina, of the Universidad Nacional de San Agustín. My gratitude also goes to Dr. Humberto Núñez Borja and his family for their warm hospitality. I owe much, as numerous citations will attest, to two deceased Arequipans, Fray Víctor M. Barriga and Dr. Santiago Martínez. They devoted their lives to southwestern Peruvian history and their careful research in local, national, and international archives was an inspiration.

I am indebted also to members of the Instituto de Estudios Peruanos, to Professor Franklin Pease G. Y. of the Pontificia Universidad Católica del Perú, and to the staffs of the Biblioteca Nacional del Perú, the Archivo Nacional del Perú, the Museo Nacional de Historia (Lima), the Archivo Departamental de Arequipa, the Biblioteca Pública de Arequipa, the Convento de Nuestra Señora de Mercedes of Arequipa, the Archivo de la Catedral de Arequipa, and the Archivo General de Indias. During the last several years, many people at Vanderbilt University Library have helped me immensely.

The Social Science Research Council and the American Council of Learned Societies, the National Endowment for the Humanities, Vanderbilt University, and the American Philosophical Society extended generous financial support and encouragement. Professor Hugh M. Hamill, Jr., has always provided invaluable suggestions and succor. My thanks also go to many of my colleagues in Vanderbilt's Department of History, who read versions of the manuscript. I am indebted to Professors Samuel McSeveney and James Lockhart for their careful readings and judicious advice. This book would have been but a dream had my family not given so much of their time and understanding: my special thanks to Deb, Michael, and Trefor.

Landowners in Colonial Peru

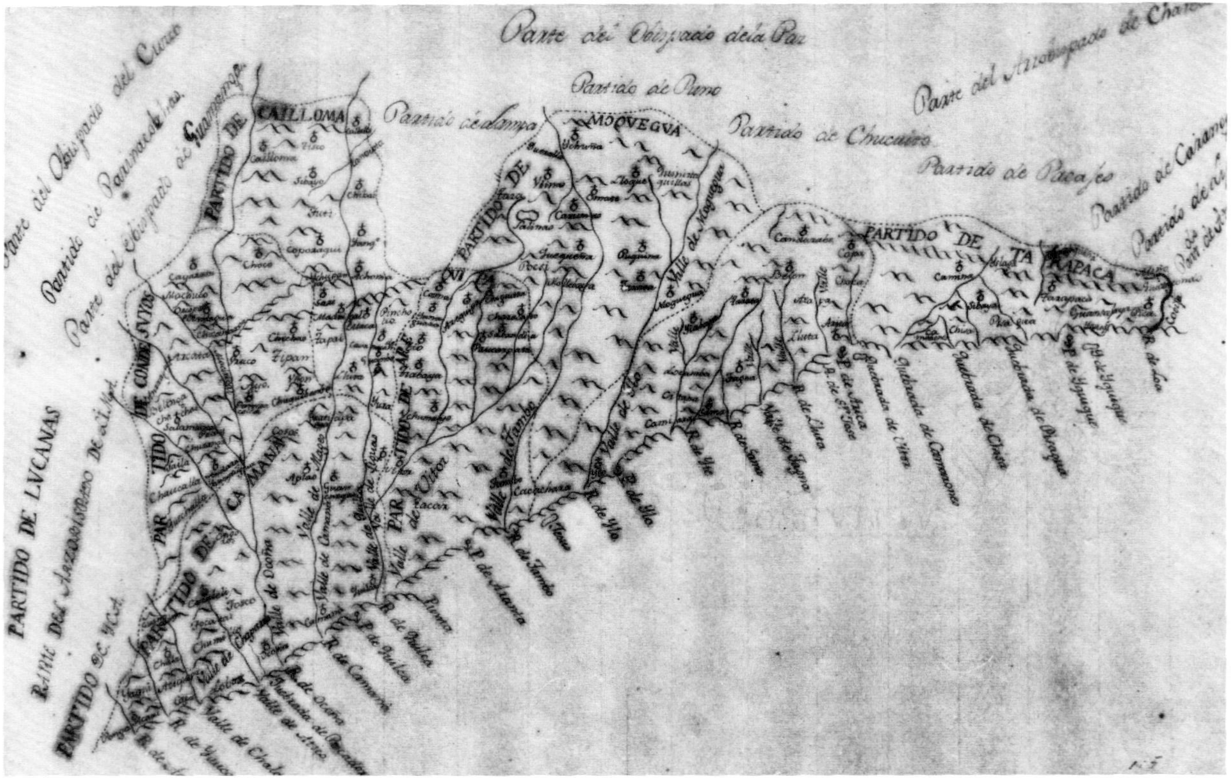

Plate 1. Bishopric of Arequipa

Introduction

Arequipa heróica y legendaria, llamada por el Manco de Lepanto la ciudad de eterna primavera; uno de nuestros eminentes literatos la denominó—Esparta por el valor guerrero de sus hijos; Atenas por la inteligencia de sus hombres notables; Roma por su espíritu e influencia en la historia del Perú.

————Fray Víctor M. Barriga

Arequipans have always been a proud people. Although some have occasionally claimed too much for their city and its inhabitants, there can be no denying Arequipa's importance to modern Peru and its significance in Peru's history since the mid-sixteenth century. Arequipans are probably best known for their unusually active role in national affairs and for their pugnacious political style, a style that, during the nineteenth century, earned their city the sobriquet "daughter of volcanoes and mother of revolutions." Jorge Basadre, one of Peru's most distinguished historians, attributed the unique political behavior of Arequipans to their geographic isolation, racial and cultural homogeneity, and deep reverence for the church.[1] His observations recall those of travelers, including James Bryce, who visited the city during the early 1900s. Bryce not only commented on the large number of "Spanish" families in the population, but also added that, because Arequipa had so long been cut off from the outside world, there has been "nothing but local interests . . . to occupy men's minds."[2] Surprisingly, neither Basadre nor Bryce included another oft-repeated explanation of the self-confidence and independence of Arequipans: their freedom from "the irritant of inequality that engenders in the poor hatred for the rich." A number of Arequipans, in turn, attribute this equality to the region's peculiar land-tenure patterns, the extensive subdivision of the countryside.[3]

The allegation that land in southwestern Peru has traditionally been dispersed among numerous residents contrasts sharply with the popular notion that Latin American rural proprietorship has until very recently been characterized by a very few owning extensive tracts and most others possessing only tiny parcels or no land at all. Admittedly, research findings during the last generation have challenged this view by suggesting that it is overdrawn. Moreover, many historians now believe that the large landed estate, the hacienda, became a predominant institution in much of rural Spanish America only after the early 1800s, a development due in part to the "liberal" legislation that sought to provide Indians with full legal rights. Ironically, these measures proved counterproductive: they dismantled the protection the state had formerly accorded many landowners and enabled the more powerful to strip proprietors of their tracts. Simultaneously, some nationals and foreigners who were anxious to produce for internal and world markets made more accessible by improved transportation and communication encouraged large landholding.[4]

Yet, even when we recognize that much of colonial Spanish America could not possibly have been integrated into world markets, and that other factors, including royal protection, permitted many to hold and retain lands, there still has been a tendency to consider the hacienda an important form of non-Indian land tenure after the late 1500s.[5] Indeed it was. Its existence in valleys of central and southern Mexico as well as in areas to the north, for example, has been carefully documented.[6] Haciendas also flourished within the Viceroyalty of Peru, early on along the Pacific coast in places such as the Puangue and Jequetepeque valleys, and later in the highlands. Best known are the haciendas of the Jesuits, scattered throughout Peru, but generally located near urban centers.[7]

Haciendas evolved in these areas because of accessible colonial markets. As Manuel Burga and Robert G. Keith have demonstrated, certain colonists consolidated holdings in valleys close to Lima beginning during the late sixteenth century, when that city's population expanded. Much the same happened at various stages in Mexico. David A. Brading has documented the emergence of haciendas in León in response to the Guanajuato mining boom; Herman W. Konrad has studied the development of Santa Lucía, a Jesuit estate in the Valley of Mexico, as Mexico City's population grew; and Eric Van Young has established the growth of large landed estates surrounding Guadalajara as landholders responded first to the colonial demand for livestock, and then to the need for food in urban centers of central New Galicia.[8]

But what landholding patterns existed in colonial areas where the hacienda did not dominate the countryside? A number of studies carried out over the course of the last generation have pieced together patterns in some regions where Indians outnumbered other groups.[9] Less well known is the situation in areas of colonial Spanish America, especially of South America, more heavily populated by non-Indians. I studied southwestern Peru because it seemed an ideal area for some answers. The region, particularly its coastal valleys and the interior Arequipa Valley, had long been regarded as a place where the Indian population was small soon after the Spaniards arrived in the late 1530s. Moreover, the Southwest enjoyed the reputation of having had much of its land dispersed equitably among non-Indians. My research did not substantiate such equality in landholding, but it established that most properties within the coastal belt and the Arequipa Valley were small and medium-sized farms, rather than large estates. This mix of farms emerged in part because of the restricted access of Arequipans to colonial markets after the early 1600s and their limited local consumer market. It also resulted from the crop choices of landholders, from colonists' slender capital resources, and from regional labor shortages. The character of holdings in this region points up the diversity of land-tenure patterns in the Americas.[10]

This study not only describes the nature of Spanish landownership in the Southwest, it assesses the effects of landholding patterns on society. The connection between land and society has long been regarded as a most important aspect of the colonial and national experiences of Latin Americans. Consequently, the social world that developed within rural estates has been examined closely.[11] My focus, however, is not on the society that evolved within southwestern farms, but on the impact of landownership on the broader society of non-Indians, most of whom lived in the city of Arequipa. In considering this broader context in a general manner, many have suggested that landholding imbalances resulted in or significantly contributed to social stratification. Certainly that is the case in studies of Peru. Histories are replete with references to landowning oligarchies, and there are also frequent discussions of political movements and rebellions spawned by the desire to loosen the grip that forty or so families have had on Peru's society, economy, and polity.[12]

Yet, despite the importance often attached to rural proprietorship in determining non-Indian societal arrangements, little is known about how landholding came to play such a critical role. Suggestions were made from time to time that the early Spanish immigrants brought to the New World a predisposition toward equating social preeminence with possession of major landholdings, a mind set that, once transferred, simply persisted.[13] That view has increasingly been challenged, especially by historians who argue that Spaniards turned to land when it benefited them financially.[14] Financial considerations did motivate Spaniards during the late 1540s as they appropriated and developed rural land in southwestern Peru. But the desire for economic gain was intertwined with social ambition then and throughout the colonial period. The relationship between land and social concern developed in Arequipa, and very likely in many other parts of the Americas, because social status could not rely principally on birth as it did in Spain: there were too few nobles in the colonial Spanish population. Status at first therefore depended on selection by political authorities for a prestigious position, such as that of being a grantee of Indians, and, later, when such selection was limited, on marriage to a well-regarded spouse and on leading a distinguished lifestyle. When impressive marriages and an aristocratic lifestyle became the hallmarks of social distinction, possessing wealth proved critical to preserving or improving social status. And wealth, for a variety of reasons, rested on the returns that colonists received from selling the products raised on their land.

This study, then, examines two processes in the history of Arequipa: the various ways Arequipans owned and exploited the countryside, and the social repercussions of their landholding. I develop these from Arequipa's founding in 1540 through the late seventeenth century. I could, of course, have extended consideration of both to the end of the colonial period or even to the present, but several reasons argued against my doing that. One constraint, frankly, was time. Reconstructing the economic and social history of Southwesterners demanded extensive archival work, particularly in notarial records. Lengthening the chronological coverage, even to the early 1800s, a frequently used though arbitrary date preferred by some colonialists who study rural history, would have necessitated several more years of fieldwork, a luxury I could not indulge in. But more importantly, the late 1600s conclude the formative years in the life of Arequipans. By then, non-Indians had interests throughout southwestern Peru and had established a particular agricultural economy. Subsequent developments, at least until the late nineteenth century, modified this economy and the patterns of land-ownership only slightly. Further, the period to the late 1600s also set the broad limits within which future social changes took place. Arequipa's landowning families remained a social elite; they intermarried extensively and were willing to incorporate only prestigious outsiders. Differences in the social status of such families continued to reflect their differing abilities to appropriate, primarily through landed wealth, the accepted symbols of preeminence.[15]

1. Indians, *Encomenderos*, and Arequipa's Early Rural Economy

Venidos los españoles . . . [n]o hallaron oposición en los naturales, antes sí todo el alivio, que por entonces pudieron apetecer. Los granos de maíz, las papas, la quinua y habas fueron suficientes, y les sobraron para socorrer a otras distancias.
————Doctor Don Francisco Xavier de Echeverría y Morales

. . . y por ser cosa notoria que con las guerras y alteraciones pasadas y avidas en estos dichos Reynos quedaron los naturales disminuidos cansados y faltos de comyda . . .[1]
————Lic. Pedro de la Gasca

In late 1540 La Villa Hermosa de Arequipa was no more than a camp. The only signs of a Spanish presence were fifty or so settlers, a gallows and a cross (symbols of new authorities in the Southwest), and boundary markers for a future plaza, streets, house plots, and public buildings. Beyond these markers, the Spaniards had staked out certain nearby lands for farms.[2] During the ensuing year, residents concentrated on building adequate shelters and procuring enough food to survive. The settlers besieged the Spanish artisans, especially carpenters and masons, with requests for their services, and the demand drew others from throughout Peru to the town. A few farsighted colonists must have rejoiced that they had brought Indian and black slaves familiar with construction and could thus avoid the hectic bidding for Spanish workmen. Spanish artisans acted mainly as supervisors and left the labor to Indians, whose numbers in the *villa* expanded gradually as colonists secured additional workers from local Indian officials. Many colonists soon had small gangs at their disposal and housed them in crude dwellings within and around the town site. Construction proceeded steadily, but inadequate funds and a law requiring that housing be completed by March of 1541 resulted in hastily erected shacks.[3] Finding food was no less difficult. Many colonists probably seized whatever they could from local Indians, for they had little opportunity to plant crops or to organize regular deliveries of native foodstuffs. Efforts to supply the community by importing Spanish products through rude ports on the Pacific proved disappointing. Such trade was minuscule, prices prohibitive.[4]

Most settlers in Arequipa had probably foreseen such difficulties, the usual consequences of settling a new area. After all, they were seasoned colonists, many having lived elsewhere in the Americas for some time. No doubt they looked forward confidently to the end of these inconveniences and a more normal life. It is impossible now to know what they expected that life to be, but perhaps a goodly number looked to an urban setting, one in which they could practice their previous occupations. Indeed, many would carry on as city-based artisans, merchants, churchmen, and the like, as would other Spaniards throughout Peru.[5]

Yet some clearly wanted more. Life in the Americas, they knew, given the example of many other settlers since 1492, offered a chance to prosper if they could mobilize the Indian community. From the 1540s to the 1560s, Arequipa's colonists consequently directed much of their attention to the area's native residents. Some employed Indians in their homes and shops, or on small farms. A privileged number of Spaniards, however, simply consumed and sold native artisanal goods, crops, and livestock. They also insisted that Indians introduce European crops and livestock on native lands, for such a conversion proved lucrative to the colonists, given Spanish tastes and the irregular shipment of Old World foodstuffs. Their interest in the countryside laid the foundation for the community's agricultural economy.

The Southwest at Settlement

Southwest Peru comprises two broad geographical zones: the coast and the highlands (see map 1). The western chain of the Andes, which parallels the Pacific approximately forty kilometers inland, delineates the coastal belt on the east, and the Acarí and Azapa rivers form the northern and southern boundaries, respectively. Within this zone, low-lying, narrow terraces run along most of the coast, which is cut off from the interior by hills—the remains of a pre-Andean mountain range—that average six hundred meters in altitude. Only from the Atico River to Camaná and around the well-known headland of Arica do these hills reach the Pacific Ocean. Broad desert plains lie to the east of this coastal range, inclining upward until they meet the Andes.

The principal sources of water in the coastal belt are several rivers that

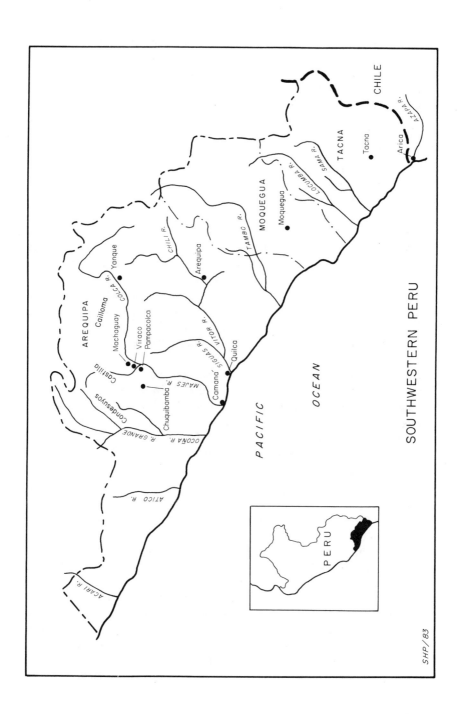

SOUTHWESTERN PERU

SHP/83

flow swiftly down from the Andes on a westward course and underground streams that occasionally form pools. The Ocoña, Majes, and Tambo rivers run through deep valleys as much as two kilometers wide; the Vítor, Siguas, Acarí, and Atico rivers cut narrower gorges while traversing the plains and threading their way through coastal hills. These hills receive additional moisture during the coastal winter months (May to October) from mist that settles mostly on the seaward slopes. The green vegetation the mist supports contrasts sharply with the dull gray and brown of the adjacent slopes and plains.[6]

From the plains the eastern highlands appear to be a wall. This zone—now the provinces of Condesuyos, Castilla, and Cailloma—is extremely rugged, with imposing Andean peaks of over forty-five hundred meters. Occasionally, the mountains are relieved by highland plains, the broadest lying near the present border between the departments of Arequipa and Puno, and to the east and northeast of the Misti volcano. Heavy rains from December to April, along with melting snow and glaciers, feed countless streams and rivers. Two major river systems dominate the Southwest's highland zone: the Colca, which snakes its way from the Cordillera de Quilca through canyons in Cailloma and Castilla; and the Río Grande, whose origins are in still-remote La Unión province.[7]

At the time of the Spaniards' arrival, most Indians lived along these major highland rivers, their tributaries, and the rivers of the coastal belt. The Southwest was sparsely populated in comparison with many other regions of Peru; the Indians totaled at least 110,000.[8] They were most heavily concentrated in the Colca Valley and that of the Río Grande. Indians who lived in these valleys and along tributaries of the Colca River and the Río Grande resided in small and dispersed settlements. For example, those found in the valley formed by the Huacone River, which flows into the Colca, lived in the town of Chuquibamba and in twenty villages, each housing from sixty to two hundred dwellers and sprinkled over a twenty-kilometer stretch. Similar residence patterns prevailed in the Arequipa Valley and along the coastal belt's rivers. Fewer towns were located on the highland plains; instead, most natives lived in hamlets and smaller compounds with one or two families.[9]

When the Spaniards settled the region, most Indians in the coastal valleys were farmers. Each family made use of one parcel of land, generally devoting it to maize, chilies, cotton, and coca. Because the area had been part of the Inca empire, these small plots often abutted others set aside for the support of the Inca and the Sun, the administrative and religious establishments.[10] Yet, given the shortage of arable land, only a small percentage of the total appears to have been assigned for these purposes, in contrast with patterns elsewhere in Peru.[11]

Another imprint of the Incas on the coastal economy was the presence of irrigation works, but these were not as sophisticated as those Europeans found along the coast to the north of Lima. Whereas southwestern rivers have as much annual water volume as northwestern ones—the Majes River, for example, normally exceeds the Jequetepeque, and even the smaller Vítor carries twice the water of the Moche River—technological and climatic factors hampered irrigation. High valley walls and an evaporation rate higher than that of upper Egypt made it difficult to divert water onto the plains. Indians therefore confined their canals (*acequias*) to the valleys, although they kept even these small. Because of frequent floods and earthquakes and shifting rivers, it would have been foolish to build elaborate irrigation works.[12]

Many highlanders also farmed, particularly those living in the lower-lying valleys of Condesuyos and Castilla and on sunny slopes along the Colca River as far inland as the present town of Yanque. They could grow maize, although sierra (highland) farmers devoted most plots to tubers, principally various types of potatoes, and to grains, such as quinoa, that resist cold temperatures common at the higher elevations. Unlike coastal families, those in the highlands did not farm one parcel, but ordinarily cultivated several plots scattered at various altitudes and with different exposures to the sun so that a number of crops might be grown. Interspersed among these holdings were lands of the Inca and the Sun. Extensive terraces on mountain slopes and irrigation canals suggest that Indian authorities, including the Incas, made efforts to increase farmland, as they did elsewhere.[13] At the highest elevations, where farming proved impossible, Indians relied on ranching and grazed llama and alpaca herds on the grasses common to the plains.[14]

Indians throughout the Southwest also depended on local resources for their normal diet. Those within the coastal belt relied on a variety of wild fruits and plants, salt- and fresh-water fish, and prawns from the rivers. They ate little red meat except that from domestically raised guinea pigs. Indians in the sierra also gathered wild fruits and plants and consumed meat only sparingly. They employed alpacas and llamas mainly as beasts of burden and as sources for wool.[15]

Yet Indians did not survive solely on the resources found close to their homes. Parties often foraged far from villages for weeks at a time. Communities also established permanent outposts from which the settlers regularly exchanged goods with those left behind. Indians from Cailloma and Condesuyos, for example, set up colonies in the Arequipa Valley and along the lower reaches of the Vítor, Siguas, Majes, and Ocoña rivers. Less known are the colonies of coastal Indians, such as those established by villagers based along the Ocoña River who settled in the lower highlands around Chuquibamba, and those of the Acarí Indians in the sierra, which served as bases for farming and grazing.[16] Although many of these colonies antedated the Inca empire, the Incas encouraged colonization in order to relieve densely populated areas, scatter rebellious peoples, and introduce loyalists into a region. Their settlements probably also enriched the empire by providing scarce goods.

The best-known site of Inca colonization in the Southwest is the Arequipa Valley. According to legend, the valley was almost uninhabited until the twelfth-century campaigns of Mayta Capac. When his captains passed through the region on their way home from a victorious campaign, Arequipa's available farmland and mild climate so attracted them that they asked to be allowed to settle. The Inca agreed and ordered over three thousand highland families to join them.[17] These highlanders apparently came from nearby Cailloma, yet Inca (and pre-Inca) colonization at times relocated peoples great distances from their homeland. By 1540 groups from Lake Titicaca could be found in many parts of the Southwest. Their settlements generally lay to the south of the Tambo River and served to supply highland communities with coastal crops and wild fruits, with guano used as a fertilizer, and with pastures for sierra animals annually driven west.[18]

The Distribution of *Encomiendas*

The Southwest's sparse population and humble economy initially discouraged Spanish colonization following the conquerors' arrival in Peru and their capture of the Inca Atahuallpa in 1532.[19] A few parties from Cuzco scouted its eastern sierra during the mid-1530s, and others probed along the Pacific from Lima, Governor Francisco Pizarro's colonial capital, founded in 1535.[20] In 1537 Diego de Almagro entered the area by way of the Atacama Desert after a difficult Chilean campaign, crossed the coastal plains and rivers, visited the Arequipa Valley, and then exited over the highlands to Cuzco.[21] Almagro thereafter challenged Pizarro's claims to southern Peru and provoked a civil war, which forced Spaniards to postpone further exploration of the Southwest. Following Almagro's defeat at Salinas early in 1538, quarrels among Pizarro's followers over the paltry spoils as well as the resentment of Almagro's supporters threatened a new round of revolt. In an effort to channel the frustrations, Pizarro and his captains arranged a series of expeditions into unconquered areas. They planned these so as to establish Spanish towns strategically placed to control more Indians. One expedition founded San Juan de la Vitoria, later popularly known as Huamanga, between Lima and Cuzco, and another began the settlement of present-day Bolivia.[22]

The opening up of the region to the south of Cuzco created communication problems. Since the early 1530s, Lima had been linked to interior southern Peru by two routes. One took travelers up along the Rimac River, or through an adjacent valley, across the Andean range to an Inca road that lay within Peru's intermontane valleys. That highway headed southward, past the future site of Huamanga, to the Pampas River. Beyond Uranmarca it ran through Andahuaylas, crossed the Abancay River, and proceeded eastward to Cuzco. The other route, which went south from Lima over the coastal plains as far as the Nazca River, traversed deserts relieved by only occasional river valleys. Several paths scaled the difficult highlands east of Nazca; the most popular cut through the provinces of Lucanas, Aymaras, and Chumbivilcas. Spaniards veered north at Totora, crossed the Apurimac River close to Catabambas, and approached Cuzco from the south.[23] Although established and projected settlements near Lake Titicaca might be tied to Lima by these routes and a connecting trail from Cuzco across the highland plains, it made more sense to develop a shorter route through southwestern Peru to the Pacific. From there Lima could be reached by sea. Pizarro decided to establish such a route, and to ensure its protection and use, he scouted possible sites for a town in the area during a brief trip in mid-1539. When he returned to Cuzco later that year, he had not determined the location for a town, a decision he left to a commission. It eventually decided on a spot near the coast, alongside the Majes River.[24]

A number of Spaniards who had accompanied Pizarro to the Southwest and had settled in a makeshift village in the Arequipa Valley entertained reservations about the Majes site. This initial opposition soon proved well-founded; given the blistering heat of late summer and constant mosquito attacks, the new residents must have found La Villa Hermosa de Camaná inappropriately named. Fearing its abandonment, local authorities forbade anyone to leave without permission.[25] As many at Camaná fell ill, particularly those Indians brought down from the sierra, local leaders decided to secure Pizarro's permission to move. Early in June, Pizarro instructed Garcí Manuel de Carvajal, his lieutenant in the area, to canvass the settlers on their views about the comparative advantages of a settlement at Camaná or in the Arequipa Valley. Concerned specifically about the effects of either location on the health of highland Indians, Pizarro made clear that any move should be executed rapidly lest the whole southern enterprise collapse. Those at Camaná met in the newly erected church on 20 July 1540 and, after a brief discussion, chose Arequipa. Carvajal concurred and ordered their removal within twenty days. The transfer went smoothly, and, on 15 August 1540 they formally founded the new town of La Villa Hermosa de Arequipa.[26]

The transfer may have salvaged Pizarro's plan for a southwestern settlement but a number of Spaniards probably would have stayed on in Camaná had the governor insisted. It had been common practice throughout the Americas since the 1490s to distribute Indians to certain settlers; few Spaniards considered a house plot and a farm sufficient inducement to settle. After the commission selected Camaná, Pizarro accordingly granted unassigned Indians to some Spaniards. (Several colonists had earlier received allotments of southwestern natives while living in Cuzco. Pizarro required that these men emigrate to Camaná or lose their Indians, and most complied.) Because the grantees, known as *encomenderos*, had vested interests—access to their Indians' labor and produce—few probably would have left Camaná no matter what hardships they might encounter.[27]

Pizarro had proceeded deliberately when he assigned grants (*encomiendas*) of southwestern Indians (see Appendix A). Not surprisingly, he awarded Indians to a brother, Gonzalo, to his cousin and former page, Pedro Pizarro, and to his secretary, Alonso Rodríguez Picado. He also preferred men like Juan Crespo and Lucas Martínez Vegaso, who had been born in Trujillo, his Spanish birthplace. Others who shared his Extremaduran regional origins, such as Juan de la Torre and Garcí Manuel de Carvajal, were singled out, as were men such as Andrés Jiménez, Pedro de Mendoza, and Alonso Ruiz who could date their association with Francisco Pizarro as far back as the Inca's capture at Cajamarca. Many of the remaining *encomenderos* had arrived in Peru after Cajamarca, but had been loyal to him for some time before they received grants. Gonzalo de Aguilar, Pedro Godínez, Gómez de León, Lope de Alarcón, and Juan Ramírez had helped defend the colony against Indians bent on undoing the Spanish conquest. They and other grantees had actively supported Pizarro thereafter when Diego de Almagro attempted to challenge his claims to southern Peru.

But most of the men recruited by Pizarro to be Arequipa's *encomenderos* were not prominent Spaniards in early Peru. Pizarro chose mostly from among the lesser distinguished settlers in Lima and Cuzco. Few very important people would have left these cities for the isolation of Arequipa. The more prominent of the Pizarro followers who moved to the Southwest were men such as Gómez de León, who served as one of Pizarro's captains in the war against Almagro and who participated in negotiations on the delicate issue of boundaries between their holdings, and Francisco Rodríguez de Villafuerte, who fought actively and was at the decisive battle at Salinas that ended the uprising. Not unexpectedly, the likes of Rodríguez de Villafuerte settled in Arequipa only temporarily and later drifted back to Cuzco.[28]

Pizarro also accommodated several Almagro supporters. Their selection as *encomenderos*, so soon after Salinas, was a brilliant stroke. No doubt he chose former enemies in hopes that lingering resentment would end. Yet, when selecting from Almagro's supporters, Pizarro applied more rigorous standards than he used in choosing allies. The men had to have had truly distinguished Peruvian careers and some social status. They included Pedro Barroso and Francisco Noguerol de Ulloa. Barroso had been a captain of Pedrarias Dávila in Nicaragua during the 1520s and had reached Peru in 1535. He moved on to Cuzco, joined Almagro, and became an official during Almagro's ill-fated Chilean expedition. He later fought for Almagro in the civil war and served as an *alcalde* (judge) of the town of Chincha. Noguerol de Ulloa had left for Chile by sea on Pizarro's orders to resupply Almagro's expedition. After returning to Peru, he achieved dubious renown as the man responsible for captured Pizarro supporters in Cuzco.[29] Such impressive service overcame their Almagro connections, especially when the men showed an inclination to settle differences with the governor, Barroso by accompanying Pizarro to Arequipa in 1539, and Noguerol de Ulloa by going to Camaná shortly afterward. But for men of lesser distinction in Peru and with an Almagro background, *encomiendas* were out of reach, even for a university graduate like Alvaro Marín. They would have to prove their loyalty further before earning grants.[30]

Pizarro by no means distributed an equal number of Indians to all of these men. Instead, he rewarded unequal accomplishments by assigning more Indians to those with more distinguished service. Thus, a Pizarro supporter and Trujillan like Martín López de Carvajal, with participation only in the Indian siege of Cuzco to his credit, received a small grant of only 287 tributaries. In contrast, Lucas Martínez Vegaso, who had been at Cajamarca and Cuzco in the early 1530s, was the recipient of 1,637 tributaries. Complications inevitably arose when Pizarro was forced to distinguish between persons with strong cases for a good-sized grant.[31] Andrés Jiménez, for instance, appeared to be in line for at least as sizeable an *encomienda* as Pedro de Mendoza, since both had served at Cajamarca; and Jiménez had picked up additional honors by returning to Spain and securing from the Crown a captaincy as well as a seat on Lima's city council. That he received a smaller *encomienda* suggests that Pizarro was unimpressed by status achieved through Crown reward and ultimately valued Trujillan roots and his close association in Peru with a man.[32]

Interestingly, in judging the various men, particularly his civil war partisans, Pizarro did not have to face any complication arising out of differing social standing. Those selected as *encomenderos* were socially homogeneous and unprepossessing by metropolitan standards: most were drawn from the families of commoners and reared in Spanish towns and cities; apparently none came from peasant stock and only a handful from the lesser nobility.[33] Pizarro did draw a line in that he did not assign Indians to artisans, men like Diego Martín, a carpenter, Francisco Sánchez, a blacksmith, Juanes Navarro, a tailor, and Pedro Irés, a crier.

Yet, beyond this, a man's occupational background was unimportant. Many in the group, men like Lucas Martínez Vegaso, Pedro de Mendoza, Lope de Alarcón, and Juan de San Juan, are aptly described, in James Lockhart's words, as "men of affairs" who had dabbled in a host of business ventures while in Peru, from speculating in imported and Indian goods to managing the business and financial concerns of other Spaniards.[34] A minority identified themselves as merchants. Luis de León, from Valdepeñas, had received a license to travel to Peru in 1534, and in 1535 was joined by a brother, Juan, who migrated with royal permission to sell slaves and make loans. They worked together in Lima until the late 1530s, when Luis moved to Arequipa. Another brother, Nicolás de Almazán, joined Luis there shortly thereafter.[35] Gonzalo de Aguilar came from Segovia, one of a Castilian family with extensive business interests in the New World. By 1540 the family had transferred its base of operations from Santo Domingo to Lima and came under the direction of Gaspar de Cuéllar. Gonzalo and his brother, Alonso de Aguilar, were probably sent to Arequipa because its location between Lima and southeastern Peru seemed to promise that the town would become a major trading center. One additional *encomendero*, Hernando Alvarez de Carmona, was a notary.[36]

As in several other regions of the New World, the preconquest administrative structure facilitated the task of rewarding settlers of unequal merit.[37] Perhaps Pizarro became aware of this native structure during his visit to Arequipa; grants of Indians dating from January 1540 refer to it often. At conquest, the Southwest was a part of the Inca empire's western quarter, known as Cuntisuyu.[38] The Incas designated each of the major coastal valleys within Cuntisuyu a province. They organized highland provinces, on the other hand, around important ethnic groups: for example, the upper Colca Valley was the province of the Collaguas; provinces to the south of the Colca Valley were the provinces of the Ubinas and Carumas.[39] In the populous highland valleys, where several ethnic groups often resided near each other, the Incas subdivided the provinces. The province of the Collaguas, accordingly, included three segments: those of the Yanque Collaguas, the Lari Collaguas, and the Cabanas. At least two segments made up the province of the Ubinas. Smaller administrative units existed throughout the Southwest down to the local community level.[40]

A complication in the Indian administrative structure resulted from the subdivision of each ethnic group into two branches: the *hurinsaya* and the *hanansaya*. Because of this moiety-like arrangement, each ethnic group possessed two officials from the local to the provincial levels.[41] Viraco, a highland valley town, provides a good example of this organizational scheme. During the early 1500s, the town's residents, all members of one ethnic group belonged either to the *hurinsaya* or to the *hanansaya*. Each branch had an official (*curaca*). Each of these *curacas* was a subordinate of an official with jurisdiction over a larger number of Indians. Viraco's *curaca* of the *hanansaya* reported to Chaumullo, who was an official responsible for over eight hundred Indians. The town's other *curaca* was under the authority of Yucuramullo. Chaumullo and Yucuramullo reported, respectively, to the *curacas* of the *hanansaya* and *hurinsaya* for the province of Condesuyos. (At each level, Indians customarily regarded the *curaca* of the *hanansaya* as the principal authority.) Although some correspondence existed between administrative units and specific territories, particularly at the higher level, the system rested on the subjects of *curacas*. Chaumullo's happened to be located within villages and towns of one valley, yet those of Yucuramullo lived not only in many of these same settlements, but in a fishing village on the coast near Camaná.[42] Thus, the tendency of Indians to disperse as they colonized produced a very complicated administrative map, especially in areas such as the southern coastal valleys, where many highlanders settled. Even in other places, the need for suitable farmland and pastures scattered the native population.

Recognizing that each coastal valley had a predominant official (the *curaca* of the *hanansaya*), but that these officials had varying numbers of Indians under their authority, Pizarro simply assigned to each Spaniard of less distinction a *curaca* who had few subjects.[43] Whereas a more distinguished Spaniard could generally expect an *encomienda* with a larger number of Indians, all of whom lived in one valley, Pizarro occasionally split the natives of a coastal valley. He would base his grant on the *hanansaya* and *hurinsaya* division at the provincial level in those cases when a valley's population was unusually large and its agricultural economy was impressive, such as in the Tacna region or along the Río Grande and the Majes River.[44] Pizarro deviated even further from standard practice in his allotment to Lucas Martínez Vegaso. Vegaso's Indians (over sixteen hundred adult males) were subjects of many provincial *curacas* to the south of the Tambo River. In this case, Pizarro probably abandoned his inclination to confine each *encomendero*'s Indians to one valley, because each valley in this stretch of the coastal belt often supported only a few residents: combining them all under one *encomendero* avoided minuscule grants. Pizarro also included many of the Indian colonists in the region in his grant to Martínez Vegaso. This arrangement proved inconvenient for Martínez Vegaso and forced him to administer the grant through many *curacas*, but he was compensated by having Indians whose villages lay close to the known silver deposits of Tarapacá.[45]

Another type of *encomienda* joined Indian subjects of a coastal valley *curaca* with a group residing in the interior. Miguel Cornejo, for example, received Indians of the *hanansaya* residing in the Vítor and Quilca valleys as well as some from the Arequipa Valley. Similarly, a grant to another Spaniard merged Indians of the Tambo Valley with others living in Pocsi.[46] Since no apparent ethnic or administrative link existed between these Indians, Francisco Pizarro probably combined them mainly to provide the Spaniards with some natives living close to their Arequipa homes for convenience in securing labor. He distributed the remaining Arequipa Valley Indians, predominantly of highland origin and ethnically diverse, in two ways. He lumped together many of the small ethnic groups, whose roots lay outside of the Southwest, to make up several grants. Had he not, the *encomiendas* would have been too small, and dissatisfied recipients might have emigrated. As it was, the combined Indians hardly sufficed, and their *encomenderos*, generally the least distinguished settlers given grants, later had problems. Other valley Indians, offshoots of ethnic groups such as the Collaguas based in the highlands closer to the new Spanish town, Pizarro assigned with their parent group.[47]

In the more densely populated highland valleys, Pizarro created grants of impressive size. Spaniards valued these *encomiendas* not only because of the numerous Indians, but also because of the diversity of the native sierra economy. Not surprisingly, these grants went to the governor's closest associates and to supporters with noteworthy careers in Peru, some of whom he could not have expected to spend much time in Arequipa. Thus, Francisco Pizarro assigned to his brother, Gonzalo, the *curacas* of Yanque Collaguas, providing him with over four thousand adult males. Alonso Rodríguez Picado, one of Pizarro's secretaries, and Juan Flores, a Pizarro partisan and distinguished warrior, shared the Lari Collaguas, one receiving the Indians of the *curaca* of the *hanansaya*, the other those of the *curaca* of the *hurinsaya*. Pizarro also employed the *hanansaya* and *hurinsaya* split when he granted the neighboring Cabanas.[48] In distributing Indians living throughout Condesuyos and Ubinas, the governor bestowed to various Spaniards the *curacas* with jurisdiction over segments of each province. Consequently, each recipient was allotted Indians of both the *hurinsaya* and the *hanansaya* of a segment. The 1540 grants specifically mention the *curaca* of the *hanansaya* following the Indian custom of considering him the major administrative figure at each level.[49]

The Early *Encomienda* Economy

After the distribution of grants, southwestern *encomenderos*, like others throughout the colony, enjoyed a relatively free hand in dealing with their Indians. Francisco Pizarro and the royal government virtually ignored relations between the Indians and the Spaniards for some years. The only standing legislation was a 1537 order that introduced a plan (first implemented in the more closely governed colony of New Spain) by which the governor was to appoint for all Spanish settlements officers to examine the number of Indians granted each *encomendero*, to evaluate the quantity of their lands and other holdings, and to determine the amount of tribute natives had paid before the Spanish conquest. The order further required that royal officials draw up lists of future tribute limited to reasonable amounts of local crops, livestock, and products. These tribute lists were to be left in each Indian village and residents notified of their content. Any attempt to collect more than was specified or to require alterations in the Indian economy would incur a fine; a second offense was to be punished by loss of the *encomienda*. But the instructions were not enforced in remote Peru, and most settlers at Arequipa in 1540 had probably forgotten about the order, if they had ever heard of it.[50]

During the first years after Arequipa's founding, therefore, the *encomenderos* generally visited their Indians' villages in order to reach agreements with the *curacas* on the tribute required. By early 1541, Indian officials were already arranging for the collection and delivery of native goods to *encomenderos* at Arequipa or other sites.[51] *Encomenderos* not only provisioned their expanding households with such products, but also sold them to pay for services and to buy local and imported wares. The value of tributes to grantees should not be overestimated, however; Indian goods had limited uses in a small community incapable of absorbing all it received. Even those *encomenderos* who turned to outside markets or sold to merchants realized only modest gains. Peru remained a young and underpopulated colony with few Spanish consumers; often tributes of grantees living elsewhere in the colony duplicated Arequipa's. The town's major outlet was apparently Chile, accessible by sea, where Spaniards still involved in conquest had not succeeded in organizing local Indians to meet their needs.[52]

Dissatisfied with the returns from such tributes, *encomenderos* sought more lucrative possibilities. At first they channeled native labor into building urban homes, generally leasing out their Indians to other colonists. Some formed small businesses, often with artisans, and employed their Indians in preparing lime, making adobe bricks, cutting stone, and supplying other construction materials. Soon prospecting fever hit. *Encomenderos* hired agents from among those who had no Indians and sent them out into the countryside, with a few black slave laborers and several natives. Most agents searched near villages of the *encomendero*'s Indians, but they discovered only a few small deposits of silver in Ubinas and limited gold along the Ocoña River. The reserves of Tarapacá provided the only mining opportunity, but its remoteness prevented most *encomenderos* from working them. Southwestern Peru surely must have disillusioned those who dreamed of an El Dorado.[53]

As another venture, *encomenderos* turned to agriculture and encouraged their Indians to raise European foodstuffs to meet the healthy colonial demand. To introduce crops and livestock, as well as to organize production on their Indians' lands, *encomenderos* contracted with Spanish agents. The arrangement worked out by the Extremaduran Garcí Manuel de Carvajal, whose *encomienda* included Indians in the Camaná Valley, was typical. In mid-1541, he hired a Spaniard, Juan Gallego, to work with his Indians for a year and provide him with twenty chickens and some pigs. Gallego's contract stipulated that he breed these and direct local Indians in fishing expeditions, wheat cultivation, wood collection, and anything else he saw fit to do. In return, he would receive a third of the wood and half of the fish, chickens, pigs, wheat, or any other harvested crop. Men like Juan Gallego were invariably illiterate, of humble social station, and often so initially mistrusted that their contracts included a fine for leaving their posts.[54]

Staggering costs for seed and animals hampered efforts to introduce crops and livestock. Nevertheless, a few *encomenderos* made some headway through the mid-1540s, despite the resumption of civil war. Discord followed Governor Francisco Pizarro's assassination in 1541 by a group of disgruntled Almagro supporters. Shortly after the defeat of the Almagrists, a more serious and protracted rebellion, brought on by the publication of the Crown's New Laws, engulfed the colony. These measures forbade Indian slavery and called for the eventual abolition of the *encomienda* system.[55] Although Arequipa's *encomenderos* and residents fought actively in both uprisings—generally siding with the Pizarro followers in the first and with the Crown's opponents in the early years of the second—the local economy sustained little damage until 1546. Indeed, it appears to have functioned uninterruptedly and to have benefited, because the conflagration was confined elsewhere and the combatants needed supplies. The constant demands of colonial authorities on Arequipa for products, the lack of local food shortages, and the low prices for crops in the area suggest that rural production expanded.[56]

Arequipa's good fortune ended abruptly, however, when some locals switched their allegiance from Gonzalo Pizarro, the leader of the colony's rebels, to the Crown. Worried by this defection and the more serious threat posed by the coming of Licenciado Pedro de la Gasca, an ecclesiastic appointed by the king to end the rebellion, Gonzalo's supporters demanded that Southwesterners supply fighting men, money, and food. Arequipa's citizens chose instead to revolt and set up a government loyal to the Crown. Serious warfare followed, with forces of both sides ravaging the area and contributing to minor Indian uprisings. The followers of Gonzalo Pizarro subsequently mauled the royalists at Huarina, to the east of Arequipa. Among the results of this warfare was a sharp rise in food prices in the city: for example, prices for wheat and maize stood four times higher in 1547 than in 1544. Where once Arequipa had had sufficient foodstuffs to trade in the colony, scarcity was now common. No doubt many citizens rejoiced when the royalists finally prevailed at the Battle of Jaquijaguana in April 1548 and brought the rebellion to an end.[57]

The Postwar *Encomienda* Economy

Following the war, La Gasca reassigned numerous *encomiendas* left vacant by battle casualties and the removal of traitors. Significantly, as events would reveal, President La Gasca only occasionally combined former grants when he reassigned Indians, but chose instead to apportion natives as had Governor Pizarro and his successors. Because La Gasca generally selected Spaniards who had lived in the Southwest for some time as the new grantees, it proved possible to revive the *encomienda* system rather quickly.[58] The new *encomenderos* soon familiarized themselves with their Indians, secured funds to purchase seed and livestock, found and hired field agents, and established ties to wholesale merchants. Wartime disruptions did demand that the Indians be given some time to recover, but La Gasca judged that a year of moderate tributes and services would suffice.[59] Most *encomenderos* during that year probably expected their grants to be very profitable within a short time, for Peru's economic future appeared promising. Silver had been discovered in Potosí (in present-day Bolivia) in 1545, and the start of mining there suggested that it would emerge as a major highland town capable of absorbing many rural products.[60] The cessation of hostilities also brought a flood of immigrants to Peru, and their presence boosted the demand for foodstuffs in many colonial towns and cities. Particularly noticeable was the emergence of a major market in Lima, now becoming the colony's administrative and trading hub. Southwesterners were well aware of their important position in Peru. The development of mining in Potosí was fortuitous, since Arequipa lay astride the main transport route between Lima and Charcas; Pizarro's intention that the city become an important trading center could finally be realized. The point was not lost on others as well, and commercial activity in the city expanded rapidly as agents of Lima business firms and independent merchants flocked there. The subsequent selection of Arequipa in the mid-1550s, prior to the founding of a royal treasury, as the royal entrepôt for Potosí silver before shipment by sea to Lima, confirmed the city's newly developed commercial importance.[61]

Some Arequipan *encomenderos* immediately responded to the new market opportunities by setting up import firms to buy Spanish wares in Lima and Panama for sale in the Southwest and the Peruvian highlands. But these ventures demanded a great deal of capital and could be risky, for importers might flood markets.[62] Although some continued their investments, most eventually left such trade to wealthier commercial firms and turned to the countryside, because agriculture promised better returns than ever before. Such new elements in Arequipa's population as merchants, people hoping to seize opportunities at the new way station, and various royal functionaries had transformed the city. At the least, these newcomers meant an expanded local consumer market for *encomenderos*, but they also meant that the merchants became major buyers of crops and other rural products and shipped these commodities inland. During one year, Juan Moreno invested over 4,000 pesos in maize and Indian clothing. Other merchants vied for coca and several other indigenous crops.[63] Of importance too was the demand for the native livestock necessary to transport Spanish imports and regional products. The traffic between Chule and Quilca, Arequipa's ports, and the city was occasionally so heavy that Arequipan authorities allowed the temporary use of Indian bearers.[64] In short, then, Arequipa became a major trading center, and *encomenderos*, by virtue of their access to Indian foodstuffs, livestock, and artisanal products, enjoyed growing profits.

Encomenderos' successes naturally led to further demands on their Indians during the 1550s. Although native goods commanded decent prices, Spanish foodstuffs garnered even better ones. As a consequence, *encomenderos* encouraged Indians to pay tributes in Old World crops and livestock, a conversion that had been anticipated in the late 1540s. At the conclusion of the Gonzalo Pizarro rebellion, Licenciado La Gasca had not only redistributed Indians, but also had finally tackled the job of drawing up tribute lists for Indians in Peru, as suggested in the 1537 royal order. In 1549 he appointed several of Arequipa's citizens to visit Indian towns in the region and draft tribute lists: Garcí Manuel de Carvajal and Hernán Rodríguez de Huelva visited Machaguay in Condesuyos, and Bachiller Miguel Rodríguez de Cantalapiedra and Martín López de Carvajal inspected two grants in the Arequipa Valley and the Cabanas in Cailloma. They were supposed to count all adult males who could work in each village and then suggest appropriate tributes, but they followed less rigorous procedures. In at least one instance, they relied completely on an *encomendero*'s son for information on Indians and production. That they did is hardly shocking, since they too were *encomenderos*.[65] The lists drafted during this period provide a good indication of what Spaniards expected of Indians. The items most commonly noted were crops, livestock, and products associated with the preconquest economy, yet they required many European crops and livestock as well. For example, the detailed tribute list for the coastal Indians at Hilavaya, granted to Hernán Rodríguez de Huelva by La Gasca, specified 500 fanegas (1.5 bushels each) of wheat, 15 pigs, 50 sheep and goats, various Spanish artisanal products, and a host of native goods.[66] Such lists, therefore, sanctioned past demands by *encomenderos* that Indians convert to Old World agriculture.

As they had done earlier, *encomenderos* did not rely only on tributes for Old World products. Since Peruvian royal officials waited until the late 1550s to enforce the Crown's order that *encomenderos* no longer use Indians as personal servants, Southwesterners employed natives as farmers and herders. Some of the lands on which these Indians worked were located in the Arequipa Valley and belonged to *encomenderos*, but many grantees also regularly exploited Indian tracts. As a result, wheat and grapes, to name but two introduced crops, soon spread to Indian lands in the vicinity of many towns and villages. These plantings and the breeding of European livestock were important factors in the decline of prices in Arequipa during a period when the city's population grew and interregional trade became a major preoccupation. No better measure of the decline exists than the course of wheat bread prices: in February of 1551, the municipal council determined that twenty-two loaves should sell for a peso; by May, it had lowered the price to twenty-eight loaves a peso, because of increased production. Through 1556 bread remained cheap by local standards, rising to twenty loaves a peso for a brief interlude that year only because of crop damage. Nevertheless, even then bread stayed inexpensive compared with prices in the town during the 1540s. Similarly, beef and pork were now less costly than in the pre-1548 days.[67]

Encomendero reliance on their Indians' rural economy would continue for many years beyond the 1550s—a few grantees profited immensely from their Indians through the first quarter of the seventeenth century. Still, by the 1560s, signs of weakness in the *encomienda* economy began to appear. Tributes fell gradually but steadily, a development accompanied by recurrent Indian complaints of excessive exactions.

Such difficulties were not unique to Arequipa's *encomenderos*; grantees throughout Peru and Middle America also eventually confronted declining revenues. In explaining the *encomienda* crisis, historians of other regions have emphasized the catastrophic consequences visited on Indians by the spread of Old World diseases. Recurrent illnesses and staggeringly high death rates made it impossible for Indians to meet former tribute obligations.[68] Southwestern Indians, especially those living within the coastal belt, were similarly struck down. According to colonists, the Indian population in the coastal zone dropped by 90 percent between 1540 and 1570, a loss only too evident in the many abandoned farms and villages.[69] Recent research, particularly that of Noble David Cook, suggests that their estimate was somewhat exaggerated; my calculation, arrived at by using lists of tributaries in 1540 and the early 1570s, indicates that the population decline ranged from 30 percent to 50 percent.[70] Although disease was clearly the principal cause of this demographic nightmare, the depopulation of the coastal belt may also have resulted from out-migration. Coastal Indians fled to escape tribute burdens; such highland groups as the Quinistacas and the Omates abandoned their coastal colonies, south of the Tambo River, and retreated inland, probably after sensing the dangers of living in the lowlands. At least one group of highlanders explicitly recognized how unhealthy life was in the lowlands, and when ordered to serve in a coastal inn, as they had under the Incas, they refused, citing numerous instances of sierra Indians who had become ill after journeying to the coast.[71]

The *encomenderos* responded to the loss of natives and decreasing Indian production in part by doing without and by recording their Indians' deficits. Since they no doubt realized that the shortages could never be restored, some excused the debts, and a few even gave their Indians greater resources, such as livestock and property that they owned in the countryside and in the city. These donations, often written into wills, provided some communities with rental or sales income, which they used for tributes.[72] Despite these paternalistic gestures, the Indians generally had to borrow to pay for a portion of the tributes due *encomenderos*.[73] Tribute pressures also forced several communities, mainly those in the coastal belt, where disease took its greatest toll, to sell off abandoned lands. And, after the late 1550s, when *encomenderos* lost their legal access to personal services, Indians hired themselves out so that they might use cash instead of goods to fulfill their obligations.[74]

Local *curacas*, often in an attempt to improve the appalling condition of their subjects, repeatedly detailed the pernicious effects of Spanish pressures on the Indians.[75] Motives of course varied: some *curacas* seized on economic opportunities much as the *encomenderos* did, by plunging actively into Old World agriculture and using lands surrounding Indian villages for wheat, European livestock, and even vines.[76] They apparently launched these ventures on abandoned lands, with their remaining subjects obliged to work the properties. Whatever their motives, *curacas* encouraged attempts to dislodge *encomenderos* from their privileged position, especially in the late 1550s and early 1560s, when it appeared that the Crown intended to tighten regulations on Spanish grantees. Arequipa's *encomenderos*, and others throughout the Americas, had tried for years to establish the right of perpetual inheritance of their grants, but the royal government now dashed their hopes. As *encomiendas* fell vacant, at the death of a holder (grants normally were held for the life of the original recipient and an heir) or when a grantee returned to Spain and remained there beyond the time permitted, the Crown chose to administer the Indians for itself. The royal government also ordered a review of *encomienda* titles and used defects to challenge the holders' rights to Indians. In 1562, aware of the Crown's moves, native leaders banded together to oppose the *encomendero* demand for perpetual titles and requested that Indians be allowed to live under their traditional authorities and pay tributes, mainly in gold and silver, directly to the king.[77] The royal government rejected this plan, although for a few years it took over some additional *encomiendas*, including a number of the more valuable ones, such as that of the Collaguas, once held by Gonzalo Pizarro.[78] To the distress of many Indians, Crown control brought no relief from tribute burdens, for the tribute list requirements remained, including those that specified Old World foodstuffs. Officials collected the tributes and then auctioned them off.[79]

Encomenderos were no doubt relieved when the Crown's incorporation of grants proved temporary. Yet they still faced problems. Tributes declined generally, with a particularly alarming reduction in that portion that Indians paid in European crops and livestock. In 1571, for example, the *encomendero* of the Hilavaya Indians expected to receive substantially less than what was called for in the 1549 tribute list. With the exception of sheep, which would exceed the required amount, Old World livestock and crops were to be in very short supply.[80]

The effect of disease on natives, of course, contributed greatly to this development, but it appears that the Indians also abandoned European agriculture. The natives, aware of the region's critical shortage of arable lands, may have viewed such land use as a threat. More than one community must have balked at devoting parcels to unknown crops for fear of catastrophe. These fears can only have been heightened by the realization that some groups, particularly those in the Arequipa Valley, no longer insured against inadequate harvests by storing produce during good years. Before the conquest, such reserves had depended on crops raised on Sun and Inca lands, but these lands had been stripped from the Indians to accommodate the colonists.[81] And work demands by the Spaniards contributed to the refusal by Indians to modify the native economy, as those demands made it difficult for Indians to tend their fields. Finally, Indians may simply have refused to plant foreign crops in the amounts required because of their unfamiliarity with them and because noncompliance offered a way to frustrate new overlords. By the early 1560s, therefore, the *encomienda* system no longer supplied the Spaniards as well as it had during the 1540s.

Conclusion

Writing some time ago, José Miranda characterized New Spain's *encomenderos* as businessmen who plunged into assorted ventures because of their access to Indian labor and tributes.[82] Since then, others investigating *encomenderos* elsewhere in the Americas, including in early colonial Peru, have concurred in Miranda's judgment. As James Lockhart has shown, Peruvian *encomenderos* ranged broadly in their economic pursuits: they were involved in activities from urban trade (generally channeled through agents) to mining. Only a few historians now suggest, as did many before Miranda, that "feudal" concerns motivated the *encomenderos*, that certain Spaniards held their grants primarily for prestige, political power, and economic subsistence.[83]

The Arequipa case provides little evidence of such an *encomendero* mentality among those who settled early colonial Peru. What is striking about Arequipa's *encomenderos*, then, is not that they had a penchant for business, but that they largely restricted their concern to agriculture so soon after settlement. Nothing in the backgrounds of these colonists presages their New World economic ventures. They grew up in urban areas and, during their pre-Arequipa days, avoided agriculture. The decision to concentrate their Indian labor on farming and herding was simply forced on them. They happened on an agricultural native economy, and their attempts to develop alternate business interests failed, generated unacceptably low returns, or proved too risky.

Encomendero exploitation of the countryside proved astute. As colonizers bent on maximizing opportunities for financial gain, they would strike out into unfamiliar territory. They soon insisted that their Indians not only supply them with American crops and livestock, but also raise Old World foodstuffs. They then marketed these locally and throughout the colony.

Yet, far sooner after the initial settling than in other regions of Peru and Middle America, southwestern *encomenderos*, especially those with Indians along the Pacific coast, faced severe declines in tributes.[84] The early arrival of a crisis in Arequipa's *encomiendas* was not brought on by special

Crown restrictions on local grantees, by fiercer native resistance, or, most importantly, by proportionately greater Indian losses to Old World diseases. Instead, its timing was due to the area's small Indian population base at conquest and the manner in which natives were distributed to Spaniards. Francisco Pizarro had attempted to establish economically viable *encomiendas* by avoiding minuscule grants. But most Spaniards received only a modest number of Indians. Such allotments had been necessary to attract sufficient settlers in 1540 to an area not prized by Spanish colonists. When the Indian population began to drop, no attempts followed to consolidate Indians into larger grants, although there were opportunities to do so during the civil wars and at their conclusion; pressures from claimants on leaders like La Gasca would not allow for that. The Spaniards may also have felt that Indian resistance would become more dangerous if they stripped *curacas* of their authority when regrouping Indians. Thus, as the Indian population dropped and natives refused to adapt to Old World agriculture, the ever-shrinking *encomiendas* supplied meager returns. The decline in tributes and in produce raised under the supervision of Spaniards threatened the region's early colonial economy and forced *encomenderos* either to accept declining returns or to restructure production.

2. *Chácaras* and *Estancias* in Early Arequipa

Nuestra tierra de Arequipa, ni es blanda y cariñosa siempre, ni siempre dura; ni por fácil para producir enerva al hombre, ni por ingrata lo desalienta ni le quita la ilusión y la esperanza del fruto abundante, que es la gloria del trabajador.

—————Jorge Polar

In 1540 ownership of rural lands by Spaniards in the Southwest was neither a route to wealth nor a sign of social status; it was a necessity. Francisco Pizarro had recognized the colonists' need for land and had directed local officials, as he had done elsewhere in Peru, to distribute tracts to all residents when a town was founded, if possible. He apparently expected such properties to be just large enough to sustain their owners— particularly those who had no Indians—while they lived in the *villa*.

The governor's intended role for land use and land ownership was short-lived in the Southwest. At first, some settlers neglected their holdings and lived off the agricultural products they gathered from Indians or bought from a few colonists. Later, especially by the 1550s, many colonists decided to devote their rural land to crops and pastures so that they might trade agricultural goods in colonial markets. As they converted properties to these purposes, the countryside held by Spaniards increasingly came under the control of a narrow segment of Arequipa's population.

The Arequipa Valley in 1540

The Arequipa Valley was and is a magnificent oasis. At almost 2,500 meters above sea level, mountains enclose it on three sides. The peaks to the north and east are particularly impressive: the beautiful conical volcano,

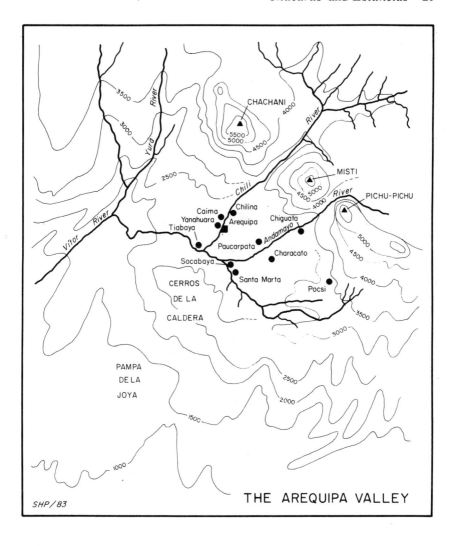

THE AREQUIPA VALLEY

the Misti, flanked by Chachani, a snow-capped mountain of over 6,000 meters, and rugged Pichu-Pichu. Low, barren hills, the Cerros de la Caldera, close off the valley to the south and southwest, and to the northwest the land rises to an arid plain. The valley measures approximately 15 kilometers from beyond the Misti to the Cerros de la Caldera, and 25 kilometers from beyond the village of Caima, near the plain, to the peaks of Pichu-Pichu. The inhospitality of its surroundings enhances the valley's beauty. The overland traveler from the coast or from the northwest or southwest traverses desert; from the interior of Peru, that traveler must cross either a desolate highland plain or difficult mountainous terrain.[1]

During the late 1530s, the valley supported approximately twenty thousand Indians, who relied on farming.[2] Land distribution among the Indians resembled that of other regions in the Inca empire: most arable tracts were in the hands of individuals, each of whom farmed a plot to sustain his household; of the remainder, several segments served to meet communal needs and obligations, and other portions (the Inca and Sun lands) supported the administrative and religious establishments.

Because of the valley's aridity, Indian settlements, like those elsewhere in the area, were quite small and scattered along modest rivers. Most lay along the Chili, the valley's principal river, and to the south and east of the river, along the other important streams. The Chili originates in the Andes, enters the valley between the Misti and Chachani, and crosses its northern end on a southwesterly course through a canyon. It occasionally reaches a width of one hundred meters. Indians farmed the rich soils of this canyon, but their most important agricultural sites were on the slopes and plains near the towns of Yanahuara, Caima, and Tiabaya. Spaniards probably marveled at the fields around Caima, since they lay well away from and above the Chili and were irrigated by a major canal that brought water from some distance upriver. Below Yanahuara, the Chili runs through a broad plain dotted with Indian farms.

The Andamayo, another important river, enters the valley between the Misti and Pichu-Pichu. It first flows through a hilly section where Indians worked lands principally in the small clearing around Chiguata. The river eventually makes its way to the plains that lie between the towns of Paucarpata and Characato, also valued by preconquest Indian farmers. A number of streams descend from the hills near the town of Pocsi, to the south of Characato, and run through small valleys with rich soils. These streams feed into each other, flow through a broad plain on which the village of Santa Marta is located, and then meet the Andamayo River near the town of Socabaya. Beyond Socabaya, the river runs through the lovely Guasacache Valley to join the Chili River near the town of Tiabaya. The Chili then veers northward, leaves the Arequipa basin through a narrow and serpentine passageway, and eventually joins the Yura River to become the Vítor.[3]

Any Spanish settler admiring the valley on a summer's day from an elevated vantage point like Caima must surely have been struck (as was an Arequipan writer some time ago) by the contrasts: green fields bordering rivers that snake their way through gorges and defiles, countless irrigation ditches, vegetation fanning out occasionally onto the plains; barren brown or grayish hills and flatlands set off the rest of the valley floor, all enclosed by rugged and arid mountains, often with snowcaps.[4]

Land Distribution to Spaniards in 1540

Francisco Pizarro warned local leaders to damage Indians as little as possible when they distributed land to the settlers. He urged the leaders to take only Inca and Sun lands or parcels abandoned for at least three years, if they had to appropriate Indian property to accommodate the colonists. The governor further suggested that officials might exclude from ownership those *encomenderos* with Indians near the town, because they presumably could survive adequately on tributes. But the partitioners disregarded the suggestions and distributed land to all founders and also selected compact blocks of land close to the townsite (see table 1). Given conditions in the Arequipa Valley, it is highly doubtful that all the nearly 2,000 acres distributed on the plain surrounding the settlement and within the canyon on the Spanish side of the Chili River represented vacant plots or Inca and Sun lands. Since the grants make clear that much of this land had been worked and had functioning irrigation ditches, the seizure of some Indian tracts seems certain. Yet, officials tried to minimize the negative effects on Indian land tenure. They assigned noncontiguous parcels to many settlers, and several grants consisted of various plots interspersed among Indian farms.[5]

Local officials distributed land for farms unequally (see table 1). García Manuel de Carvajal, Pizarro's lieutenant governor, and the *regidor* (councilor) Hernando de Torres, his assistant in the partition, ultimately favored *encomenderos* and assigned them plots of 35 to 55 acres; everyone else received approximately 12 to 47 acres. They also made a few large grants to leading colonials like Governor Francisco Pizarro, Hernando Pizarro, and Bishop Fray Vicente de Valverde. In their only concession to Pizarro's suggestion that *encomenderos* not be favored unduly, they gave the largest parcels to men assigned the fewest tributaries.

The preference shown the *encomenderos* is understandable. The officials no doubt felt that those without *encomiendas* would be unable to use large holdings, since they would have to hire Indians, and assigning them extensive lands would waste precious resources in an area short of arable lands. Then, too, the partitioners, as *encomenderos* themselves, simply

Table 1
Original Partition of Land, Arequipa Valley, 1540

Allotment Location and Recipient	Allotment Size (*fanegadas*)*
NEXT TO THE CITY	
Francisco de Montenegro	11.0
Pedro Pizarro	11.0
Alonso Ruiz	11.0
Juan de la Torre	11.0
Antonio Beltrán	10.0
Padre Rodrigo Bravo	10.0
Lope de Idiáquez	10.0
Lucas Martínez Vegaso	10.0
Francisco Noguerol de Ulloa	10.0
Juan de San Juan	9.5
Juan Alejandre	9.0
Juan Cansino	9.0
Luis Méndez	8.0
Juanes Navarro	6.0
Francisco Sánchez	5.0
Pedro Irés	4.0
IN THE CHILI RIVER GORGE	
#Francisco Pizarro	24.0
Andrés Jiménez	14.0
Gómez de León	14.0
#Fray Vicente de Valverde	14.0
Pedro Barroso	12.0
Pedro Godínez	12.0
Francisco Gómez	12.0
Diego Hernández	12.0
García Juárez	12.0
Martín López de Carvajal	12.0
Alonso de Luque	12.0
#Gonzalo Pizarro	12.0
#Hernando Pizarro	12.0
Hernando de Silva	12.0
Gómez de Tordoya Vargas	12.0
Hernando de Torres (Cervantes)	12.0
Gonzalo de Aguilar	11.0
Lope de Alarcón	11.0
Garcí Manuel de Carvajal	11.0
Melchor Cervantes	10.0

Table 1 (continued)
Original Partition of Land, Arequipa Valley, 1540

Allotment Location and Recipient	Allotment Size (*fanegadas*)*
Pedro de Mendoza	10.0
Juan Ramírez	10.0
Francisco Rodríguez de Villafuerte	10.0
Juan Crespo	9.0
Luis de León	9.0
Pedro Benítez	8.0
Alvaro Marín	8.0
Nicolás de Almazán y León	6.0
Hernando Alvarez de Carmona	6.0
Francisco Montoya	6.0
Pedro Hernández	5.0
Francisco Madueño	5.0
Alonso de Aguilar	3.0
Diego Martín	3.0

Sources: Francisco Xavier Echeverría y Morales, "Memoria de la Santa Iglesia de Arequipa," in *BMHA* 4:11-12, 2:265; and Jorge Polar, *Arequipa: Descripción y estudio social*, 3d. ed. (Lima: Lumen, 1958), p. 95.

Notes: * There is confusion as to the size of a *fanegada*, because two measurements were used in colonial Arequipa: one by royal officials, and one by Arequipans. The former measured 288 x 144 varas, or 7.19 acres. Arequipa's *fanegada* was smaller, but its measures are not given in documents. I have concluded that it was 150 x 150 varas, or 3.90 acres, as determined from statements that the measure used for the allotments given in this table was "cuatro solares por hanega" ("four *solares* per fanega"). Four *solares* made up a city block, with a length of 150 varas per side. The allotments noted in this table are in the smaller Arequipan *fanegada*.
\# Indicates that the recipient did not settle in Arequipa.

favored the group to which they belonged: had they more generously assigned land, they might have damaged the native economy on which their tributes depended.

Why, though, did the non-*encomenderos* receive tracts of such varied sizes? The differences probably reflected the officials' estimation of each man's social standing and possibly their evaluation of the quality of the land. When favoring certain persons, Carvajal and Torres chose from among those most like themselves, men such as Alonso de Luque and Francisco Gómez, men who either had seen service in the early conquest or who were members of respectable professions. Luque, for example, was related to

Bishop Hernando de Luque, who had assisted Pizarro and Almagro with the financing of the 1531 expedition to Peru, had become a notary in 1537, had subsequently served as a notary public in Lima, southern Peru, and Cuzco, and then had been a scribe for the town councils at Camaná and Arequipa in 1539 and 1540. Their kind, they may have reasoned, had only been denied Indians because of Pizarro's unwillingness to create minuscule *encomiendas*. Thus they should be treated like *encomenderos* in the land distribution. (Most of these men did receive Indian grants later, as such fell vacant.)

In distinguishing among artisans, leaders applied the same standards as Pizarro had in determining an *encomendero*'s importance and the size of his grant of Indians. Thus Juanes Navarro, who had fought during the 1530s, received approximately 24 acres; Diego Martín, without such service, received only 12. And Carvajal and Torres allotted larger parcels to older brothers when assigning farmland.[6]

Early Spanish *Chácaras* and *Estancias*

Despite the imbalance in landholding, most interested colonists initially exploited about the same amount of nearby land. *Encomenderos* usually lacked interest in their outlying Arequipan properties. Because they possessed Indians, such men preferred to exploit farms near the villages—and the accessible labor—of their tributaries. Other colonists only developed enough land in the Arequipa Valley to meet household needs.

Spanish proprietors developed their lands rapidly and easily. Most founders did not work their farms, or *chácaras*, as Arequipans came to call them. Instead, they oversaw laborers from the *villa*—the most common pattern—or delegated that responsibility to a poorer Spaniard.[7] Each used only a handful of workers. Laborers feel into two categories: those employed in small gangs for short intervals to plant and harvest crops; or those employed permanently (from one to several workers, depending on the size of the farm) to weed, tend, and protect crops, clean and maintain ditches, and irrigate the land. They only occasionally used black or imported Indian slaves. Peruvian Indians, almost exclusively, worked the *chácaras* from the outset.

Methods of procuring these Indians varied according to the owner's position. *Encomenderos*, with direct access to labor, received workers through the various regional *curacas*. They encountered some difficulty at first, because several grantees had Indians living far from the town, but they readily solved this problem by having temporary workers travel to the *chácaras* when needed and by settling a few other Indians permanently in the valley. For example, Francisco de Hinojosa brought six families to his *chácara* from highland Machaguay, the residence of many Indians under his control.[8] Those without *encomiendas* normally negotiated employment terms with *curacas* when hiring laborers. The laborers were supposed to receive wages and daily food allowances during these early years, but in all likelihood they received only food. Any other payments went to the *curacas*. This practice, common throughout Peru, eventually led the royal government to insist that each worker be paid directly, but the order was loosely enforced for over a generation.[9]

Spaniards, including *encomenderos*, also used other Indians, whom they described as *yanaconas*. The designation originally applied to a preconquest servile group in Peru; in Spanish Arequipa, as elsewhere, it referred also to Indians who had broken away from their communities after 1532. Spaniards settling in the town brought *yanaconas* with them. Unfortunately, their relationship to these Indians is unclear, though *yanaconas* appear to have worked for no wages, and Spaniards considered them permanently attached to particular colonists. Such workers offered *chácara* owners a stable labor force unencumbered by communal obligations and free of conditions imposed by *curacas*. The Indians, in turn, gained access to land and the time to work on it, and avoided tribute. Despite these advantages, their small number before the 1560s suggests that procurement of laborers from local *curacas* posed no major problem.[10]

The *chácaras* on which these *yanaconas* and hired Indians worked consisted of little more than open fields and irrigation canals. Only a few had crude, straw-roofed shacks, made of sticks, to house laborers and provide storage facilities. Instead, most Indians resided either near the town in compounds, as preferred by municipal officials, or on the house plots of farm owners. Colonists stored crops in their urban homes.[11]

At the outset, *chácara* owners emphasized Peruvian crops, particularly maize, since seed was readily available and Indians were familiar with its care. By 1541 they also grew wheat, which did so well that the town's curate managed to collect the tithe on it during the following year. Despite prohibitive import costs, some colonists soon added other Old World foodstuffs, such as grapes and olives. Still, the valley never became a center for diversified agriculture, because the settlers and their descendants found other local areas better-suited to the crops they chose to emphasize when European seeds and plants became cheaper. The valley fields thus continued throughout the colonial period to grow mainly potatoes, maize, alfalfa, and wheat.[12]

The early Spaniards also raised livestock in the Arequipa Valley. Since town leaders clearly did not expect all settlers to develop herds, they made no community-wide distribution of lands for this purpose. Most colonists had only a few animals for personal use and consumption, or as many as they could care for on a town common and on their *chácaras*. Beginning in 1541, those few colonists interested in raising livestock for market received exclusive rights to blocks of land for grazing and corralling.[13] These blocks, commonly referred to as *estancias* through the late seventeenth century, were originally as modest as 550 meters along the Chili River, but sufficient for pasturing small animals such as goats and sheep. In general, the Spaniards located their first *estancias* several kilometers from Arequipa, toward Tiabaya, on land that lacked irrigation canals. But since each bordered a river, animals could feed on the vegetation along the banks during the dry season from March to December, when natural pastures on the plains proved insufficient. Although ordinances drawn up at Camaná stipulated that owners build their corrals at least 1,400 meters from neighboring corrals, from common pasture lands, and from Indian farms and villages, the requirements could not be enforced in the Arequipa Valley, because of population density near the rivers. Nevertheless, farmer complaints of damage to crops were rare during the early 1540s, which suggests few *estancias* and a modest number of animals.[14]

Few *chácara* owners engaged in commercial agriculture. Arequipa's founders traded only agricultural commodities obtained from Indians through the *encomienda*. Because many colonists had only a half-hearted interest in agriculture, several claimed their tracts only when goaded by municipal authorities. None complained of land shortages. Rural property was plentiful, since some land recipients, including prominent colonial leaders, had no intention of residing permanently in the Southwest and were soon anxious to dispose of their shares.

Land Scarcity

Colonists in Arequipa became more interested in rural lands after the mid-1540s. The outbreak of civil war thrust the Southwest into the role of a food supplier for colonists elsewhere.[15] Following the war, that role continued as immigrants to Peru expanded urban markets. The demand for food raised in the Southwest contributed to price inflation in Arequipa throughout the 1550s. Local prices for wheat bread and most meats, for example, were high by Peruvian standards, often one-third above prices in Lima.[16]

Locals responded rapidly. Despite high prices, residents who had the means purchased Old World animals from those willing to deliver at the settlement; others, attempting to lower costs, either traveled or dispatched agents to procure livestock and seed in Lima and several colonial centers. The resulting growth in the number of small animals was startling: two Arequipan partners, for example, had over 650 goats by 1552; another pair owned more than a thousand head in 1557.[17] Although the number of larger livestock increased more slowly initially, it expanded impressively, which contributed eventually to a decline in prices. Cows, which had sold for around 65 pesos in 1550, dropped to 10 pesos in 1560 and to 2.5 pesos by 1575. Increases in crop production cannot be measured as accurately in the late 1540s and throughout the 1550s, but the gradually falling retail price for items such as wheat bread, even as the city's population expanded, proves that farm owners had also begun to raise greater quantities of European foodstuffs.[18]

This interest in farming and animal raising created a host of problems for the community and its surrounding Indian residents. A flood of complaints about the trampling of crops, the overuse of pastures near the city, confusion over livestock ownership, and the breaking of irrigation-canal walls forced the municipal council to revise the ordinances on *estancias*. These new regulations reserved an area of 4 kilometers around the city, which, if not farmed, made up a common; those who previously had had grazing rights within this circle could retain only their corrals. Beyond the common, city officials apportioned specific pastures and required corrals to be at least 2,000 paces from Indian lands, villages, and neighboring corrals. Compliance with these requirements did not absolve an owner from responsibility for any harm caused by his animals to surrounding crops, buildings, irrigation ditches, or pastures. In cases of crop damage, the aggrieved parties were to be compensated with seed or with shares of the offending livestock. The *cabildo* (municipal council) later established monetary fines.

Before long, the *cabildo* realized that animals actually caused relatively minor problems. The major damage resulted from *estancieros* and their hands who broke *acequia* (irrigation ditch) walls to divert water and improve their pastures during the dry season. Given irrigation's critical importance to farming, the council moved swiftly and ordered that any Spaniard caught destroying an *acequia* or impeding water flow be punished by a 50-peso fine and two-months' banishment from the vicinity of the ditch. An Indian or black was to receive one hundred lashes for a first offense and double that thereafter. Other measures required the branding of cattle and horses, as well as the segregation of various animals. The *cabildo* reserved the most stringent regulations for swine, which had to be kept 5 kilometers from all other animals and well away from irrigation canals because of their alleged danger to health.[19]

The *cabildo* also attempted to handle other problems plaguing farm owners. During the late 1540s, it adopted Licenciado Pedro de la Gasca's ordinances on water use. Anyone who possessed property alongside an irrigation ditch was now responsible for cleaning the portion adjacent to his land and keeping the *acequia* deep enough to prevent floods. When a ditch ran through vacant land, all beneficiaries had to share maintenance costs. The ordinances also created a committee of leading citizens to determine water rights and to record their awards in a book kept by the *cabildo*. To insure that each *chácara* owner received the assigned share, the committee required the placing of a hollowed-out stone that regulated the flow of water where the farm's *acequia* met the main canal. Although these ordinances never eliminated disputes, they did prevent a powerful few from monopolizing the valley's water supply and also enhanced the value of holdings, since water rights were transferable at sale.[20]

All of these regulations, however, failed to address the community's central problem in the early 1550s—the shortage of land.[21] Given the emerging zest of Spaniards for commercial farming and ranching, no one could confine Spanish landholding to that small portion of the Arequipa Valley from Chilina to Tiabaya along the Chili River (see map 2).[22] At first the *cabildo* responded mainly by apportioning new grazing sites to colonists from lands near towns like Pocsi and Chiguata, well away from the area farmed by Spaniards. Such allotments succeeded temporarily in relieving some of the pressure and helped satisfy Spanish farm owners' recurrent claims of damage to crops by the larger herds.

Yet the new sites posed problems. Surely Indians in these towns must have been quite unhappy at having livestock so close to their fields. And *estancieros* could also only use the land for part of the year, since the assigned pastures had no irrigation canals.[23] They adjusted rather rapidly by availing themselves of the vegetation on the coastal hills, which is at its best during the Arequipa Valley's dry season. Many successfully petitioned the *cabildo* for grazing land on the hills and valleys to the south of Camaná. Such grants were possible in large part because of Indian depopulation within the coastal belt.[24]

The *cabildo* could not so easily satisfy those who wanted farmland. Demand for *chácaras* centered on the Arequipa Valley, particularly the section closest to the city, because proximity enabled owners to oversee their properties while residing and working in the city. Few, especially among the post-civil-war newcomers, could afford to hire a manager for a more distant tract.

But there was little available arable land near Arequipa to distribute to Spaniards. With the exception of those parcels assigned to the founders, land continued to be held by Indians. Significantly, the valley's Indian population had declined less precipitously than in the Southwest's lowlands in the decade since the city's founding. With the altitude and climate shielding them from some diseases, their numbers declined about 10 percent, a pattern that continued for another generation.[25] Consequently, arable land could be provided the settlers only if the *cabildo* or other colonial authorities chose to strip the Indians of their holdings. Such a course was refused by these officials. Indeed, from the early 1540s, the *cabildo* granted land only when it could justify the action on the grounds that the land either had been unworked for some time or had formerly been of the Sun or the Inca.[26] The council even denied the petitions of powerful men, like Pedro Pizarro, for uncultivated tracts, because Indians argued that they might require the property in the future. Naturally, the *cabildo* would not allow Spaniards to misuse its infrequent grants to land. When an agent of the prominent *encomendero* Lucas Martínez Vegaso sought to use an *estancia* grant to infringe on the traditional croplands of some Indians and the matter was brought to the council's attention, it had the property remeasured and returned some land.[27]

Although the city governors could have provided unirrigated tracts to petitioners, they did not. The prohibitive costs of building major *acequias* made this pointless. Only a few irrigation projects of that type would be tackled later during the colonial period, and in nearly all instances they involved either a group of wealthy Arequipans, a religious order, or the city government. No one was prepared to take on the task during the mid-sixteenth century: the *encomenderos* had sufficient irrigated land or, like the others, insufficient funds.[28]

Those who wanted property had to purchase it, but sales were slow and resulted mainly from the death of an heirless founder or a decision by a landowner to emigrate. Prices invariably were high, a condition aggravated by land speculation.[29] The shortage drove some residents to squatting or even to farming on house plots or in the streets.[30] Eventually, as might be expected, it led to legal squabbles over rights to many holdings. In an attempt to gain some control over the deteriorating situation, municipal officials argued strongly in the early 1550s that settlers should not appeal such disputes to colonial officers other than the city's governors, who had granted the land in the first place. The *cabildo* also forbade donations and sales to religious orders on the grounds that these "did not have the [financial] possibility of cultivating the land and also had no livestock."[31]

Recognizing that the problem had to be dealt with more adequately, the municipal council yielded to the land-hungry with a major distribution of tracts. In 1557 it dispatched a commission headed by Hernando Alvarez de Carmona to search for lots in less densely populated Indian areas. The commission scouted the remote portions of the Arequipa Valley and along the Vítor River and found available parcels around Socabaya and in the upper Vítor Valley. The *cabildo* subsequently designated parcels in the Arequipa Valley as an additional common and had the others measured by Martín López de Carvajal into farm plots of 25 acres in preparation for a general distribution.[32] Their small size suggests that these plots, like many of those provided the 1540 settlers, were intended to provide for only an owner and his family. The Vítor land went primarily to newcomers: only three of the eighteen recipients for which there is evidence had resided in the city for more than two years. The difficulty that had faced anyone who wanted land before 1557 is evident in this group's experience, since just three had previously managed to buy a *chácara* in the Arequipa Valley.[33]

These grants pitted community interest against that of an *encomendero*. Francisco Pizarro had assigned the Vítor Valley's Indians to Miguel Cornejo and, on hearing of the projected partition, Cornejo's family immediately challenged the move, arguing that the land rightfully belonged to their Indians. The *cabildo* rebuffed the claim in what was probably an agonizing session; as both *alcaldes* and all but one *regidor* were *encomenderos*, they must have recognized that the land grants would limit the family's ability to expand *estancias* or farms. Nevertheless, they pointed out that these were unused lands and that the Indians would not need the tract, as the Cornejos contended, since most lived at some distance and toward the coast. One cannot help wondering whether the municipal officials reached this decision solely because of the *encomienda*'s status at the time. Miguel Cornejo, who had been a fairly important figure in Arequipa as an *encomendero*, *cabildo* member, and royal treasurer, had been killed only recently. The family's affairs consequently were largely in the hands of his widow, Leonor Méndez, a formidable woman but hardly of Miguel Cornejo's stature and thus no match for a determined *cabildo*. In any case, the decision so threatened the Cornejos that several family members later approached the royal government and secured a grant to some vacant land near the section taken for the partition.[34]

Ironically—but not surprisingly—the Vítor properties proved undesirable to many new owners. Though near the Arequipa Valley, they were still almost 30 kilometers from the city and therefore hardly convenient for those who preferred urban life. Their undeveloped state also posed problems: sizeable work crews would have to be formed to clear the land and put in irrigation ditches. (Colonists did not need major canals, since the plots lay along the Vítor River.) Because the non-*encomendero* recipients could not avail themselves of cheap labor, most chose to sell, with some eventually migrating to what they no doubt hoped were better areas where they might acquire an *encomienda* or fertile land.

Yet, since the *cabildo* had forbidden immediate resale to discourage speculation, disposing of these grants required ingenuity. The most popular expedient involved creating a dummy company whereby the seller pretended to contract for the land's development while the buyer pledged to clear and level the property, dig irrigation ditches, and do anything else needed to set up a farm. The buyer also agreed to provide slaves or Indian workers, livestock, and tools, in return for which he would receive half of anything produced during the contract period. A second agreement between the same parties often followed the development contract. By its terms the recipient of the *cabildo*'s land grant sold his half share of the produce to the developer.[35] Gifts were another way of transferring holdings. In these instances, some sort of under-the-table payment was likely involved, although the records, not surprisingly, are silent on this point. Suggestively, one man who formed various development companies also figured prominently as the recipient of an unusually large number of gifts.[36] Such stratagems eventually ended—with some proprietors openly selling their grants—because municipal officials did not monitor land exchanges closely.[37]

Land Consolidation

Encomenderos, merchants, and venturers ultimately acquired most of the grants along the Vítor River.[38] The disposition of these grants highlights an important development in Arequipa's rural ownership patterns. During the 1540s most settlers had held land. Over the next two decades the situation changed markedly, though, as *encomenderos*, merchants, and venturers gained control of farms located near the city and of *estancias* within the Arequipa Valley and the coastal belt. Their acquisitions and the consolidation of rural proprietorship depended on a number of factors, from personal proclivities, to good timing, to the costs involved in agriculture.

For most colonists, livestock raising had proved too expensive. Land was the least costly aspect of the industry: an unirrigated tract with corrals and shacks, even in the Arequipa Valley, went for only 100 pesos (of 450 maravedís each).[39] A prospective *estanciero*'s major financial burden was, of course, the stock, which initially had to be imported. During the late 1540s and early 1550s, cows sold for around 75 pesos each, mares, 175, mules, 300, goats, 16, and pigs, 15.[40] Thus the sale price for a stocked *estancia* ranged from 400 pesos to 1,600 pesos.[41] In addition, high operating costs attended the industry, probably discouraging those of moderate means who might have had sufficient funds to buy some animals.

Arequipa's *estancieros* relied principally on black laborers, usually slaves, in the early years. Some blacks were more familiar than were local Indians with Old World animals; the slaves also were more immune to the diseases introduced recently to the region and often lacked social and personal ties, thus facilitating their employment on isolated *estancias*.[42] Royal regulations forbidding Spaniards to transfer highland Indians to the lowlands, known to many of the *curacas*, may also have played a role in Spanish labor choices, once transhumance became common.[43] A male slave, in good health and around twenty years old, sold for at least 300 pesos in the early 1550s, and an *estanciero* normally would have two or three such workers.[44] Since few Spaniards could afford that kind of investment, livestock raising devolved to those who could.

Ownership of farms, unlike that of *estancias*, had initially included men of different social, occupational, and financial positions, due to the community-wide partition in 1540. Although high prices for European seed and saplings may have discouraged some of the poorer landholders at first and led to sales of land, they did not substantially change ownership patterns. Most founders who had only modest means and who survived into the 1550s kept their land and concentrated on maize and potatoes, selling any surplus of these native staples in local markets.[45] Land prices, however, made it difficult for the founders, and others who migrated to the city, to acquire additional property. The city government did not distribute much land between 1540 and 1557, so prices of rural tracts in the Arequipa Valley inflated. During the 1550s, cleared parcels with irrigation canals sold for 8 to 10 pesos an acre; few small plots were available, so the average selling price for a *chácara* reached 250 pesos.[46]

Forced out of the Spanish swath close to the city, those few poor colonists who became landowners did so principally by taking over farms abandoned by Indians in coastal valleys, where, as one such settler in the Majes Valley remarked, the Spaniards had to suffer isolation, the hot climate, and ferocious mosquitoes.[47] During the mid-sixteenth century, there was enough vacant land in the more livable sierra for only a few immigrants. Seizing Indian land or squatting proved difficult for individual Spaniards in the highlands, with *encomenderos* anxious to protect their interests and the Indians willing to challenge incursions with legal action or assaults on squatters. Only a few powerful colonists won court decisions involving highland-property disputes during the sixteenth century. Those of the regular clergy, such as the Franciscans, who had been assigned to the upper Colca River valley, may also have defended Indian land interests. They helped Indians with a number of other challenges from the Spanish community.[48] Thus, cut off from further land acquisitions, poor Spaniards were soon reduced to a minor element in the landholding community.

On the other hand, some *encomenderos*, merchants, and venturers expanded their holdings. A number, of course, had been given land in the early 1540s. Like other founders, those who survived into the 1550s retained their land, and the properties provided the foundation for their dominance of farming. During the first generation, *encomenderos*, on the whole, proved less aggressive than others in acquiring additional land close to the city. *Cabildo* and notarial records indicate that some petitioned for and received parcels from the local government. Most were small allotments given to those individuals who had their tributaries far from the settlement.[49]

Each *encomendero*, it seems, requested land primarily so that he would have a local tract on which to grow household staples. The *encomenderos* who went beyond this and purchased Arequipa Valley land often had been assigned Indians after Francisco Pizarro's time. They bought land because, after 1541, the *cabildo* seldom provided new *encomenderos* with rural property, as it had at the founding. This is understandable, since a few of the men who became *encomenderos* had been founders and already possessed *chácaras*; the others arrived when rural land was becoming critically scarce.[50]

Encomenderos' lack of interest in land close to the city persisted for some time thereafter because they could usually avail themselves of parcels near the villages of Indians under their control. This practice remained unchallenged by the royal government until the late 1550s, and even then enforcement of rules against it proved difficult. *Encomenderos*, however, had only so much land at their disposal, particularly in the still-populous highland valleys, where arable soil remained at a premium. Those with Indians in the sierra, not surprisingly, tended therefore to concentrate on stock raising and used pastures to graze a mixture of Old and New World animals.[51]

A select group of *encomenderos* moved more swiftly to secure title to lands in the Arequipa Valley. Nearly all were men like Juan de Castro, whose Indians lived close to the city of Arequipa. Starting in the early 1550s, this group bought land from their Indians, generally through the *curacas*, and they were extremely careful that these transactions adhered to Spanish legal requirements. Municipal officials, including the Protector of Indians, oversaw such sales, and, as the surviving documents detail, Spaniards subjected the Indians to painstaking warnings about the irrevocability of their decisions.[52]

Although some sales no doubt involved collusion between *curacas* and colonists, or may have resulted from forceful persuasion by *encomenderos*— a practice all too common in the Americas—communities occasionally sold land voluntarily. Certain *encomenderos* appear to have been so closely acquainted with and sympathetic to their Indians that they not only bought land from them but also represented them in property suits against Spanish usurpers.[53] Most of these *encomenderos* did not secure land for immediate resale.[54] In all likelihood, they acquired Indian tracts to produce staples such as wheat and wine for local and colonial markets. Their insistence on ownership rather than use of Indian lands may have resulted from fears that, as their tributaries declined in numbers and as land pressures continued to build, such tracts in the Arequipa Valley might become vulnerable to expropriation. Legal control insured their access.

Unlike the *encomenderos*, merchants and venturers actively purchased properties in the pre-Vítor grant days. Some took advantage of the reduced circumstances of a few *encomenderos* and usually bought the *chácaras* of men who had received small *encomiendas* and who were suffering from declining tributes as Indian numbers fell. They also acquired the farms of prospective emigrants or of deceased owners whose properties city authorities auctioned to pay off debts. They purchased other farms from *curacas* of Indians in the Arequipa Valley.[55]

Yet acquisition did not always lead to permanent landownership, since speculation was common among merchants and venturers.[56] Some merchants were temporary farm owners. As agents for commercial houses in Spain and Lima, they used the land to raise goods for colonial markets or to supply a particular individual. A number appear to have used lands near the city to provide goods for Pedro de Valdivia's Chilean expedition, after his business agent visited Arequipa. Although most merchants possessed land and exploited it as part of their expected business duties, a few did so without the approval of their superiors, probably in order to supplement their income.[57]

The more permanent merchant landowners very often became involved in stock raising and farming simultaneously.[58] Most probably were not agents of merchants based elsewhere; quite likely, they settled in Arequipa because the region proved more open to men of limited circumstances than did a center like Lima. Possessed of business skills, they established short-term partnerships with *encomenderos* and other colonists to raise the capital needed to buy land and livestock. As we shall see, some of these business alliances developed when merchants and venturers married into the families of *encomenderos*. A few enjoyed the good fortune of being related by blood to respectable citizens. Diego Bravo, for example, followed his brother, Padre Rodrigo Bravo, the city's first curate, to Arequipa and soon was dabbling in various trading ventures and in farming. In less than three years, he had accumulated four *chácaras* and owned at least 90 acres of prime land close to the Spanish settlement and several *estancias* where he grazed Old World livestock.[59] But his holdings were no more impressive than those of others who had come to control Arequipa's countryside a generation after the founding and who were now acquiring property in the Vítor Valley.[60] Few of Arequipa's landowners possessed huge tracts yet, but they did own increasingly valuable holdings.

Conclusion

Arequipan attitudes toward land changed dramatically between the early 1540s and the mid-1550s. Whereas many founders had regarded ownership of rural land rather cavalierly—so cavalierly, in fact, that some required prodding before they confirmed their rights to tracts distributed by town leaders—many colonists later scrambled for any available property that could be farmed. That Spaniards grew more interested in Arequipa's land should be no surprise. After all, the acquisition and use of rural property by Europeans remains a central theme in Latin American colonial history. But it is notable that land became important to southwestern colonists so rapidly.

Land's importance reflected several new purposes. To some, it became a valuable source of household staples—not a mean thing in an area where foodstuffs, particularly European ones, remained expensive. Others responded to agriculture's increased profitability. Spaniards in Arequipa enjoyed a growing demand for their livestock and crops unusually soon after the founding of their town. Their unique economic position when compared to that of settlers elsewhere in the Americas owed much to the region's escaping the ravages of battle during the early years of the civil war and to the combatants' need for supplies. Subsequently, *estancieros* and *chácara* owners found markets among postwar immigrants to Arequipa and the settlers of the newly developing centers in Chile and Upper Peru, areas advantageously located with regard to transport accessible to Spaniards in the Southwest. The southwestern experience substantiates the notion that Spanish colonists opted for capitalist ventures when circumstances made them possible.[61]

But southwestern settlers encountered some obstacles in their efforts to expand agriculture. Through the late 1550s their *estancias* and *chácaras* remained confined to a small section of the Arequipa Valley, along the Chili River, and to enclaves in the valleys and hills of the coastal belt. As in sections of Mexico at another time, agriculture suffered because of a shortage of arable lands; desert covered much of the Southwest. Then, too, like portions of highland South and Middle America well into the nineteenth century, Indians retained many of the region's best lands.[62] Early-colonial Indian farmers and herders survived in the Southwest because powerful colonists protected them. Some *encomenderos* as well as municipal and religious authorities responded to legal and moral strictures against dispossessing Indians of land. Others followed the dictates of economic self-interest. *Encomenderos* soon recognized the certain damage to their tributes if other Spaniards appropriated their Indians' land. (Perhaps this inducement needs to be highlighted among *encomenderos* elsewhere.) Native resistance and the unwillingness of colonists to live a rustic existence far from the city of Arequipa also discouraged Spanish land acquisitions.[63] Only when the native population began to decline severely, a situation evident in lowland Arequipa by the late 1550s, were there openings for the further spread of Spanish agriculture.

A varied group acquired land during the early years. The *encomenderos'* involvement is surely not unexpected, given their known association with a host of profitable business ventures throughout the Americas upon the founding of urban centers. What is remarkable is the extensive participation of so many other colonists in Arequipa. Indeed, they appear to have been the most active group. Non-*encomendero* founders, merchants, and venturers acquired land, some for temporary use, others more permanently. Further research must establish whether such broad involvement characterized the early years of Spanish agriculture elsewhere.

But broad participation in landholding in Arequipa did not mean that all settlers shared the countryside equally. By the mid-1550s, arable tracts increasingly came under the control of the wealthier, the better-connected, and the more-enterprising colonists. The dominance of such colonists would be the foundation of their subsequent consolidation of additional southwestern land.

3. Wine Estates and Landowners

La principal grangeria q' tienen los vs° son las vinas y el vino que dellas se saca . . . por ser los valles y tierras de su distrito acomodadas.

————Anonymous

The 1560s and the two succeeding decades were crucial in the economic history of Spanish Arequipa. Responding to the growth of consumer markets at Lima, colonial Peru's administrative center, and at the burgeoning mining site of Potosí, Southwesterners established an agricultural commercial economy in the coastal valleys to the west of the city of Arequipa. The exploitation of those valleys was primarily the work of some *encomenderos*, men who had the financial means and, given continued problems with their Indian grants, the incentive. Others participated as well, including venturers and a few merchants, generally those who had already invested in lands of the Arequipa Valley during and after the civil wars. Most emphasized the production of wine on small estates. The commercial economy they fashioned would endure through the eighteenth century; the landholding patterns along the coast persist to this day.

The Beginnings of Commercial Agriculture

Several small rivers running from the Andes to the Pacific traverse Arequipa's largely desert coastal belt, and it was along these rivers that Spaniards established their farms. Differences in soil and water conditions—there is a fairly high alum content in some rivers south of the Tambo—as well as colonial market opportunities and the individual preferences of landowners insured diversity of land use throughout the 1500s and 1600s.[1]

Thus a traveler crisscrossing the area after the mid-sixteenth century would have found parcels devoted to wheat and alfalfa, as well as to indigenous crops like chilies, maize, and potatoes. Spanish colonists also introduced fruit trees in many of the valleys, put in olive groves on the coastal hills, where winter mists provided some moisture, and raised various Old World animals wherever possible.[2]

Nevertheless, despite regional specialization, after the 1560s all rural ventures paled compared with viticulture. At the end of the sixteenth century, during which Arequipans enjoyed one of their most prosperous periods, wine from the western valleys, the heartland of the Southwest's commercial economy, had an estimated value of 1.5 million pesos (of ca. 300 maravedís each) per year.[3] By then, much of the other agricultural production within the coastal belt merely supported the wine economy.

Peruvian colonists relied almost exclusively on Andalusian wine for several decades after the conquest, but suffered from irregular shipments and high prices. Officials in various colonial centers sought to make the wine that did arrive available to as many Spaniards as possible by regulating prices, but their efforts failed, and sellers openly disregarded price ceilings. A lack of uniform prices in the colony aggravated matters; wine at inland markets, such as Cuzco's, was consistently dearer than at coastal settlements, a difference due not simply to transport costs but also to demand.[4] Merchants, constantly lured by these potential profits, moved wine to the interior, a practice that occasionally backfired when too many shipped to the same spot simultaneously.[5] Attempts to prevent the inland flow through trade restrictions proved as ineffective as did price regulation.

Because Arequipa was positioned on a major colonial trade route, its settlers naturally became aware of this lucrative commerce. Wine sold in the city from the late 1540s to the early 1560s regularly commanded higher prices than at Lima, which encouraged coastal shipments to the south.[6] As might be expected, the imports failed to satisfy local needs, because merchants funneled much of the wine through Arequipa to the highlands.[7] The potential benefits of a local wine industry may have been responsible for the request by settlers in the early 1540s that the Crown provide them with lands suitable for vineyards. The king sent an order of compliance, but hostilities prevented its execution.[8] Still, the explicit royal support for local viticulture would not be forgotten.

No precise time or place can be pinpointed for the emergence of the Southwest's wine economy. It probably began simply as an effort by some residents to insure their domestic needs; a few attempted plantings during the 1540s within the gardens attached to their urban house plots and in *chácaras*. After the Gonzalo Pizarro uprising, settlers became more active, concentrating vines on lands around the city, and by the mid-1550s they had productive vineyards near Tiabaya and Socabaya.[9]

Encouraged by the industry's possibilities, *encomenderos* instructed stewards to put in vines on lands near the villages of their Indians, and thus wine making spread to the lower elevations of surrounding highland valleys and to small, scattered, isolated plots throughout the coastal belt, from the Acarí River to the Atacama desert. These vineyards, particularly those in the highlands, proved of no long-range significance. Soil and climatic conditions hampered productivity and eventually forced their abandonment. Interestingly, *encomenderos* entrusted a few to Indians in hopes that the proceeds would help relieve tribute burdens, but, although the Indians did maintain several, they normally leased them to Spaniards.[10]

More organized efforts at viticulture date from the late 1550s. The wine economy then shifted to the valleys of the coastal belt west of the city. Desert plains and rugged hills between Arequipa and these sites hindered access by city-based owners, so they normally visited their properties only during pruning and the harvest.[11] But this location offered several advantages. The coast had a hot, dry climate akin to Andalusia's best wine districts. Marketing wine was easier from here than from highland valleys or more remote coastal locations: llama and mule trains reached the city of Arequipa and its Pacific ports in a few days.[12] Owners also found that they could shift needed workers to their vineyards from the city or surrounding *chácaras*. Later, colonists discovered that, by having grouped their estates in compact blocks, they were able to defend them when brigands began roaming the countryside.[13]

The first wine estates evolved from the 1557 *cabildo* land-grants along the Vítor River. The city council had intended that these parcels serve as *chácaras* for recent immigrants and relieve land pressures, but most recipients disposed of them. The following example suggests one way in which such land might have become wine estates. Employing the common ruse that he was contracting to develop lands for several recipients, Antón de Castro, a merchant, managed to buy three tracts in violation of the *cabildo* ban on sales and then acquired a fourth through donation. These were soon purchased by Diego Hernández de la Cuba, a newcomer to Arequipa who had secured an *encomienda* after the Gonzalo Pizarro revolt. Hernández de la Cuba, in turn, accumulated other properties until he had a block of ten parcels, which he sold to Francisco Madueño, who finally put in a vineyard during the 1560s.[14]

Colonists gradually expanded from their foothold on the upper reaches of the Vítor River into surrounding coastal valleys by acquiring much land from Indians—a development linked directly to the destructive effect of diseases. Indian *curacas*, at times acting on their own and in some instances for their communities, sold off lots and justified the transfers by claiming that the land was no longer needed. Many added that such sales helped them meet tribute loads, and more than one impartial observer concurred, commenting on the abandonment of Indian villages and lands in the wake of epidemics. (Naturally, some of these sales were for personal gain, but disguised by convenient pretexts.)[15]

Aware of the depopulation, the *cabildo* and, less frequently, the viceregal authorities, granted abandoned land to colonists who petitioned for it.[16] Additional property became available because of viceregal efforts to reduce Indian settlements. The Crown first pressed its Peruvian representatives to consolidate Indian villages during the 1560s, a process that culminated in the serious efforts of Viceroy Don Francisco de Toledo. Arequipa was drawn into the drive during the 1570s, especially after the viceroy's brief visit. The initial implementation of the new policy brought on a rash of Indian-land sales.[17]

Indians, however, retained some land along the Vítor, Siguas, Majes, and Tambo rivers through the late sixteenth century. The efforts to resettle them lasted only a few years: many Indians were unaffected; others who had been moved drifted back to their former holdings. Most Indians along these rivers farmed small plots adjacent to vineyards.[18] Some Indians even expanded their properties. Several *curacas*, living in these river valleys and in more remote ones to the north and south, built up fairly sizeable farms and raised crops for market.[19] But their successes should not disguise the broad trend: Spaniards dominated the lowlands. Significantly, viticulture's coastal orientation preserved highland Arequipa for Indian farmers and herders—a reprieve that would last, save for exploitation by royal functionaries, *encomenderos*, and occasional squatters, until the mid-seventeenth century.[20]

Arequipa's *Encomenderos* and Viticulture

Encomenderos possessed more vineyards than all other Southwesterners during the initial years of viticulture. By the late 1560s, almost a decade after the first vines were planted in the coastal belt, seventeen of the region's thirty grant holders certainly owned estates; another four probably did.[21] A few had the advantage of knowing their Indians well and so had acquired tracts fairly easily from them. Three of the four families that had held Indians in the western valleys since 1540 eventually owned estates on lands that had once belonged to their tributaries. One estate sprang from a *cabildo* land-grant that bordered a number of Indian farms. The Indians' *encomendero* first bought the property from the Spanish recipient and shortly thereafter purchased several of his natives' surrounding plots, thereby creating an estate. The other two *encomenderos*, as well as several relatives, also acquired land from their Indians, mainly through sales. None of the three *encomenderos* assumed that their grant of Indians included legal rights to land; consequently, they followed the appropriate Spanish legal formulas when purchasing tracts.[22]

Encomenderos had more important advantages than that of knowing potential Indian sellers. Their possession of *encomiendas* had provided them with the means to acquire and develop land. These men and their families had for years (some since 1540) profited by selling tributes and by exploiting cheap Indian labor. Some ventures, from modest mines to textile mills and construction companies, rested on their access to Indians and the gains they realized by marketing tributes. The experience of the Cornejos illustrates the extent to which these and other activities could benefit an *encomendero* family. Miguel Cornejo received a fair-sized (by Arequipan standards) *encomienda* from Francisco Pizarro, which included Indians in the Vítor and Arequipa valleys. (In the 1540s Spanish officials calculated that his adult male Indians totaled six hundred; Viceroy Toledo's assistants, prone to be more precise, enumerated 736 tributaries.)[23] A commoner like most other founders, Cornejo was not well off when he arrived in Peru. With his share of the treasure collected at Cajamarca and resources from his *encomienda*, he began to build up his interests in the Southwest.[24] A number of years after Cornejo's death in 1554, his mother-in-law, Juana Muñiz, temporarily oversaw the running of that part of the estate left to three of his legitimate minor children (table 2). Over the course of almost two years for which there are records, the estate's gross income was 5,624 pesos, 7 tomines. The largest single amount, derived mostly from mortgages on rural properties, provided nearly 2,100 pesos from interest and some repaid principal. Probably much of the capital for these loans had come from the sale of tribute goods. The *encomienda* continued to be a valuable source of revenue, yielding close to 1,900 pesos over the same period from tributes. Outlays for religious instruction—the only expenses incurred for the grant— totaled 170 pesos. The expenses while Juana Muñiz acted as guardian did exceed income by nearly 920 pesos, but the family hardly faced penury. The Cornejos could have cut back on such expenses as the purchase of European clothing and livery for black slaves. What is most important here is that the Cornejos, like many other *encomendero* families, poured a significant percentage of income into acquiring land and establishing vineyards along the Vítor River.[25]

Not all *encomenderos*, of course, throve on the proceeds from their grants, and thus a small minority could not avail themselves of the new

Table 2

Assets of Miguel Cornejo's Three Legitimate Children, 1569-1571

		Type of Asset		
Money	Labor	Real Estate	Livestock	Business Interests & Material Possessions
12 loans, of more than 12,407 pesos	8 black slaves	Houses in city of Arequipa	Cows, goats, sheep, mares on coastal hills near Quilca	Silver objects
		Shacks on outskirts of city (for Indian workers)	Oxen, horses in Vitor Valley	1 ship, docked at Quilca
		2 *chácaras* in Arequipa Valley		1 sugar mill with implements
		1 vineyard in Tiabaya (ca.20,000 vines)		2 wagons
		1 *chácara* and fruit farm with implements in Vitor Valley		
		Plot of land in Vitor Valley, for wheat		

Source: Eduardo L. Ugarte y Ugarte, ed., "Memoria y cuenta de Da. Juana Muñiz, vecina de Arequipa, sobre sus nietos hijos de Miguel Cornejo, 1570-1571" (unpublished, Arequipa, n.d.).

opportunities in viticulture. Some simply received too small a grant to accumulate the funds needed to take the plunge. As might be expected, a few others bungled their affairs. Pedro Godínez, for example, developed a number of *chácaras* and *estancias* during the 1540s. But although he subsequently added a tile works, financial problems engulfed him, forcing him to dispose of some urban property. By the early 1560s he even negotiated to sell his *encomienda*. He never managed to recover and survived mainly by speculating modestly in Indian goods purchased at government auctions.[26]

Unlike Godínez, most *encomenderos*, recognizing their temporary reliance on Indian tributes, shifted their energies and resources to viticulture. The declining value of their *encomiendas* was obvious: colonists talked frequently about Indian depopulation and also of the Crown's continued efforts to limit tributes. If some had missed the government's steady course to restrict *encomenderos* from the 1540s to the 1560s, they could not ignore royal intentions when Viceroy Don Francisco de Toledo visited the city. Toledo and his assistants had the Indian population counted and new tribute lists prepared.[27] The new lists scaled down the tribute allotment per Indian. They also favored indigenous crops and products over Old World commodities, and even allowed partial tribute payments in silver and gold.[28] Viceroy Toledo's measures struck at the common practice of requiring that Indians work on lands near their villages under the direction of *encomenderos'* agents. The success *encomenderos* had enjoyed in raising non-Indian foodstuffs had largely depended on this device, because of the Indians' greater willingness to work on these lands than to devote their own to unfamiliar crops. Royal policy, supported by the increased presence of district officers—*corregidores* and their lieutenants—in the countryside, now limited such work to the production of specific crops in prescribed quantities.[29]

The position of Arequipa's *encomenderos* eroded even further in the years that followed, as the Crown continued to uphold the principle that a grant's total obligation had to be revised when the population fluctuated. Additional, dramatic declines in the Indian population of the coastal belt occurred during the remainder of the century as epidemics, such as measles and smallpox in the 1580s and early 1590s, assaulted the natives.[30] Consequently, many coastal *encomiendas* yielded practically nothing. One in the Majes Valley, for instance, whose tributaries dropped from 164 to 51 between 1573 and 1594, provided the *encomendero* at the end of the century with only 53 pesos, 5 tomines and 3 granos of silver; 31.5 baskets of chilies; 25 baskets of coca; and 12 pieces of native clothing per year.[31] Given the paltry returns, a number of *encomenderos* eventually no longer bothered administering their grants, but simply rented them out.[32] The impact of the population losses was tempered somewhat because cost-conscious royal officials refused to monitor tribute payments regularly, a practice that enabled a few *encomenderos* to squeeze slightly more from their Indians.[33] Most communities handled this extra burden by borrowing gold or silver and raising cash through land sales or by working for Spaniards.[34] Thus, by the late 1500s, many *encomenderos* had the option either of making do with a few tribute goods that they might sell and decreased cash payments, or of finding another way to survive. Most turned to agriculture.

Arequipa's *encomenderos* by no means shifted to viticulture in concert. Those with highland grants hesitated. They continued to receive sufficient tributes to support their families during the late 1500s because diseases had not yet methodically reduced the Indians.[35] Nor did these *encomenderos* suffer as much as those with lowland Indians when royal officials emphasized indigenous products in the post-Toledo tribute lists. Climatic conditions and limited arable lands in the sierra had made it difficult for those with grants to introduce non-Peruvian crops, so they had adjusted by marketing native products. To their benefit, developments after the mid-sixteenth century increased the value of several highland commodities. Shipments of regional foodstuffs and of Spanish imports from Arequipa to Cuzco and Potosí caused a demand for pack llamas, the mainstay of many communities at higher elevations in Condesuyos and Cailloma. Indian clothing—another zonal staple—also became an important marketable commodity, following silver strikes at Castrovirreyna (immediately north of the Southwest) and then Cailloma, for miners needed protection in the inhospitable climes.[36]

Nevertheless, *encomenderos* of highland Indians eventually encountered grave difficulties that also encouraged their participation in viticulture. With the opening of the silver mines in the vicinity during the late 1500s, the Crown insisted that sierra Indians serve there and assigned such work greater priority than that required for tribute payments.[37] The situation worsened as the highland Indian population began to decline more severely during the seventeenth century and as *corregidores* and their assistants, at times in league with some *curacas*, habitually skimmed off a portion of the tributes.[38] Even some priests assigned to the area, increasingly seculars now, required that Indians labor for them as farmers, shepherds, and weavers.[39] *Encomenderos* could not stop such practices. Although officially committed to preventing the abuses, the Crown prosecuted only occasionally because of the cost and the influence of *corregidores* on powerful friends in the bureaucracy.[40] Often the best that an *encomendero* could hope for was that his interests might be tampered with only slightly or that he might share in the illegal activity. An *encomendero* foolish enough to challenge a *corregidor* on his home ground could run into trouble. Not surprisingly, at least one *encomendero* preferred to handle his complaints by dispatching an agent, only to have his emissary arrested and then embroiled in drawn-out litigation.[41]

Before matters reached this stage, most highland *encomenderos* embraced coastal agriculture, a decision perhaps influenced by further royal tinkering with tributes. During the sixteenth century, Arequipans held *encomiendas* with compositions determined in 1540 by Francisco Pizarro. Crown officials only occasionally divided grants, usually into two parts, to create new *encomiendas*.[42] Moreover, they did not disturb the rule that each grantee receive all tributes from his Indians. Payments to priests as well as to Indian and royal officers were built in over time, but these were for services, and the *encomendero* alone generally received the remainder.[43]

During the late 1500s and increasingly thereafter, royal measures forced *encomenderos* to share proceeds with others by tacking on recipients when grants passed on within a family or were reassigned. The beneficiaries might be institutions, such as a religious house or a hospital, but more commonly they were either men whom the Crown felt deserved a reward for signal service as administrators or military captains, or the widows or children of such men. On most occasions, these beneficiaries chose not to reside in the Southwest. This dispersion of revenues diminished the *encomenderos'* shares so much that many began to search for alternate sources of income.[44]

Other Early Estate Owners

During the 1560s, other Arequipan colonists sensed viticulture's potential. The most important non-*encomendero* developers of coastal lands proved to be venturers, men like Diego de Herrera and Francisco Madueño, who had recognized the value of farming the Arequipa Valley as colonial markets expanded in the 1540s. Some profited enough from their initial holdings and other investments to be in a position to acquire coastal tracts. Madueño, who, as previously noted, bought ten plots for an estate in the Vítor Valley, paid for this land with 300 pesos and sixty-two hundred roofing tiles. Venturers who did not have such resources turned to relatives. For example, Diego de Herrera's father-in-law, the merchant-*encomendero* Francisco Boso, helped him buy and develop an estate. Others, very often the mestizo sons of *encomenderos*, received land and the opportunity to exploit it from parents. In one instance, Diego Cornejo, given a share of family property, opened that tract and put in several vineyards. Finally, some Spaniards who married into *encomendero* and venturer families also acquired lands from in-laws; others probably received financial assistance that enabled them to purchase rural property and establish estates.[45]

Merchants, who, like venturers, had not shunned rural enterprises after the founding, avoided the rush to viticulture. Perhaps the delay in returns on capital dissuaded them: vines only became productive seven years after planting. *Chácaras*, in contrast, yielded earnings almost immediately: they only had to wait out the growing season for maize and wheat; in the case of livestock raising, profits followed gestation by only a matter of months.

The financial commitments required in establishing and operating a vineyard (discussed below) probably prompted merchant fears. An asset such as an estate might be seized should the merchant run into difficulties with creditors or customers—not an unusual happening, given the highly volatile market conditions of early colonial days.[46] The merchants' penchant for temporary residence was no doubt a factor also, so that the few who did buy in decided to forego merchant habits and become full-time landowners. Usually, like Juan de Quirós Vozmediano, they hesitated at first, waited until wine markets developed or vines matured, then bought developed lands.[47] Nor did other merchants ignore the industry altogether. Some, such as Andrés de Argüello, indulged in land speculation, buying tracts and disposing of them shortly afterward,[48] but most, acting as middlemen, bought what they could of the region's wines, brandy, grapes, and raisins in order to ship them, often through their own transport companies, to local and viceregal markets.[49]

The Opening-up of the Coastal Valleys

Although most persons who became landowners were well off by regional standards, they only slowly acquired land and built their estates. This financial conservatism was prudent, given the colony's limited markets and fluctuating prices. Such was the habit of Juan de San Juan, whose holdings at the time he began developing a wine estate are indicated in table 3. He minimized risks by owning a few *chácaras* in the Arequipa Valley (where he grew crops with a local demand), by renting urban properties, and by maintaining a profitable mill as well as livestock. As an *encomendero*, Juan de San Juan could also rely on such tributes as were still available, an advantage not enjoyed by many estate owners.[50]

Potential viticulturists of the 1560s and 1570s faced considerable costs. The undeveloped tracts in the Vítor Valley, which the *cabildo* had apportioned, sold for 40 to 50 pesos each. Land usually had to be cleared and *acequias* dug; some parcels also required leveling for irrigation. In one

Table 3
Assets of Juan de San Juan, late 1550s

Labor	Real Estate	Livestock	Business Interests
8 black slaves	3 *chácaras* in	100 cows	1 mill
Encomienda of	Arequipa Valley	1,000 pigs	
Arones Indians	Several houses on	500 goats	
	city plot	12 mares	
	Half of estate on	6 oxen	
	Ocoña River		
	(grapes and figs)		

Sources: BNP, ms. Z1264 (1562); ADA, Valdecabras, 9 November 1551, Torres, 21 February 1556, Hernández, 8 June 1556, Muñoz, 1 February 1557 and 29 October 1561.

instance, it took 928 man-days to prepare the property and begin the planting of forty thousand vines. The developer only employed eighty laborers, which suggests that Indian farmers had just recently abandoned the land.[51] Other Spaniards recruited much larger gangs—figures of as many as one thousand Indians are cited—solely for this initial clearing. Given the standard day rate of one real per worker, the expenses involved were significant.[52] Moreover, landowners had to purchase vines at exorbitant prices, since, like some seed and livestock during the early postconquest days, they imported them from Europe.[53] Because of their unfamiliarity with viticulture, prospective vineyard owners also recruited costly specialists. Unfortunately, little is known about the origins of these men whom Arequipans apparently found working for other colonists in coastal areas of middle Peru.[54] Favorable contracts and rumors of opportunity probably convinced them to emigrate to the South. Determined to moderate their investments, most estate owners did not pay their specialists a cash salary, but preferred to share profits from the land during the contract period (often seven years). Some provided a part of the developed property as well, when an agreement expired.[55]

The following example illustrates another cost-saving scheme. Juan de Pedroso, an immigrant with agricultural skills, secured a tract in the Vítor Valley in the late 1550s. After acquiring an adjacent plot, he negotiated with a backer in order to develop the land. His association with Diego García de Villalón lasted for six years, and, by the terms of their agreement, Pedroso promised to reside on the land for the life of the company and to do all required to improve it. He could not work on anyone else's property, and, should he purchase more land, the men would hold the parcel jointly. During the first three years, Pedroso had to put in as many fruit trees as he could, plant fifty thousand vines, and open up some land for a vegetable plot. García de Villalón, in turn, provided the capital needed for vines and fruit tree saplings and supplied the necessary tools and laborers, including Indians to clear the land and three black slaves for permanent work. They agreed to divide the harvest each year after meeting their expenses. Following the sixth year, each would get half the holding. García de Villalón, like many other merchants, eventually sold his portion.[56]

Specialists seldom endured as important regional landowners. One of the best records available on landholders in the region dates from 1583, when the Mercedarians, based in the city of Arequipa, compiled a list of proprietors along the Vítor River. As an attempt to regularize payments for one of their number handling pastoral duties in the valley, the friars assigned a monetary contribution to each owner in 1583 (Appendix B). Since some of these assignments were as low as 2 pesos per year, the list is very likely a complete profile of non-Indian owners in this valley.

A survey of notarial records from the late 1570s through the 1580s makes this seem even more probable, since the names of no other proprietors appear, save a few who had sold out to someone on the 1583 list or who had acquired tracts after it was drawn up.[57] The document reveals that most specialists who had held property a decade earlier no longer did so. Perhaps most had sold out for generous sums; as will be noted, Arequipan interest in viticulture persisted strongly throughout the last third of the sixteenth century and Arequipans bought land at high prices.

Time and local exposure to the wine industry also had an important effect on specialists' landholding. Over the generation that elapsed between the introduction of vines and the compiling of the Mercedarian list, others—often the mestizo sons of early settlers, but also some Spanish immigrants and even black freedmen as well as Indians—gained experience working in the vineyards. By the late 1570s, consequently, a developer rarely had to hire an outside specialist or trade land for an expert's services. Instead, he simply contracted with a local, who generally would work for a reasonable salary.[58]

Land, Labor, and Marketing in the Early Wine Economy

Most southwestern coastal belt estates ranged from 50 to 75 acres.[59] Their owners could have added to them easily by incorporating surrounding, unused lands, but this made no sense because the adjacent vast stretches between the rivers could not sustain crops or animals.[60] Before the 1590s and the concern for precise identification of the boundaries of a holding brought on by royal interest in selling vacant plots, many proprietors hardly bothered to lay claim to some parcels within the valleys. They ignored land too far from the rivers (which could only be worked by building prohibitively expensive irrigation canals) and hilly sections that required grading to water effectively.[61] The rather modest size of these estates may explain why locals only occasionally referred to the properties as haciendas, but preferred to call them *heredades*. Whatever the case, "*heredad*" seems an appropriate designation to employ here, for the term "hacienda" has lost precision, being, as it is, applied loosely to various types of rural holdings in Latin America larger than a modest farm.

Estate owners, or *heredados*, as colonial Arequipans frequently referred to them, used land intensively.[62] They devoted about a fourth of their holdings to vines, commonly employing several parcels to take advantage of the best soils, access to water, and exposure to sun. Each vineyard, in turn, was subdivided into sections to accommodate various types of grape.[63] The proprietors did not simply grow grapes initially but tried to maximize profits by handling all facets of wine making. Each *heredad* therefore had its own wine press, housed the *tinajas* (containers that held four hundred liters) in which the must matured in storage sheds, and possessed other storage sheds to accommodate jugs and tools. An estate also often included a building with ovens and other equipment to distill wine for brandy. Since the *tinajas* and the jugs used to transport wine were made on some estates, there might also be a workroom with potters' wheels, kilns, and vats for heating the pitch that lined these earthenware containers.[64] Constructing such buildings cost little: all structures were roughly built, with walls made of cane collected along the river banks and plastered with mud. The equipment stocked in an estate, being scanty, also required only a moderate investment. On Francisco García's estate during the 1590s, for example, there were two sickles, one saw, and twelve hatchets for clearing debris and vine pruning; several shovels, two hoes, and a plow were on hand to tend the fields. A few other tools, such as pliers, hammers, and chisels, were kept for building repair and other needs. After the early years, tools became quite reasonable, since *heredados* could purchase them from local artisans rather than rely on Spanish imports.[65]

The rest of the property supported the owner and his enterprise. *Heredados* frequently reserved a small parcel for raising oranges, guavas, peaches, apples, limes, and pomegranates. They occasionally put in olive trees as well, although most preferred sites on the coastal hills, because of better yields there.[66] Each estate also contained an alfalfa field and a *chácara* where vegetables, corn, and wheat were raised. The fruit grove and *chácara* supplemented the owner's income through local sales but served mainly to reduce costs by sustaining his family and workers; alfalfa fed the oxen used in ploughing and the horses and mules needed for transport.[67]

Arequipans rarely worked on or supervised their estates. Most *heredados* lived in the city, generally journeying to the coastal valleys only during the harvest and when workers pruned the vines (March and May). Their temporary residence explains, in part, why so many possessed no more than a crude country home. Don Francisco Zegarra's *heredad* in the Vítor Valley, for example, was furnished during the 1590s with a bed, several mattresses, blankets and bedspreads, a table and tablecloth, and a chest. His Arequipa home, in contrast, had such items as silver cutlery, candlesticks, numerous beds and cushions, tables, trunks, bureaus, chairs, rugs, and braziers. It also contained fine clothing, including many things of European origin. Like other *heredados*, Don Francisco Zegarra endured a rustic existence while in the field.[68]

Some owners, particularly the Jesuits, later constructed imposing rural structures and furnished them elaborately. Plate 2 reveals the accommodations on a seventeenth-century Jesuit *heredad*, which included cells (*celdas*) for the brothers assigned to the property, a drawing room (*sala*), a chapel (*capilla*), a kitchen (*cocina*), and a veranda (*corredor*). The main complex overlooked a patio that had on one side the storage sheds (*bodegas*), the wine presses (*lagares*), the storage and potter's sheds (*ollerías*) as well as ovens (*hornos*). The workers' living quarters and an *acequia* bounded the other sides of the patio. (These structures appear in the lower half of plate 2, which is a detailed drawing of the left-middle portion of the diagram above it. The diagram is a good illustration of what a Vítor Valley estate looked like. The vineyards lay adjacent to the river; an *acequia* ran between the vineyards and the living quarters. A wall-lined lane, or *callejón*, divided the Jesuit property from that of its neighbor. A road, the Camino Real, connected the *heredad* to Arequipa.)[69]

A shack close to the owner's housed the estate's manager, or *mayordomo*, who supervised the day-to-day operations of the *heredad*. Landowners usually hired such men on one-year contracts to keep accounts, guard equipment, and oversee laborers during the harvest, the pruning of vines, and the wine making. They received lodging, food, and wine as well as a cash salary. Owners avoided the need to come up with the salary all at once by spreading payments. They customarily advanced a small sum and then paid the remainder quarterly or biannually. A good administrator on an average-sized *heredad* (ca. 60 acres) could expect as much as 320 pesos (of ca. 300 maravedís each) during the late 1500s, an impressive annual salary that revealed the crucial role such men played. Skilled *mayordomos* retained a strong bargaining position throughout the sixteenth century, even though their numbers increased as others learned the trade from Spaniards. Provisions in their employment contracts required that *heredados* pay

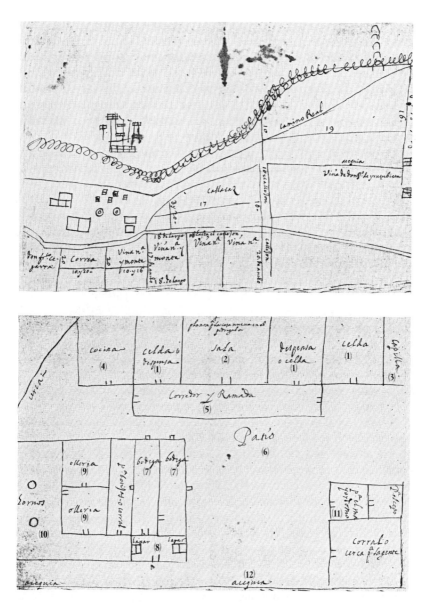

Plate 2. Jesuit *Heredad*, Vítor Valley, 1650s

Key: (1) *celda*; (2) *sala*; (3) *capilla*; (4) *cocina*; (5) *corredor*; (6) patio; (7) *bodega*; (8) *lagar*; (9) *ollería*; (10) *hornos*; (11) workers' living quarters; (12) *acequia*

Source: ANP, Compañía, Títulos, leg. 3 (1628-1652).

salaries on time and that, if they failed to do so, they had to pay double. Nor could owners dismiss managers without reasonable cause. At times, a particularly talented *mayordomo* received exceptional benefits: some had their clothes cleaned and were given lard as well as candles; a few got a mule or a horse. The fear that good managers might leave in search of better conditions or a higher salary led to a contract clause that stipulated that they must remain on the estate (except for trips to procure labor) and that failure to do so meant that they lost the portion of the year served.[70]

Indians constituted most of the rest of an *heredad*'s work force during the late 1500s. Estate owners employed temporary gangs at harvest, often recruited by negotiating with *curacas*. Sources are vague on the areas tapped for laborers, but a few hint that managers usually traveled up the coastal rivers into Condesuyos.[71] Royal decrees excluded drafted Indian workers from estate labor. Not enough Indians to support such a system lived within the coastal belt when the industry got started. In addition, Viceroy Toledo specifically exempted highlanders during the 1570s.[72]

Nevertheless, Arequipans attempted to devise a labor draft. During recurrent crises, especially after one of the region's earthquakes, viceroys relaxed the laws forbidding highlanders from working in the lowlands. Arequipans petitioned to prolong the span of these temporary exemptions, no doubt hoping that the draft would thus become permanent.[73] When their pleas gained only a few extra months, they resorted to other expedients. The most common was to divert Indians assigned as drafted laborers for the farms in the Arequipa Valley, a practice that continued into the seventeenth century despite the objections of some native leaders.[74]

The only legal draft secured by *heredados* was implemented to transport wine to inland markets. During the 1580s viceroys assigned highlanders from Cailloma and Condesuyos to such work from time to time. Don Fernando de Torres y Portugal regularized the system in 1591 by ordering the *corregidores* of Cuzco, La Paz, Chucuito, Cabana, Los Collaguas, and Arequipa to provide Indians—5 percent of those available after the Potosí draft had been met. Royal officials assigned these Indians to colonials who required that the natives bring their llamas to the headwaters of the coastal rivers, load the wine, and transport it to interior Peru.[75]

Other Indians served as wage laborers on the *heredades*. An average-sized estate had a dozen year-round workers who lived on the property and planted, tended vines and crops, cared for livestock, and irrigated.[76] This force included women (generally the mates of male Indian laborers), who not only worked in the field but also did household chores for the *mayordomo* and *heredado*. Like native wage laborers on the *chácaras* of the Arequipa Valley, colonists probably hired these Indians through *curacas*.

Later, during the seventeenth century, they recruited more and more from among those who had abandoned their Indian homes. By the 1560s and 1570s, such workers signed on annually. Owners regularly promised to provide enough cash to cover their tribute obligation, clothing, religious training, and medical attention. Some workers also received food or a small parcel of land to farm. In the latter case, Indians normally built their hovels near these plots. Wage workers thus cost estate owners very little initially. An *heredado* who fed a healthy Indian for a year would expend around 25 pesos.[77] Since the Indians had usually been farmers, the colonists encountered little difficulty when they introduced them to the *heredad*'s field work. Nonetheless, certain chores, such as brandy making, shoeing horses, carpentry, making and fixing tools, demanded the skills of itinerant specialists of Spanish origin. Soon, though, Indians and mestizos replaced the Spaniards. For example, Indians from Caravelí, a region where pottery had flourished before the conquest, adapted their talents to making *tinajas* and jugs.[78]

Arequipa's *heredados* depended on few outsiders during the early years. Even in marketing their goods, most forged direct ties with retailers in Arequipa and at markets throughout Peru. Sometimes they simply bartered wine and brandy for needed commodities and services. *Heredados* often handled their own transport as well, either by using their livestock and workers, by availing themselves of drafted laborers, or by contracting with a carrier. In exceptional cases, owners had boats that delivered their wine to markets along the Pacific coast.[79]

The relatively low cost of land and labor, the self-sufficiency of *heredades*, the small investment required in buildings and equipment, and the owner's control of marketing made sixteenth-century Arequipan estates quite profitable. Average-sized holdings could accommodate some thirty thousand vines on 15 to 20 acres. Their yield in a good year, depending on the grape strain, might be converted into six thousand *botijas* (earthen jars that held eight liters) of wine. If wholesaled at 4 pesos each, an average price for common white and red wine during the late 1500s, this volume of production would bring in a gross income of 24,000 pesos (of 8 reales each).[80]

Conclusion

Viticulture's sudden emergence in the Southwest during the generation after the 1550s was but a continuation of the colonists' early interest in commercial agriculture. The expansion of Peruvian markets following the civil wars combined with local factors encouraged Arequipans to exploit the countryside further. A particularly important local development that encouraged agriculture was the increased availability of land, the result of Indian depopulation and resettlement in the lowlands. That coastal agriculture became synonymous with viticulture owed much to peculiar regional conditions. The soil and climate in the valleys to the west of Arequipa proved ideal for grapes, but not for extensive livestock raising or for crops such as wheat. Of course, Spanish dietary preferences, a colonial shortage, and wine's greater imperishability than many other rural products encouraged the industry as well. Arequipans, then, were among the first settlers to fashion a local economy that concentrated on raising special products of European origin for colonial markets.

During the early days, the wine economy attracted a variety of people. But viticulture's financial demands soon forced out those of modest means. *Encomenderos* remained an important group within the landowning community. *Encomendero* rural proprietorship was hardly unique to the Southwest. Mario Góngora, for example, has painstakingly reconstructed their involvement as *estancieros* in Chile.[81] Significantly, some *encomenderos* in both Peru and Chile built their estates on land acquired from their Indians. This was natural enough: given agriculture's promise, grantees turned to the landholders they knew best—their tributaries and *curacas*. No evidence exists that any southwestern *encomendero* assumed that a grant of Indians included legal rights to land; consequently, any who sought to own property that belonged to their Indians followed the appropriate Spanish legal formulas when purchasing a tract.

In Arequipa, however, undue importance should not be attached to an *encomendero*'s close ties to his Indians when considering Spanish land acquisition. Although a few *encomenderos* did have Indians who lived in the coastal belt and from whom they acquired land for *heredades*, most had Indians who resided elsewhere. The great majority of grantees therefore purchased land from Indians of other *encomenderos*. Yet, almost all *encomiendas* proved extremely valuable assets to potential estate owners. The exploitation of Indian grants, no matter their location, provided *encomenderos* with the capital necessary to take up viticulture. Only a few others in the community, venturers and merchants who had invested in agriculture during the 1540s as well as those connected to people of means, could participate alongside the *encomenderos*.

Heredados proceeded slowly as they established and developed their estates. They balanced investments over several enterprises and contained costs by making their *heredades* as self-sufficient as possible. In this respect, Arequipan landowners acted much like proprietors elsewhere in Spanish America. Both James Lockhart and Herman W. Konrad have emphasized the enduring importance Spanish estate owners gave diversification and risk spreading. The techniques served to protect the landed from the vagaries of market forces, so often a problem during the colonial period. Only at a later time and in a few places would certain estate owners devise other approaches, such as price fixing or holding back crops from market, to safeguard their interests.[82] In sixteenth-century Arequipa diversification and risk spreading functioned well, guaranteeing *heredados* a decent return on investments.

4. *Encomenderos*, Landowners, and Society in Sixteenth-Century Arequipa

*Los que poseen estas tierras [del Perú] son los mas ricos y
antiguos descubridores y conquistadores del Reino y sus hijos y
descendientes y otras personas aquien estos las han vendido y
todas las tienen Rompidas Labradas plantadas y mejoradas e con
edificios y algunos han hecho mayorazgos con facultad de vm^d
porque al principio entraron todos en ellas sin ninguna contradi-
cion dando los virreyes y governadores muchas gracias y ayuda.*
————Viceroy Don García de Mendoza

It has become increasingly common, as Magnus Mörner has observed, for
colonial historians to emphasize economic interests as primarily responsible
for Spanish exploitation of the American countryside.[1] Indeed, such a
perspective informs the preceding chapters. This approach contrasts with
the older view that the settlers' rural concerns, particularly their ownership
of land, largely reflected status needs. The early colonists, the argument ran,
sought property because they identified social prominence with major
landholding, an identification they carried over from the Old World.
Although the Arequipan case provides little evidence to uphold this
contention, it does suggest some extremely important relations between land
and society. From the 1540s to the 1590s, land use by *encomenderos* served
to reinforce and prolong their acquired social preeminence. And, after the
1550s, the development of coastal *heredades* also made possible modifica-
tions in the Southwest's non-Indian social structure and allowed for the
incorporation of newcomers and the social advancement of some
descendants of early non-*encomenderos* in the community and in the
Spanish world.

Spanish *Encomendero* Society of Early Southwestern Peru

Arequipa's Spanish founders were a mix of commoners and minor nobles (*hidalgos*). The group's social status was typical of the early colony. As James Lockhart has noted, Spanish Peru's settlers were seldom high nobles before the civil wars of the mid-1540s.[2] Admittedly, Arequipa had fewer *hidalgos* than centers like Cuzco and Lima. The regional origins of Arequipa's colonists also matched those of settlers elsewhere: the largest contingents came from Andalusia, Old Castile, and Extremadura.[3] Occupationally, they included as did Spaniards in other settlements, men of affairs, merchants, notaries, churchmen, and artisans. Later arrivals, those reaching the city through the early 1550s, did not significantly alter the population makeup, but simply expanded the subgroups already present. The only notable exceptions were the women who began to arrive in large numbers after 1548, a development common throughout the colony once the violent infighting ceased.[4]

Despite their rather homogeneous background, Arequipa's early colonists by no means lacked social distinctions. From the outset, the *encomenderos* stood out as especially favored, as did other men assigned Indians elsewhere in the Americas from the 1490s on. In general the size of an *encomienda* and the quality of its resources translated into the degree of social prestige enjoyed by a recipient. The various political posts held by the *encomenderos* also reflected the distinctions among Spaniards. Although grantees as a group monopolized local governmental offices for several generations, the better-rewarded won the best posts. Pizarro initially appointed them to serve as *regidores* and *alcaldes* of the town; later they perpetuated their position by controlling annual elections. Some secured additional political power during the early years by filling local offices in the colonial bureaucracy, principally in the royal treasury.[5] Nevertheless, despite the gradations in their ranks, all *encomenderos* were conscious of their unique stature in the community and soon placed further distance between themselves and others. They dropped such socially ill-regarded labels as "merchant," which some had used previously in characterizing themselves.[6] More importantly, several strove to be quite selective when they chose spouses.

Only a few marriages were possible in the new town during the 1540s, for males predominated. Moreover, many had wed before arriving in Arequipa but had left their wives in Spain or in older New World settlements. Most remained separated from their spouses until after 1548, largely because of civil strife. They lived, as did most bachelors, with Indian concubines brought to the Southwest.[7] Those *encomenderos* who did marry during the early years preferred Spanish women from respectable families, meaning a spouse from another *encomendero* family or from the family of a colonial official. Such a match was arranged, for instance, by Captain Diego Hernández, who wed María de Mendoza, the daughter of Cristóbal Dervas, an early governor of the city. After Dervas died, another *encomendero*, Captain Francisco Noguerol de Ulloa, married his widow. Frequently the early marriages revealed the affiliations of settlers and Peruvian conquest leaders: all three husbands just mentioned, for example, had at one point been associated with Marshal Diego de Almagro; families of Pizarro's supporters as well intermarried in several cases.[8]

Despite the *encomenderos'* desire to base their marriages on such associations, as well as on business partnerships and even on common regional origins, they could not afford to be too choosy, given the shortage of Spanish women in the colony. Still, most avoided marrying into the families of merchants and artisans. Men like Miguel Cornejo and Alonso Rodríguez Picado wed women like Leonor Méndez and Juana Muñiz, whose major recommendations were Spanish birth and legitimacy; neither woman would have the stature to merit consistently the respectful designation "doña." These marriages illustrate in yet another way the *encomenderos'* limited choices. The men were not of equal local prominence, since their *encomiendas* differed in size and value, but they married sisters, the daughters of Alonso Méndez and Juana Muñiz.[9]

Events of the 1540s dictated that Arequipa's *encomendero* community would undergo constant change in its composition. The initial changes, following the assassination of Governor Pizarro in mid-1541, were minor. Although the new governor, Diego de Almagro's son, stripped the original grantees of political power, he chose to respect the *encomiendas* of Pizarro supporters.[10] During the civil war that ensued, most of Arequipa's *encomenderos* avoided the conflict, waiting until shortly before the rebellion's end to oppose Almagro openly.[11]

Yet, because a few finally committed themselves and fought in the decisive battle at Chupas in 1542, alterations in the *encomendero* community followed.[12] Two grantees, Captain Andrés Jiménez and Gómez de Tordoya Vargas, were killed at Chupas, and Licenciado Cristóbal Vaca de Castro, the new royal governor, reassigned their Indians. Jiménez's went to his son; Hernando de Silva received those of Gómez de Tordoya Vargas. Silva, already an *encomendero*, had been one of the few to voice opposition to the Almagro government set up in 1541 and had had his grant seized; he later joined the Pizarro faction in fighting in Cuzco. Only three other Southwesterners, Gómez de León, Garcí Manuel de Carvajal, and Juan de la Torre, received new Indians in grants that recognized their resistance to the rebels.[13]

Licenciado Vaca de Castro's six other assignments of Indians in the Southwest introduced into Arequipa's *encomendero* aristocracy new elements, Spaniards who had accompanied him to Peru and colonists from elsewhere who had fought well. For instance, Captain Alonso de Cáceres came with the judge to serve as a royal accountant; Lope Martín valiantly scouted Almagro's troops and positions before Chupas. All save Martín soon moved to the city of Arequipa. None except Cáceres came from a better social background than the important original *encomenderos*. This and the moderate size of the assigned grants apparently eased the newcomers' integration into Arequipa's elite.[14]

More radical changes in the ranks of the *encomenderos* resulted from Gonzalo Pizarro's subsequent uprising. At first Pizarro did not tamper seriously with local grants. He had no cause to do so, for most Arequipans supported his opposition to the Crown's New Laws. In a town meeting they voiced their determination to ignore the orders and then joined his forces in ousting the newly appointed viceroy.[15] Those who showed less enthusiasm Pizarro handled astutely by allowing them to live in Arequipa peacefully. He stripped the *encomiendas* of only a few irreconcilables and exiled them to La Villa de la Plata.[16]

Nevertheless, events soon led to a hardening in the attitude of Pizarro's officials. By 1546 opposition to Pizarro's revolt surfaced in the colony, including armed resistance under Diego Centeno's leadership in southeastern Peru. When Gonzalo Pizarro's army crushed Centeno's forces, Centeno fled to Arequipa where he was almost certainly apprised of hiding places there by Luis de León, an exile who had supported the viceroy.[17] Suspecting some of Arequipa's *encomenderos* of aiding Centeno, officials harassed them and on occasion removed their Indians.[18] As royalist resistance escalated, the civil war entered a violent stage. Aware of the royal government's determination to end the rebellion, many Arequipans openly switched sides, joined Centeno's new army, and summarily replaced Lucas Martínez Vegaso, Pizarro's lieutenant in their city. Quickly the *encomenderos* dispatched Garcí Manuel de Carvajal to Licenciado Pedro de la Gasca, the new president of the Audiencia of Lima, to assure him of their loyalty to the king.[19]

Southwesterners paid a heavy price for their defection. Pizarro met Centeno's forces in the Battle of Huarina and routed them;[20] the governor's troops subsequently removed the wives and relatives of several royalists from La Villa Hermosa to Cuzco.[21] To this day Arequipans recall, in a familiar poem, the damage visited on the city:

Yo la villa más hermosa

> *De Arequipa, la excelente*
> *Lamenté sólo una cosa:*
> *Que en Huarina la rabiosa*
> *Se acabó toda la gente.*[22]

Despite the heavy costs, survivors slowly made their way to Andahuaylas, where they joined La Gasca's army.[23] In April 1548 the two sides met in the valley of Jaquijaguana, where the royalists, aided by mass desertions of former Pizarro partisans, prevailed.[24]

By the end of the 1540s, Arequipa's *encomendero* population had significantly changed from that at the founding; only ten of the more than thirty men assigned grants by Francisco Pizarro survived and just five of those had their grants pass on to sons, widows, or relatives.[25] Most losses probably resulted from battles: twelve of the thirty-four who held *encomiendas* when the rebellion began in 1544 were killed.[26] The civil war pruned the *encomendero* ranks in other ways. At least two men, Lucas Martínez Vegaso and Hernando de Torres, lost their grants (the former temporarily) because of their complicity in the rebellion. Another, Hernando de Silva, settled elsewhere in Peru because his singular service to the royalists earned him a larger *encomienda* in the non-Arequipan highlands. Others left Peru, possibly frightened away or weary of the turmoil, gave up their grants and returned to Spain.[27]

With so many *encomiendas* vacant, La Gasca had a difficult task assigning them. He wisely attempted to isolate himself and avoid the intense lobbying that was sure to occur, but a few hopefuls still managed to press their cases in audience. The men he selected and those his successors chose for southwestern grants were a varied lot.[28] A small number of the original *encomenderos* enhanced their position. For example, Francisco Noguerol de Ulloa, who had met most requirements for a major *encomienda* in 1540 but had been denied such a grant because of his Almagro affiliation, now was assigned the Yanque Collaguas to reward his active support of the Crown. This *encomienda*, formerly held by Gonzalo Pizarro, was the best in the region, and replaced his grant of the Ubinas, which went to Garcí Manuel de Carvajal, Arequipa's early leader and wartime ambassador to La Gasca's *audiencia*. Significantly, a handful of founders, men like the notary Alonso de Luque and the merchant Nicolás de Almazán, who had missed out on grants in 1540, secured Indians as well, generally because they had switched to the royalist side early or had played leading roles late in the war. Hernando Alvarez de Carmona, to cite another, had helped plan Lucas Martínez Vegaso's capture and removal to Cuzco.[29] Men other than the founders filled the remaining vacancies. Most whom La Gasca selected had come to Peru before Gonzalo Pizarro's uprising. Hernán Rodríguez de Huelva, for example, an immigrant from Panama in 1542, resided in Arequipa during the early years of the civil war, then went to Cuzco, and later joined Centeno to fight at Huarina. After the defeat there, Rodríguez de Huelva fled to the royalists in central Peru and fought at Jaquijaguana.[30] Notably, few wartime arrivals to Peru secured grants, despite the flood of such men during the final years of the rebellion. The only newcomer who managed to win an *encomienda* in the Southwest, Diego Hernández de la Cuba, did so in an unorthodox way—by convincing an *encomendero*'s widow to marry him rather than her husband's nephew, to whom she had previously committed herself.[31]

Social Developments in Postwar Arequipa

Following Gonzalo Pizarro's defeat at Jaquijaguana, the social distinctions that raised Arequipa's *encomenderos* above others in the community sharpened. *Encomenderos* could now select spouses whom colonists judged suitable to an *encomendero*'s social position. The conclusion of the rebellion brought an influx of Spaniards to Peru, and, by then, the marriage pool had also broadened, because the children of some *encomenderos* who had managed to marry or maintain Spanish households during the early postconquest years had reached maturity. A spate of marriages followed in Arequipa: single *encomenderos*, some now quite old, finally wed, as did most widows, including the many left husbandless by the bitter civil war battles. Although the grantees with the most tributaries generally garnered the best marriage partners, almost all did well. Juan de San Juan and Juan de la Torre, for example, married sisters, Doña Lucía de Padilla and Doña Beatriz de Casillas, respectively. (Juan de la Torre's former wife, Ana Gutiérrez, had not been a "doña.") Lucas Martínez Vegaso's bride, Doña María Dávalos Ribera, was the daughter of Nicolás de Ribera, a notable citizen of Lima and an *encomendero* who could date his participation in the Peruvian conquest back to Gallo Island in 1527. Nicolás de Almazán y León wed Doña Olaya Merlo de la Fuente, the aunt of a judge in Lima's Royal Audiencia. Widows like Doña Ana Chacón, Juan de Andagoya's widow, married Licenciado Miguel de Cuéllar, a resident of Lima who had once served as Arequipa's *corregidor*; Doña María Rodríguez wed Captain Pedro de Melgar; and Francisca Navarrete, once married to Alonso de Buelta, was betrothed to Captain Francisco de Grado.[32]

Strikingly, most Arequipans chose to marry outsiders. Most *encomenderos* and widows seemingly regarded marriage among their kind in the Southwest as socially suspect. Colonial opportunities were such that they could wed into the more prominent families of leading Peruvian *encomenderos*, recently arrived nobles, or well-placed royal officials. The same pattern prevailed among the *encomenderos'* few legitimate peninsular-born and American-born children who wed during these early years, except those whose fathers had died before their marriages. Diego Hernández's son (Diego Hernández de Mendoza), for example, chose Doña María de Guzmán, the daughter of another *encomendero*, Hernando Alvarez de Carmona. Although the match was between unequal families—Hernández's *encomienda* not only was larger than that of Alvarez de Carmona, but also had been assigned to the family by Francisco Pizarro—a very generous dowry of 12,000 pesos smoothed the way. He wed Doña María because he lacked contacts elsewhere, and he probably did not receive much help from his mother and stepfather, with whom he was squabbling. His sister also married in Arequipa, though to an immigrant, Juan de Castro Figueroa.[33]

Despite the outside marriages, Arequipa's social elite did not become substantially larger during the late 1550s and throughout the 1560s, because of the increasingly popular habit of grantees, most often those with the more valuable *encomiendas*, of residing outside the Southwest. A few, like others during the pre-civil-war days, returned to Spain—some for a sojourn that became permanent, others intending to stay. Although several may have traveled home to marry and handle affairs, men like Captain Francisco Noguerol de Ulloa must also have relished displaying their new wealth.[34] Another handful, though technically remaining citizens of Arequipa, chose to live for long periods in Lima, attracted no doubt to its viceroys, *audiencia* officials, their relatives and hangers-on, as well as to Spanish nobles who had previously shied away from chaotic Peru. The major *encomenderos* of the Southwest surely were at ease in such circles. Conquest and wartime feats in addition to their impressive Indian grants and recent distinguished marriages helped overcome humble social origins. By settling in the colony's capital, they could best promote their economic interests and other ambitions. Nor was residence outside Arequipa restricted to males. Widows of some *encomenderos* spent much of their lives in Lima, often marrying prominent Spaniards of that city.[35]

The exodus of *encomenderos* and widows, along with the marriages to non-Arequipans of those who remained, modified the character of Arequipa's upper society. Two distinguishable subgroups can be identified: one comprised the few surviving major *encomenderos* granted Indians in 1540 and those assigned important *encomiendas* shortly thereafter; the other included the remaining grantees. Whereas persons in both subgroups might cooperate in business ventures and share political power in the municipal government, those in the latter subgroup clearly were socially inferior. It is hardly conceivable, for example, that a Diego de Peralta Cabeza de Vaca and a Martín López de Carvajal regarded themselves as equals.

Cabeza de Vaca, after all, had fought in conquest battles, had been a royal supporter and a captain during the civil wars, and had married Doña María de Robles y Solier, the daughter of a Lima citizen who had also been a captain in early Spanish Peru. (After her husband's death, Doña María's mother had wed Captain Alonso de Cáceres, an Arequipan *encomendero* who had an impressive social background and who became a *corregidor*.)[36] Martín, on the other hand, of mean background, had secured a modest grant primarily because he was an Extremaduran. Although a remarkable man who served the city in many posts and enjoyed some success in business, he never fully transcended his humble social origins and married a woman of unprepossessing lineage.[37]

Yet another development widened the social gulf between *encomenderos*. As noted previously, Arequipa's population had been predominantly male through the late 1540s. The postwar years saw the addition of females, a number of whom were young women settling because they had married aged *encomenderos*. Within a decade, most were widowed and soon remarried. In choosing second spouses, these widows introduced a new group to the city's social elite, Spanish bureaucrats like the *corregidor* Licienciado Gómez Hernández.[38] The extent to which bureaucrats penetrated Arequipa's society is vividly illustrated by an incident in 1575. In that year, twelve women responded to a call for support of the Crown's war effort against European enemies by contributing jewelry and other personal effects. As befit their prominent station, they made substantial donations: the highest was valued at 3,560 pesos, the lowest at 130 pesos; a number of donations ran well over 500 pesos. Nine of the women were married to *encomenderos* and, significantly, at least four of their husbands enjoyed the position as a result of having served as royal officials in the Southwest.[39] Arequipans invariably considered such royal officials members of their city's upper social tier, despite some having married the widows of minor *encomenderos*. That they were so regarded reflected on their lineages, impressive by colonial standards: several could trace their roots to Peruvian conquistadores of major import; others had or were presumed to have noble blood. Some had begun their colonial service after arriving in the retinues of President Pedro de la Gasca and his viceregal successors—associations that enhanced their stature in Peru. The men often were licentiates who practiced before Lima's Royal Audiencia.[40]

Non-*Encomenderos* and Early Arequipan Society

Given the *encomenderos*' growing concern for social position, it is not surprising that few married or allowed their legitimate relatives to marry non-*encomenderos* in the community. Only three of Arequipa's merchants or venturers—Francisco Madueño, Antonio de Llanos, and Diego de Herrera—managed to scale the social barricade cutting off *encomenderos* from others in the city during the first generation after settlement. Their success was possible, at least in part, because each was financially well off. That appears very probable in Antonio de Llanos's marriage to María Zermeño, Tomás Farel's widow. As a self-declared merchant during the 1550s, Llanos traded in imported wines, sugar, and Indian tribute goods. After his marriage, he dropped some of his overt commercial dealings, built up his land assets by acquiring a number of *chácaras*, and increased his stature locally by securing the post of royal treasurer. By the 1570s, he had become one of Arequipa's most prominent and wealthiest citizens.[41]

Madueño and Herrera were well-to-do when wed, but hardly on a par with Antonio de Llanos. Each owed his marriage to other circumstances; Madueño's, for example, grew out of his association with Diego de Almagro. After participating in Arequipa's founding, Madueño handled some business affairs for a number of *encomenderos* who had been partisans of Almagro. Later, when one died, Madueño was entrusted with the care of his children. Two years later Madueño married the *encomendero*'s widow, María de Mendoza, a Spaniard who now occasionally used the designation "doña." Madueño by then was no longer a minor figure in the city of Arequipa, having served as chief constable, plunged into several lucrative business ventures, and become an officer of the mint in 1551. He would do well after marriage, too, becoming a royal treasurer, subsequently serving as a *corregidor* in Camaná and later Arica, and expanding his interest in land by purchasing and developing farms in the Arequipa and Vítor valleys. It appears that he funded some projects by drawing on the tributes of the Indians held by his wife's first husband, which were turned over to him through an agreement with his stepson's tutor.[42]

Diego de Herrera, like Antonio de Llanos, came to Arequipa after the founding and immersed himself in commerce. He was farsighted enough to recognize the possibilities that ranching and agriculture offered and soon invested in both. Like many *encomenderos*, merchants, and venturers of the 1540s, Herrera formed a partnership to share costs. His main associate was Francisco Boso, the holder of a small *encomienda* of Indians at Characato. Their alliance proved to be a fortunate one, for, after several years, Herrera married Boso's daughter, Madama Polonia. Such a match between a venturer and an *encomendero*'s daughter was highly unusual, although Boso was something of a misfit: of Italian origin, he clung to the habits of his merchant days. His marrying of a daughter to Herrera accords with merchant practice of solidifying economic ties with personal ones; later, he would wed a second daughter to yet another merchant.[43]

But these cross-group marriages were exceptional. *Encomenderos* and their legitimate relatives seldom tied themselves to others in the community. Some local landowners and other wealthy non-*encomenderos* therefore sought out the illegitimate children of *encomendero* families. Such unions began in 1540: the merchant Diego Gutiérrez, for example, managed to marry Constanza Rodríguez, the illegitimate daughter of the *encomendero* Juan Crespo. Until the 1550s, few such opportunities existed, given the male dominance in the colonial population.[44] Whereas the chances for these unions improved at mid-century, when many of the *encomenderos*' illegitimate mestizo children reached marriageable age, only a handful of matches followed. The established merchant-landowners now shunned the mestizas. Age differences—wealthy men in the city were generally much older than the mestizas—probably played only a minor role in discouraging their unions, since marriages of unequal ages were common. Perhaps the reason was that unmarried men hoped to do better, following the example of Antonio de Llanos, or that many merchants viewed residence in Arequipa as a temporary business expedient. Although marrying an illegitimate mestiza would generally enable a merchant to acquire land through a dowry, such gains must have been judged insufficient. Better to marry within merchant circles, solidify profitable commercial alliances, and advance a career. Whatever the reasons, most merchants avoided mestizas and remained in Arequipa only a short time.[45]

The illegitimate mestizas wed incoming Spaniards, a diverse lot of artisans, self-proclaimed merchants, venturers, and professionals. Such men lacked the opportunities available to established merchants and thus regarded the *encomenderos*' illegitimate daughters as a godsend. The mestizas, with dowries that often included rural land and cash, promised not only immediate rewards to the poorly connected, but also future financial support from in-laws, entry into a profession, and even the chance to buy into a family's holdings on favorable terms. Several cases illustrate well how critically important these marriages could be to immigrants who generally could offer only their Spanish blood in return. Two men, Gaspar Hernández and Juan de Vera, wed sisters, Beatriz and Leonor, the daughters of Alonso de Luque, who had served as a notary in the city before acquiring an *encomienda* during the 1540s. Both bridegrooms also practiced as notaries, and Vera eventually emerged as an important landholder as well.[46] When Pedro de Artaño arrived in Arequipa, he identified himself as a merchant and soon married María de San Juan, one of Juan de San Juan's illegitimate daughters. His father-in-law had been one of the more active *encomenderos* in accumulating *chácaras* and *estancias*. Eight years before his death, Juan de San Juan agreed to sell most of his holdings to Artaño for 12,000 pesos. Although Artaño pledged to raise the full sum within eight months, he apparently never did, and the debt remained outstanding when the *encomendero* died. Significantly, Artaño kept the property.[47]

Usually *encomendero* parents provided for their illegitimate mestizo sons as well. They often gave their sons a *chácara* or *estancia* when they became adults and encouraged them to marry Spanish women. Seldom were they able to make such marriages, however, since the few young, single women, if legitimate, were averse to unions with illegitimate mestizo sons and preferred Spaniards. Thus mestizo sons usually ended up marrying illegitimate mestizas, most often the daughters of *encomenderos*, and overseeing lands that those daughters possessed, thereby creating a new layer of non-Indian landowners.[48] Notably, they controlled less land than did *encomenderos*, venturers, or merchants, and also received smaller tracts than those given to legitimate children by the few *encomenderos* who had such offspring during the early colonial years. Yet the mestizos managed to secure a foothold in a region of scarce resources, became knowledgeable agriculturists, and, like Diego Cornejo, the illegitimate son of Miguel Cornejo who married the mestiza daughter of another *encomendero*, they occasionally emerged as fairly important figures within the community. Elvira de Carvajal, Diego's wife, was sometimes accorded the "doña" later in life; their daughters always were granted the honor.[49]

Of course, this preferred role for mestizos was at times rejected by children who chose instead to live and associate primarily with Indians. Typically, Pedro Bernal de Cantalapiedra, the son of Bachiller Miguel Rodríguez de Cantalapiedra, made little use of the *chácara* he received and survived mainly as a petty trader in the mountainous interior. He dealt with *curacas* of his father's *encomienda* whom he supplied with horses and livestock in exchange for wheat and maize. He lived with an Indian woman and fathered a son, to whom he willed in 1571 his few belongings: a cape, shoes, a mattress, and a blanket.[50]

Social Differentiation among Second- and Third-Generation Elite Families

Having cut itself off socially from other non-Indians in Arequipa, save for ties through mestizo children, the *encomendero* community continued to reinforce those subdivisions within its own ranks during the next two generations. The disuniting of these *encomendero* factions after the 1560s was most apparent in the marriages of children. As might be expected, no cross-subgroup unions took place apart from those instances in which a child of a lesser *encomendero* wed an illegitimate offspring of a major family. Such was the case with Martín López de Carvajal's eldest son, the heir to an *encomienda*, who married Guiomar Maldonado, the illegitimate daughter of

Captain Francisco de Grado.[51] Those of the upper social tier enjoyed better options in selecting spouses, and, like their parents, frequently chose from the best that the colony offered. Alonso Rodríguez Picado, for example, who succeeded his father as *encomendero* of the Southwest's largest grant, owned extensive rural properties, including some vineyards, and later became a general and married Doña Mayor de Sarabia, the daughter of a judge in Lima who became president of Chile.[52]

Others looked beyond the families of colonial administrators and Lima's important *encomenderos* to Spain. In 1574 Diego de Peralta Cabeza de Vaca dispatched six of his children to Toledo, where they were cared for by a sister and her husband; Pedro Pizarro and his wife Doña María Cornejo did likewise. The children fared extremely well. The Pizarros flourished under their grandfather's tutelage, and four of the five sent abroad are known to have married. One daughter, Doña Luisa, even wed a knight in the Order of Santiago. The emigration alternative was, nevertheless, inordinately expensive. Diego de Peralta had had to put up 20,000 pesos to sustain his children initially; the Pizarros had laid out 32,000 in 1561 to found an entailed estate (*mayorazgo*), composed of rural lands near Salamanca, for their eldest son, and had endowed one of their daughter's marriages with an additional 18,000 pesos (of 450 maravedís each).[53]

There were other costs. In many instances, families remained divided as children settled in Spain or reemigrated to other colonial areas. It is hard to ascertain whether these *encomenderos* and their wives, many of whom had left their own parents, gave this consideration much weight, but if they did, most must have derived some solace from the knowledge that their children were under the care of relatives and from the success of their efforts. We can only imagine the reactions of the Peralta Cabeza de Vaca family as they followed the later careers of sons and daughters. One, Doctor Don Alonso de Peralta y Robles, became apostolic inquisitor in Mexico City and then archbishop in Charcas; a brother, Doctor Don Matías, served as judge in Quito's and Mexico's *audiencias*; and two sisters, Doña Francisca and Doña Petronila, entered a nunnery in Seville.[54]

Nevertheless, for some important *encomendero* families, it may have been the desire to avoid such separations that led to marriages in the city. Qualms about such marriages were no doubt dispelled by the first generation's marriages. Founders of Arequipa who had been granted *encomiendas* had already solidified their families' social position by marrying prominent women; the children born to widows of the early *encomenderos* after they remarried also had two parents—mothers and their second husbands—of distinguished stature, as did offspring of grantees assigned *encomiendas* by La Gasca and the viceroys.[55]

But Arequipa's society at its highest levels—all legitimate descendants of *encomenderos*—did not become inbred through intermarriage up to the late sixteenth century. Instead, the elite steadily incorporated additional colonial bureaucrats, members of their families, and associates. Marriage often confirmed the incorporation. The trend recalls that of the immediate post-civil-war days, but there were differences. Many more newcomers were involved, and the outsiders overwhelmingly tended to be Spaniards who had recently arrived in Peru. Significantly, the social import of this new wave of immigrants proved different as well. Whereas marriages to newcomers had generally raised the status of Arequipan spouses belonging to the lower tier of *encomendero* society, that was no longer automatically the case. The immigrants' social status was more diverse.

The flood of newcomers resulted primarily from changes instituted by the Crown after the 1540s in hopes of increasing royal control over the colony. Several measures expanded the colonial bureaucracy and staffed it predominantly with Spaniards who had few ties to Peru. The royal government judged colonials, who had built up local interests, as less reliable. As the new appointees took up their posts and became familiar with conditions in the Southwest, especially the region's wealth still available through *encomiendas* but even more so through wine estates, they soon shared the locals' estimation that Arequipa's countryside offered decent returns on investments. A few only dabbled in the local economy while in office, trading in wine and tribute goods, and then left. Many more decided to settle.[56]

As might be expected, some who remained bought rural properties. The *corregidor* Doctor Don Cosme Carrillo, for example, purchased a tract along the Majes River with twenty thousand vines; Pedro de Valencia, a public trustee, bought and developed a coastal *heredad*.[57] It may be that some hoped eventually to secure an *encomienda* through a viceregal grant or through marriage, as had Spaniards earlier, but few succeeded. The turnover in *encomenderos* was now much less rapid—wars had ended and the male-female imbalance no longer existed. In addition, the viceroys tended to assign the few grants that fell vacant to persons with better connections in Lima.[58] Perhaps disappointed at the closing of this option, such men nevertheless stayed on in the Southwest as landowners, and their economic success led to the arrival of more relatives and associates who soon participated in the agricultural economy as well. Thus, not only did the likes of the *corregidor* Licenciado Gómez Hernández settle, purchase land in the Siguas Valley, and eventually build one of the region's most productive *heredades*, but so did his brother, Gómez de Tapia, who exploited land in the Vítor Valley. Similarly, Diego Martínez de Ribera, a natural son of the *corregidor* Señor Licenciado Alonso Martínez de Ribera, acquired rural property after migrating.[59]

The magnitude of the influx and the extent to which the newcomers came to own important holdings is suggested by the 1583 Mercedarian survey of landowners in the Vítor Valley (see Appendix B). Whereas *encomenderos*, venturers, yeomen, and a few merchants had been the proprietors a generation earlier, they now shared control with at least nine landowners who were either royal functionaries or former officials, or who had ties to such men before reaching the Southwest.[60] Among the twenty-nine *heredados* with Vítor holdings were Juan Ramírez Zegarra, who had served in Arequipa as *corregidor* during the 1560s, and Rodrigo de Orihuela, an accountant in the Royal Treasury. A spot check of owners in other wine-producing valleys revealed roughly the same breakdown.[61]

Economic considerations often fused with a favorable social climate in encouraging these outsiders to settle permanently. Few would live in Arequipa without marrying among themselves or locals. *Encomendero* families offered their regional wealth. Surely the acquisition of land was not the sole motivation leading immigrants to marry locals, but most appear to have been bent on trading their touches of nobility or impressive standing in the colony for land. Not surprisingly, therefore, landless *encomendero* families with modest numbers of Indians attracted them the least. Male outsiders generally gained access to rural property through endowments or by purchase from in-laws. Indirect evidence even suggests that gaining land for oneself through a spouse was only part of the calculations, for as marriages were made, relatives took advantage of the new familial bonds and also bought in. Thus, consanguinity and affinity eventually resulted in ownership of adjacent or closely proximate tracts. For example, not only descendants of Miguel Cornejo but also relatives by marriage possessed estates along the Vítor River during the mid-1580s. Gómez de Tapia, the owner of a vineyard near the Cornejo estates, was related to the Cornejo family. His brother's wife, Doña Violante de la Cerda, was Luis Cornejo's sister-in-law. Another of Doña Violante's sisters wed Diego de Porres, who also had an adjoining estate.[62]

Not all landowning *encomendero* families fared well in their attempts to tie themselves to the most socially prestigious immigrants. Although uneven wealth contributed to differences in their success, the social position of *encomenderos* played an important role as well. Naturally, the family of a major grantee and landowner like Diego de Peralta had the best options. Peralta managed impressive unions, arranging for a double marriage with the *corregidor* Juan Ramírez Zegarra for their respective eldest son and daughter.[63] For Arequipa's *encomendero* families of less stature, the most favorable matches were between their sons and the daughters of Spanish officials. Such was the case with the de la Torres, whose founder, Juan de la

Torre, was an original settler and the recipient of a respectable *encomienda* because of his support of the royalists in Gonzalo Pizarro's uprising. During the 1550s, Juan de la Torre had continued to be an important local figure and had married fairly well. For the wife of one of his sons, Hernando, then a minor, he picked Doña Catalina de Contreras, the daughter of the *corregidor* Señor Licenciado Alonso Martínez de Ribera. Although the *corregidor* regarded Hernando as acceptable (and well he might, since the youngster would become an *encomendero*), he attached stiff conditions. Juan de la Torre had to promise an endowment of 4,000 pesos plus the proceeds of a third of his goods when the couple married, a total of 22,000 pesos in 1577. Martínez de Ribera provided 6,000 pesos. Upgrading one's social position clearly could be expensive.[64]

The costs and status considerations for those, like Juan de la Torre, just below the upper crust forced most others to look toward more distant relatives of *corregidores* and treasury officials as well as their associates. For example, Marcos Alvarez de Guzmán, the holder of an undistinguished *encomienda* and the only legitimate son of the founder Licenciado Hernando Alvarez de Carmona and Leonor de Guzmán, wed Doña María de Valencia, sister of the public trustee Pedro de Valencia. But because such unions brought only limited social gains, some families turned to children of *encomenderos* in other secondary colonial centers. Luis Cornejo, an *encomendero* with a mid-sized grant and a father who had been a founder, but of unimpressive social background, married Doña Mencía de Carvajal, the daughter of a Peruvian *encomendero* based in the city of Trujillo. Whether on account of this marriage or of his leading role in the city, Cornejo eventually came to be regarded a "don."[65]

Over the course of the last half of the sixteenth century, then, Arequipa's social elite expanded, despite the tendency of some *encomenderos* and their children to settle elsewhere. Its growth was due to procreation and the incorporation of outsiders, principally colonial officials, their relatives, and associates. Rather quickly, these outsiders married locals, a development tied to their interest in land and Spaniards' control of the countryside.

The presence of outsiders proved significant to the community in ways other than increasing the size of the elite. When the town was founded, few colonists were related, a pattern that persisted for another generation as *encomenderos*, their widows, and their first children married outsiders. Although *encomendero*-landowning families continued to intermarry only infrequently after the late 1550s, their unions with royal officials and the latter's kin meant that many came to share in-laws, which diminished the familial insularity of Arequipa's leading citizens.[66] Importantly, too, finer distinctions were now recognized among those at the top of the Southwest's hierarchical society. The differences in status cannot be picked up solely by identifying the families that dominated the municipal government: posts still remained distributed among aristocrats of varying prestige, even including some newcomers, although these were a minority.[67]

The relative social positions of Southwesterners depended on a number of things. The ideal mix—one that guaranteed social preeminence—was to be the descendant of a founder who had been assigned a major grant in 1540, the current holder of an *encomienda* that continued to yield impressive financial returns, the owner of a coastal estate, and the relative of a major functionary, particularly a *corregidor*. Those not so fortunate were positioned somewhere along a continuum, their social status dependent on how closely they approximated this ideal.[68]

Land and the Society of Non-*Encomenderos* during the Late 1500s

The development of coastal estates, as noted earlier, included non-*encomenderos*, a number of whom came to own impressive properties. Fortunately, the 1583 cadastral survey of the Vítor Valley provides both the names of *heredados* and, through the individual amounts assessed annually to pay for Mercedarian pastoral duties, a ranking of the worth of all properties (see Appendix B). (Information on several *heredades* indicates that contributions were tied to the value of holdings. For instance, Don Francisco Zegarra's property had twice as many vines as Don Luis Cornejo's, so his payment was twice as much.)[69] The eight men who owned the most valuable holdings had varied backgrounds. As might be presumed, most were government functionaries, *encomenderos*, or their relatives and associates. But Diego de Herrera and Baltasar de Torres were venturers and Juan de Quirós Vozmediano was a merchant. Apparently by virtue of their landed wealth, Diego de Herrera and Juan de Quirós Vozmediano managed to achieve some distinction in the community, including election to the local government as *alcalde*.[70]

Significantly, landownership also had social repercussions. Herrera and Quirós Vozmediano saw their children married well: one of Herrera's daughters wed the son of a *corregidor*; Juan de Quirós Vozmediano's son-in-law was Francisco Pinto, nephew on his mother's side of a royal accountant. Such Arequipan landowners, acting much like *encomendero* families did when attaching themselves to outsiders, endowed these marriages with land.[71] Whereas these cases show landholding's new social value to someone without an *encomienda*, there were limits on just how far persons of their stature and their offspring might advance in late sixteenth century Arequipa. For example, Juana de Herrera's husband, Diego Martínez de Ribera, though a *corregidor*'s son, was illegitimate. He was a good catch for a venturer family—so much so that his father-in-law provided sufficient land to make him an important rural proprietor—but, unlike his legitimate half-sister, he apparently had not been sought after by an *encomendero* family.[72] (Diego de Herrera would not regret his decision, for his son-in-law was to serve as an *alcalde* and lead an illustrious life in the city.)

Landowners with less impressive holdings than a Diego de Herrera, men who had begun as small-scale venturers, merchants, wine specialists, or notaries, sparked little interest among the more imposing newcomer families. This lack of interest was not due to the inconsequentiality of their rural properties—in 1583 the mestizo viticulturist Diego Cornejo, as well as the venturer Antonio de Valderrama, possessed Vítor vineyards as substantial as and even larger than some held by *encomenderos* and functionaries.[73] Their wealth, however, could not compensate for their backgrounds. As a result, Spaniards of their group intermarried, wed arrivals with backgrounds like their own, or sought out the mestiza daughters of prominent men. Cristóbal de Torres, for example, wed the sister of another Spanish landowner, Cristóbal Hernández de Abrego; Torres's sister wed Sebastián de Monteagudo, an immigrant of limited means.[74] Antonio de Valderrama, in turn, married Luisa Rodríguez Solís, daughter of the brother of *encomendero* Alonso Rodríguez Picado.[75]

Again, land was often transferred with such unions or shortly thereafter; Sebastián de Monteagudo thus gained land from the Torres family, and Juan de Barrios acquired land when he wed into the Carvajals.[76] In-laws also often worked closely in rural ventures: Antonio de Valderrama and his brother-in-law, Antonio de Rodríguez Solís, sold wine together, as did Cristóbal Hernández and Cristóbal de Torres.[77]

Legitimate and illegitimate mestizo owners, on the other hand, chose mates principally from among their own group—ethnicity had begun to tell and consigned the males to a special social circle. For example, Melchor de Luque wed a mestiza daughter of Alonso Pizarro and María Pauca.[78] Mestizas from landowning families, especially those who were legitimate, had broader options than their brothers if they made judicious use of land endowments. They could still marry a Spanish landowner of humble social station, an incoming venturer, or even the distant relative of a functionary.[79]

Conclusion

Viewed broadly, Arequipa's society from the town's founding to the end of the sixteenth century resembled that of many Spanish colonial centers. Settlers were arranged hierarchically, with an elite composed of *encomendero* families. Arequipa's original *encomenderos*, however, exerted their influence for only a short time. Civil war battles and emigration reduced the

1540 grantees to a minority, thereby precluding the formation of a group that derived unique status by virtue of descent from founders assigned Indians by Francisco Pizarro. Indeed, the southwestern case even suggests that some historians may have overstressed the privileged position of such colonists (the *beneméritos*). Some descendants of the few original grantees who survived the 1540s received no special treatment and, instead, became members of a second tier within the *encomendero* community. Their lesser social importance often resulted from their smaller grants.

Marriage proved extremely important socially during Arequipa's early years. Settlers lacked the well-established indicators of status evident in Spain. Most colonists were much alike: they had similar occupational backgrounds and were mainly of common birth. Granted, a small number enjoyed special status in the new community because they had been made *encomenderos*, but these Spaniards required a way to reinforce their preeminence and insure its continuance among descendants. Hence, *encomenderos* chose spouses from among those respected in the Hispanic world. Although a few *encomenderos* or members of *encomendero* families journeyed to Spain so that they might marry well or acquire other trappings of social importance, most could not afford this option. The more normal course became marriage in the colony. Such unions sometimes led Arequipa's *encomenderos* to settle elsewhere, particularly in Lima, a tendency that would endure into the seventeenth century, as Fred Bronner has established.[80]

But most of Arequipa's *encomendero* families remained in their city after the 1560s. The transformation of the region's economy—the onset of viticulture—attracted a constant flow of Spaniards who provided respectable spouses. The willingness of these immigrants, especially the royal officials, to settle is reminiscent of the habits of later bureaucrats. As Leon G. Campbell and Jacques A. Barbier have revealed, many officials assigned to Lima and central Chile tended to marry into prestigious local families.[81]

Yet another parallel exists with later colonial social circumstances. As in eighteenth-century Mexico, few merchants wed Arequipans. D. A. Brading has attributed merchant endogamy in Mexico to the growing differences between economically crippled colonials and financially successful Spaniards.[82] Such a situation hardly prevailed in the Southwest, given colonists' successes in the wine industry. Merchants appear to have shunned local marriages primarily because of their habit of insuring business alliances through unions with other merchant families. A central theme in Arequipa's early social history, then, was the rather rapid conversion of an elite created by assignment to one that was hereditary, and the marriages of Southwesterners played a central role in that conversion.

Despite Arequipa's graded society, some mobility was possible for colonists throughout the sixteenth century. *Encomendero* families created and strengthened subtle differences in status among elite members as some wed more eminently than others. A faction of non-*encomenderos* also improved its social position. At first, a few rose in status through feats in the civil wars and the resultant gain of *encomiendas*. Shortly thereafter, a handful of extremely wealthy or well-connected venturers and merchants crossed the divide separating the elite from other Spaniards by marrying the widows of *encomenderos*. In the more pacific setting of the post-1550s, social advancement depended primarily on land. It remained almost impossible for a non-*encomendero* to marry into an *encomendero* family, save for someone willing to wed an illegitimate offspring, but, if one possessed important lands, there was a chance that the family of a bureaucrat might be amenable.

The rest of the non-*encomendero* community, including many who owned coastal estates, were positioned on lower rungs of Arequipa's social ladder. Growing social differences among these Southwesterners reflected not only unequal wealth, but also a gradually developing lower estimation of those of mixed race. Such attitudes emerged throughout the Americas during these years and have long been recognized as an important cause for the formation of a society of castes.[83]

5. The Wine Economy

. . . *es publico y notorio la mucha necesidad que todos los moradores desta Ciudad y sus distritos, tienen, tanto que no solamente no pueden pagar lo que deben, pero aun para comer no alcanzan ni tienen que, y . . . los que mayores y mejor heredades tienen, muchos de ellos, han . . . dicho la necesidad que padecen, y [pidiendo] muchas veces prestados, dineros y otras cosas diciendo que sin aquello no les comian . . .*

——————Don Martín Abad de Usúnsolo

Los vecinos viejos eran ricos; sus hijos son pobres porque no siguen la prudencia de sus padres, y los nietos de los conquistadores y vecinos serán paupérrimos.

——————Fray Reginaldo de Lizárraga

Arequipa's wine economy boomed during the latter half of the sixteenth century. Having built up coastal estates, *heredados* enjoyed impressive profits, the result mainly of low labor costs and favorable colonial market conditions. Like prosperous estate owners elsewhere in the Americas, many used their newfound wealth to enhance their social position by marrying well and acquiring such status symbols as permanent seats on the city council when these were sold beginning in the late 1500s. Some *heredados* also constructed more imposing urban homes and outfitted them with the best furnishings available. In addition, they began to support the church more actively and provided several religious orders with generous gifts. The orders used these to construct impressive cloisters and chapels that are still admired by tourists and remain a source of great pride to Arequipans. Many *heredados* also established chantries and promised the church a portion of their estates' income yearly in return for special masses.[1]

Established proprietors seized on the opportunity to expand their vineyards. Highland *encomenderos*, who had previously shied away from the wine industry, now joined them, given viticulture's proven profitability. Many newcomers to the region, most often government functionaries and their relatives, also invested in viticulture. A few colonists plunged into viticulture's subsidiary industries as well. Mule raising became a particularly popular venture because of the demand for transport livestock. Its expansion revived ranching, which had fallen on hard times after some initial success. *Estancieros* had concentrated on supplying the city with meat, and the consequent expansion of herds caused prices to tumble. Mule prices, however, remained stable. Each head sold for around 150 pesos between 1562 and the early 1600s. By the late sixteenth century, therefore, Arequipa's *estancieros* pushed more determinedly beyond the confines of the Arequipa Valley to the coastal hills and valleys south of the Vítor River. They found mule raising so profitable that many abandoned the extensive breeding of horses, a trend that worried defense-minded authorities in Lima and forced Viceroy Don Luis de Velasco to order *estancieros* to insure an adequate supply of war horses. He directed that a fourth of all mares be set aside to breed such horses and promised to fine violators 500 pesos or even to take away their allotment of drafted Indian labor. Despite this threat, few complied.[2]

Although many of those who invested in agriculture employed personal funds, Arequipans also used borrowed capital. During the late 1500s, most loans came from a diverse group that included religious houses, a few Indian communities, and the wealthier *encomenderos, heredados*, and merchants. In securing credit, landowners generally used their estates, other rural property, and urban holdings as collateral. The yearly interest rate on a mortgage was 7.1 percent of the principal, with payments made biannually or annually, comfortable terms for most *heredados* during the 1570s and 1580s.[3] Thus, no mention of major problems surfaces in notarial, *cabildo*, and judicial records of the period.

The financial state of the *heredados* began to weaken by the last decade of the century. Most landowners lost control of the marketing of their wine, experienced rising labor costs, and faced sharply falling prices for their goods. The agriculturists' difficulties increased at the outset of the seventeenth century when their farms sustained earthquake damage. Then increasing competition and governmental measures limited opportunities. But owners generally managed to retain their lands, passing them on to their descendants, who still possessed them during the mid-1600s.

Marketing Problems and Adjustments

The weakening position of sixteenth-century *heredados* first revealed itself in their loss to merchants of control over marketing. This development was born of success: as regional wine production reached over 100,000 jugs (*botijas*) per year in the 1580s, estate owners faced increasingly complex organizational problems. To have retained control of shipping and marketing would have required much of the *heredados*: they would have had to raise and maintain mules to carry wine across coastal deserts to the city of Arequipa and then arrange for the supervision of llama trains on the journey to Potosí or Cuzco, their principal inland markets.[4] Financing also discouraged their participation in trade, for as the wine industry grew, marketing increasingly required credit. Inland wholesalers and retailers, as well as those in Lima, often paid for large shipments with promissory notes. *Heredados* generally lacked reliable contacts in these markets and were consequently unwilling to assume the risks involved. Many no doubt feared that the buyers' notes might prove difficult to use and that they might have to sue for restitution in faraway towns.[5]

Merchants could better handle such transactions. Those based in the city of Arequipa had dealt since the 1540s in intracolonial trade, and as they had trafficked in Spanish imports and southwestern products, most had developed sure contacts and even had factors at places like Potosí. Some merchants acted as agents of traders based in Lima and thus could work through parent companies when wholesaling Arequipa's wines and brandies in the City of Kings. Most also had established transport companies or contracted regularly with independent carriers.[6] For these merchants, the developing wine industry could not have emerged at a more propitious time. During the 1570s, Viceroy Don Francisco de Toledo had threatened their livelihood by ordering that Arica serve as the southwestern Peruvian port for transshipping Potosí silver to Lima. This decision not only oriented that trade away from Arequipa, it also redirected the flow of Spanish products once sent from Lima through the city for sale in the highlands. Merchants in Lima found it simpler and cheaper to send these commodities by way of Arica on ships destined to pick up silver. The livestock that brought silver down to the port was used for the inland journey.[7]

Arequipa's merchant community expanded as others migrated to take advantage of the opportunities made possible by wine.[8] Most merchants soon positioned themselves very favorably in the wine trade and found ways to purchase wine at the cheapest prices. The productive cycle of the wine industry helped them immensely, since the second and third quarters of each calendar year were hectic and costly for estate owners. Grapes began to appear in December, ripened through March, when they were picked, pressed, and the must left to ferment in *tinajas*; the wine was ready to consume sometime from late September through November. From March to September, then, an *heredado* had to provide food, lodging, and wages for his permanent workers and manager, as well as hire temporary laborers and artisans for harvesting and the important tasks of vine pruning, *botija* making, and equipment repair or construction. Expenses could be quite high: records from quite a small *heredad* in the Vítor Valley (average yearly production of less than two hundred *botijas*) indicate a total of at least 400 pesos spent in 1592 and 650 pesos in 1594.[9] In need of cash, the *heredado* often willingly pre-sold his wine at lower prices during the first six months of a calendar year rather than wait until October or November, when the wine was ready. *Heredados* offered the lowest prices to buyers who paid in cash when the sale contract was drawn up; buyers who reached agreements before June but who promised to pay later, when the wine was delivered, did almost as well, since *heredados* could use their notes as security for credit.[10]

Purchasing wine well before a delivery date benefited merchants in another way. All wanted to get their shipments to inland centers as soon as possible, since the supply was generally quite low during the last months of a calendar year and retail prices consequently high.[11] *Heredados'* and merchants' sales records specifying delivery date and place underline this desire for speed. Those who bought before June were consistently given the earlier shipment dates. To protect against delay, merchants included a provision in such contracts that allowed them to purchase the same amount of wine elsewhere if an *heredado*'s wine was not ready when promised, with any extra cost for the wine assumed by the estate owner.

This clause also covered merchants with their carriers, since in hiring them, merchants normally were liable after three days for all costs incurred by a transporter who had brought animals to a specified *heredad*. In some instances, carriers required merchants to agree that they would pay for the entire trip even if it could not be made once the team reached the *heredad*.[12] Of course, merchants also protected themselves against carriers by penalizing those who arrived late to pick up the wine or by hiring another transporter and charging the cost to the original carrier. Naturally, failure to deliver wine on time at the specified locale meant that the carrier had to pay any difference in the market price. Sometimes the transport charge for each *botija* was lowered on tardy shipments. Finally, carriers' liability extended to all breakage and loss.[13]

Most merchants handled prepayments for wine with little difficulty. Carriers usually took approximately sixty days for trips to Cuzco, three months to La Paz, and five months to Potosí. Thus a merchant receiving wine in a coastal valley in September could have it delivered at any of these markets by February. If the wine was disposed of quickly—and the evidence suggests that it normally was—the merchant could have some cash or promissory notes back in Arequipa in time to invest advantageously in the next crop.[14]

Changes in *Heredad* Labor

While surrendering control of marketing to merchants, *heredados* had to cope with emerging labor problems. The decline in the coastal Indian population contributed to labor shortages, but it was not the sole factor. Labor scarcity also resulted from royal interference and from other options available to Indians. By the late 1500s, Indians from modern-day Cailloma worked periodically at the Potosí mines, those from Condesuyos, at Castrovirreyna. Highlanders balked at such obligations, as absenteeism made clear, but few evaded the work by escaping to the coastal estates.[15] Their reluctance had various causes, the most important being the isolation of highlanders from Spaniards after 1540 and their retention of land. Because their properties enabled them to satisfy most of their needs, highland Indians had little use for the small plots of land or the wages offered by *heredados*.[16] Consequently, estate owners increasingly bid more generously for those Indians willing to serve as wage workers. Yearly cash payments, which had ranged from 8 to 10 pesos in the 1560s and 1570s, reached 20 to 25 pesos in the 1590s and more than doubled over the next generation.[17]

The shortage compelled *heredados* to search for an alternative source of labor. Some hired among the *castas* (persons of mixed race), but their numbers proved insufficient, since they preferred to work as transporters, stewards, or in the city as artisans. Other *castas* survived in the countryside living with Indians and working on their lands, or squatting on vacant plots within the coastal belt and the Arequipa Valley. A smaller faction became brigands, stole from travelers, and occasionally rampaged through an *heredad* or Indian village. A particularly brisk traffic developed in rustling along the coastal hills; brigands drove the stolen animals south and sold them in Arica.[18]

Black slaves provided the most popular solution to the *heredados'* labor problem. Colonists had employed blacks in their *estancias* since the city's founding. A few landowners also used slaves on farms in the Arequipa Valley, and some even introduced them on their estates during the wine industry's early days. Most blacks, however, had been household servants. Owners had manumitted a number because they knew the slaves well and because of the presence of Indians to replace them.[19] Imports of blacks from Lima picked up considerably at the close of the sixteenth century. Colonists also acquired them from interior Peru and even Brazil, until, after the late

1580s, slavery was extensive in the coastal valleys. One *heredad*, that of Gerónimo de Villalobos and Hernando de Almonte, for instance, had a work crew that was almost completely black. The force included thirteen adult male black slaves, two black women, and two of their children. Most often, an *heredado* maintained a mixed force of blacks and Indians.[20]

The decision to introduce slaves must have been a hard one for *heredados*. The purchase price for a healthy adult male ranged between 550 and 700 pesos during the late 1500s and early 1600s.[21] In addition, *heredados* had to consider other costs, such as food, clothing, and medical care. They also worried about slaves' life expectancy, labor productivity, and escape possibilities. Nevertheless, slaves offered compensations, not the least of which was a more permanent and stable labor force than the Indians. This advantage was reinforced by continued threats to the supply of Indians by royal officials. Viceroys periodically announced that they would cut off highland sources on the grounds that the health of Indians was endangered by migration to the lowlands. During the 1590s, the king also forbade the assignment of drafted Indians to work in the vineyards and olive groves and insisted that Indian wage laborers be paid in cash rather than in wine.[22] The latter restrictions did not directly affect Arequipa's *heredados*, since they had no local draft and most already paid workers in cash, but they suggest the probability of constant governmental harassment.

Heredados naturally hoped to use slaves profitably. They did not simply use them as field hands, as they had the Indians, but trained them for the special demands of the wine industry. On the Villalobos-Almonte estate, one slave served as a *botija* maker, four as pruners, and another as a muleteer, thereby reducing owner dependence on expensive itinerant specialists. Scattered bits of evidence indicate that slave-owning *heredados* also leased out their blacks during part of the year. A slave skilled in making earthen containers could easily make the rounds of several estates in a year; another could prune vines in various *heredados* over two or three months; and they might do equipment repair and construction at any time other than at harvest. Such possibilities gave rise to joint ownership of slaves. In addition, some slave owners with *chácaras* in the Arequipa Valley and coastal estates shifted their blacks from one to the other over the course of a year, a practice that was possible because harvests in the two areas did not coincide.[23]

It is impossible to tell whether slaves were more expensive laborers than Indians during the late sixteenth century. A cost comparison would have to consider such factors as average life expectancy of slaves and the extent of flight and recovery, as well as the incidence of illness among Indians and blacks. Unfortunately, the records are simply too skimpy for credible estimates. At most, based on fragmentary accounts that detail expenses on two estates during the early 1600s, it appears that, if an *heredado* leased his blacks, he would have to pay more for either temporary or year-round black workers than for Indians. (The daily cost of a slave was 4 reales and that of an Indian, from 2 to 3 reales.)[24] Whatever the comparative advantages, no matter what type of worker an *heredado* utilized during the late sixteenth century, labor costs were higher than they had been a generation earlier.

Colonial Overproduction of Wine

Even as labor expenses rose, *heredados* also had to contend with declining wine prices. From the mid-1580s to the mid-1590s, the mean price for a *botija* of common wine wholesaled at an estate on the coastal strip fell from 4 pesos, 4 reales, to 2 pesos, 2 reales (see fig. 1). Merchants pre-purchasing wine on more favorable terms were partially responsible, but the drop reflected overproduction as well, for viticulture's success had encouraged excessive local expansion. What began as an industry confined principally to the upper reaches of the Vítor River spread farther within that valley and into adjacent ones. Other Spaniards invested in vineyards elsewhere. Some Arequipans migrated south and were joined by immigrants in exploiting the Moquegua, Locumba, Sama, Tacna, and Lluta valleys. Positioned close to the newly developing trade route between Arica and Potosí, producers in the valleys soon shipped their wine, wheat, corn, chilies, pimentos, and assorted fruits inland. Numerous mule *estancias* developed in this area as well. By the early 1600s, these competitors produced nearly forty thousand *botijas* of wine annually, or about 20 percent of Arequipa's total in a good year.[25]

At the same time Arequipa's *heredados* confronted challenges in Lima's markets. In 1563 Spaniards established a town, Valverde, in the Ica Valley, and soon settlers began to raise foodstuffs like those around Arequipa. An observer estimated wine production in Ica at twenty thousand *botijas* during 1572 and noted the prevalence of wheat and maize. At first Southwesterners remained unaffected by this competition, since the combined production still could not meet Lima's demand, but by the 1580s farm owners around Ica expanded, and others opened up lands close to new settlements at Pisco and Nazca.[26] The result, reflected in the import tax records kept by royal officials at Lima's port of Callao, was a substantial decline in Arequipa's coastal trade. During the 1590s, Ica, Pisco, and Nazca landowners dominated as Lima's suppliers of fruits, raisins, and wine. Although Arequipans still exported such goods northward, their trade was only a fraction of their competitors'.[27] Southwesterners no longer remained the

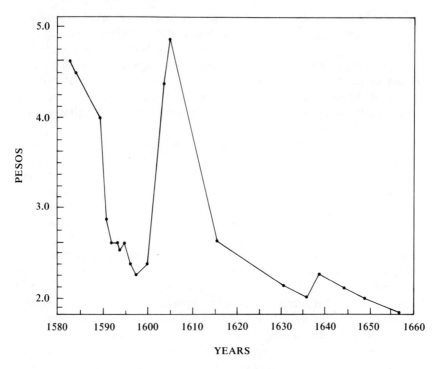

Fig. 1. Mean Prices per *Botija* of Wine Wholesaled in Arequipa's
Coastal Valleys

Source: *ADA*, assorted notarial registers.

only major producers of some agricultural goods valued highly by colonists and were losing out to competitors with better access to Peru's richest markets.

The rapid growth of viticulture in the colony concerned not just Arequipa's *heredados* but also the royal government. Since wine was a major Spanish export, colonial output threatened Andalusian producers, Spanish merchants, and even the Crown, which derived income from taxes on wine shipped to the Americas. After wrestling with the problem, the royal government decided to discourage the industry's expansion in the colonies by taxing the wine trade in the Americas.[28] In a series of decrees issued during the late 1560s, the king ordered that wine shipped across provincial lines be subject to a duty (*almojarifazgo*) fixed at 2.5 percent of its value on exit and 5 percent on entry.[29] Because most of their wine was sold within their province, Arequipa's merchants and producers only became concerned during the early 1570s, when colonial officials declared goods transported between Lima and Arequipa liable. The city's *cabildo* and several merchants took the case to court and won.[30]

In a more serious challenge to colonists, the king directed that Viceroy Toledo eradicate the industry by preventing any new plantings and by forbidding any improvements on existing vineyards. Little came of these directives, despite repeated reminders to Toledo and his successors to enforce them. In a letter to the Crown in 1588, the Conde de Villar tried to explain why officials had ignored their instructions and observed that vineyards had become vital to the colonial economy and provided cheaper wines than those shipped from Spain. He added that any attempt to destroy viticulture would provoke a rebellion, but like his predecessors, he concluded weakly that an effort would be made to inhibit production by forbidding highland Indians from working in coastal valleys. In later correspondence, the king remarked caustically on the inadequacy of this course, for, as no doubt all had foreseen, colonists continued to improve older vineyards and put in new ones.[31]

Although Philip II clearly preferred to supply the colonies with European wines—observing that this system facilitated tax collection—his viceroys made a telling point by stressing the dangers of eradicating Peruvian viticulture.[32] Therefore, he opportunistically accepted the colonial wine industry on the condition that vineyard owners legitimize their holdings by paying a fee and make new plantings only after securing a royal license. These regulations caused some grumbling in Arequipa, since many *heredados* knew that Southwesterners had received royal permission to plant vineyards during the 1540s. Nevertheless, they eventually acquiesced, a course made easier by the moderate costs of confirming titles. For example, the Crown billed owners of those Vítor Valley estates that had almost twenty thousand vines around 100 pesos and even allowed *heredados* to pay in installments. Interestingly, when royal officials registered holdings, most landowners, probably hoping to expand their plantings there if the Crown later forbade them access to land, often claimed unused stretches within the valley walls. Then, too, some may have worried that speculators might attempt to buy up the vacant plots and hold out for exorbitant prices.[33]

Besides legitimizing colonial viticulture, the royal government also instituted measures designed to further increase its revenues from the industry. Imperfectly enforced, the *almojarifazgo* had yielded less than expected. As a consequence, the Crown ordered that anyone taking wine from an *heredad* for sale or consumption register the quantity, specify its destination, and declare its transporter. Royal treasury officials were to register this information, but if unavailable, local *corregidores* could handle it. When the procedure proved difficult at the *heredad*, the closest town or port would serve as the registration center.[34] Viceroy Don García Hurtado de Mendoza, charged with enforcing this measure, refused, explaining that a challenge to powerful colonials could only spell trouble. Perhaps he was right.[35] *Heredados* were angered at being forced to legitimize their holdings and, like other colonists, furious at another tax, the *alcabala* (an excise tax). During the 1570s the Crown introduced this levy, a 2 percent tax on the value of all goods, at each sale to New Spain. It had been in effect throughout Castile for years, and in 1591 Philip II extended it to Peru, which aroused mass dissatisfaction in most cities, including Arequipa and Quito, where riots broke out. Communities quickly sent representatives to Spain to argue for its removal. Sebastián de Mosquera, Arequipa's royal treasurer, informed the king by letter that, when he notified citizens of the *alcabala*, most initially refused to pay. The tax concerned them because it raised their cost of living and also threatened wine sales by reducing consumer spending in the colony. Fortunately for the Crown, the tax did not have as severe an impact as predicted. During the 1590s, wine prices dropped only about 3 reales per *botija*, and Arequipans gradually accommodated themselves to the excise tax. A thankful monarch even praised them for their law-abiding nature.[36]

Earthquakes and Viticulture

Arequipa's wine boom was over. By the end of the 1500s, *heredados'* profits dropped as they lost control of marketing, experienced government harassment and a scarcity of labor, and faced competition from other colonial producers. They soon confronted additional difficulties: on Friday, 18 February 1600, at nine o'clock in the evening, a series of sharp quakes shook the city, followed by increasingly more violent ones later that night and during the next day. Around five in the afternoon of the nineteenth, sand and ash began to rain on the city, continuing unabated for a day. Terrified Arequipans, fearing the collapse of heavily laden roofs, camped out in the streets. The skies finally cleared by nightfall on the twentieth, but quakes persisted through Thursday of the following week and tumbled many of those buildings that had survived the initial tremors and the weight of the ash. To everyone's horror, more ash fell over a forty-hour stretch the following weekend. The eruptions of Huainaputina, a volcano to the southeast of Arequipa, not only frightened the colonists and crippled their city but also paralyzed the rural economy. A broad area, calculated by some contemporaries as radiating 90 kilometers around the city, was blanketed with up to a half meter of ash. Observers estimated that over three-quarters of the Southwest's livestock perished from the loss of pastures and that the ash destroyed almost the entire fruit, olive, and grape crop. Arequipa's average annual wine yield just prior to the catastrophe had been 200,000 *botijas*; in 1601 it amounted to 10,000 *botijas* of undrinkable wine. What reconstruction followed came to naught when Arequipa was shaken by another string of violent quakes in 1604. These also severely damaged buildings on the *heredades* and caused flooding of coastal rivers, which washed away sizeable sections of vineyards and destroyed irrigation canals.[37]

When apprised of the catastrophe, officials in Spain briefly considered eliminating viticulture in the Southwest once and for all by forbidding repairs and new plantings. Peru's viceroy and Lima's *audiencia* rejected this Draconian solution to imperial trade problems and warned that such a course would wreak havoc.[38] Instead they ordered the sending of special levies of drafted Indians from Cailloma to reconstruct Arequipa, put in food crops, and help clear the vineyards. Although highland *corregidores* never sent as many Indians as specified, and although many of those whom these officials dispatched fled shortly after arriving in the city, the drafted Indian laborers helped save southwestern viticulture. The Indians not only rebuilt damaged properties, but, with their competition, contributed to a fall in the cost of wage-earning Indian and *casta* workers, a reduction that aided *heredados* in their recovery.[39]

Other developments rescued estate owners as well. For a brief interval, their financial position was critical, because they had borrowed only recently to put in or expand vineyards and now had to meet hefty mortgage payments. The landowner-dominated *cabildo* called for a two-year moratorium on debts, but merchant-lenders immediately challenged the move, arguing that any delay would wipe them out. Because their loans to landowners served as collateral when financing trade, they would not be able to pay off debts or secure additional credit as long as *heredado* repayments remained in doubt. One merchant argued that the measure discriminated and that the region's economic health would be better served by allowing those *heredados* who could not repay to go under. The *cabildo* ignored his suggestion, and eventually most lenders recognized the *heredados'* plight and renegotiated their mortgages. They often allowed a landowner a grace period of several years and then spread payments over a longer span than that called for in the original mortgage contract. In some instances, creditors even wrote off a portion of a loan when a property had been badly damaged.[40]

Aided by such agreements, cheaper labor, and a viceregal decision to lift the *alcabala* in the region for several years, most *heredados* survived.[41] Only a few unfortunates sold out and emigrated. Probably the best-known case of emigration was that of the Convent of Nuestra Señora de los Remedios, which lost its vineyards when the Vítor River flooded. Although the nuns tried to survive in the city on the tributes from Indians in Condesuyos (assigned to them temporarily by their patroness), the returns were so paltry—2,500 pesos in five years, not the expected 10,000 ducados—that they departed for Cuzco. Some nuns of the Convent of Santa Catalina de Sena left as well, but their house weathered the crisis, thanks to a special gift from the viceroy.[42]

Merchants, some *heredados*, and even artisans bought the emigrants' property. Such people probably considered purchasing the devastated estates of others as well but could not afford to do so. Anyone hoping to buy out an indebted and crippled *heredado*, of course, needed capital or credit, and neither was readily available. The assets of most wealthy residents were either in land or in estate mortgages, difficult to liquidate, since few could buy their property or would lend when the collateral was a mortgage on damaged farmland. Buyers, therefore, settled for occasional purchases and even then, several managed only by forming partnerships to pool their limited capital.[43]

In the years that followed, *heredados* limped along, finding ways to survive. Some landowners intermittently sold small portions of their rural properties at bargain prices, preferably within their families, for capital to tide themselves over. A few prevailed on their relatives or on religious orders for loans. *Heredados* often rented parcels or their entire estates temporarily, left portions of their properties unworked for years until they had the means to redevelop them, or paid laborers in produce rather than cash.[44]

The extent to which such arrangements succeeded in rescuing *heredados* is revealed by comparing familial ownership patterns along the Vitor River in 1583 and 1620. In 1583 twenty-nine families had had *heredades*. Unfortunately, eight of these cannot be traced beyond the late 1590s. But twelve of the remainder still had their property in 1620, and an additional seven retained portions of their original estates. Only two definitely disposed of their entire holdings. (Both of the latter sold out before the earthquakes, and one of these afterward bought other rural property, which it retained.) Even if we presume that those families who cannot be traced sold out because of the destructive quakes, two-thirds survived the crisis with some Vitor land. Notably, of the seven families known to have given up portions of their estates, three passed property to the church; in one instance the land went to an order a daughter had joined and so she continued to be supported by the *heredad*.[45]

The volume of wine sales during the 1620s indicates that these *heredados* not only had managed to survive but were recovering somewhat, though there was much indebtedness. One estate owner, for example, had four outstanding mortgages with a total principal of 7,840 pesos in 1623. Difficulties in meeting interest payments for several years added 3,794 pesos to his debts, and he had, in addition, borrowed over 12,000 pesos to cover personal expenses.[46] A particularly severe contemporary critic blamed such indebtedness on the alleged laziness and lack of resourcefulness of seventeenth-century Arequipans vis-à-vis their parents.[47] That judgment seems too harsh, although there does appear to have been reluctance to reduce expenses, despite the depressed economy. Arequipa's landowning families spent, and therefore often had to borrow, in order to continue such social practices as endowing marriages, establishing chantries, and even outfitting homes sumptuously. Yet, much of their borrowing went into improvements on their estates.[48]

But as they borrowed, wine prices continued to drop, a decline due not only to their own revival, but also to colonial competition. Producers along the central Peruvian coast and in western modern-day Argentina increased their plantings and trade to inland markets during Arequipa's crisis years. The challenge of producers around Ica, Pisco, and Nazca is evident in tax records maintained by port officials. These document increased shipments to Potosí through Arica from the early 1600s on. These growers could exploit this market easily through a readily available trade channel: ships regularly journeyed between Pisco and Arica carrying mercury from Huancavelica for Potosí.[49]

Governmental decisions made competition stiffer in Peru's markets. For a brief interval during the early 1600s, the Crown remained satisfied with enforcing those taxes introduced in the 1590s. Restrictions and then a ban on trade between Peru and New Spain followed this lull, however. Initially, Arequipans must have believed that these decisions would not hurt them severely, because they did not lodge their usual vigorous complaints against measures affecting the wine industry.[50] They probably regarded the trade embargo as manageable because they no longer marketed much wine in Middle America. They depended on such commerce only for some of the pitch used to line earthen containers, and this Central American pitch was soon replaced from a local source.[51] The ban, nevertheless, had a far more important result, for those non-Arequipan producers who had previously shipped northward now turned more aggressively to Peruvian markets, and their increased sales contributed to price deflation. By the mid-1620s, the mean price for a *botija* wholesaled at an *heredad* in a coastal valley fell as low as during the mid-1590s, when Arequipa's production had been at its peak (see fig. 1).[52]

The Seventeenth-Century Wine Economy and Landownership

Many of those *heredados* who had managed to survive the catastrophic earthquakes must have hoped that the future would bring better times for the wine industry. It did not. Don Alonso Merlo de la Fuente, the solicitor general of Arequipa's cathedral, attributed the protracted difficulties to a shortage of slaves. The international disruption of the slave trade resulting from the Dutch wars against the Hapsburgs and from the Portuguese revolts, he contended, hurt *heredados* so severely that many gave up and sold their estates at low prices.[53] He exaggerated: notarial records from the 1630s to the 1660s do not reveal either a particularly pronounced slave shortage or a major round of land sales. Moreover, slave prices in the city remained quite stable.[54] Yet, his comments indicate that many *heredados* had reached the end of their rope. Although still able to procure slaves and keep their land, they were hard hit by low wine prices. Colonial overproduction and competition continued unabated, and prices fell steadily through the late 1660s, relieved only by a brief upturn during the late 1630s and early 1640s.

The tax burden also became a major concern at this point. Since the wine industry's start, *heredados* had had to cope with only one tax on production, the *diezmo*; the other levies had been on trade. The *diezmo*, a 10 percent assessment in kind on wine and on any other goods raised, supported the church. Its collection does not seem to have been a problem during the sixteenth century, despite quite substantial payments. One *heredado*, for instance, paid 400 pesos in wine in one year during the 1590s.[55]

The right to collect the tax during these years could be quite lucrative; as a consequence, many individuals bid actively when the cathedral, bishopric, and Crown portions were auctioned off. Nevertheless, *heredado* delinquency became a problem at the time of the strong earthquakes and persisted thereafter. The winning bidder for tithe collection around Arequipa in 1610, not unexpectedly, had to sign a contract stipulating that he could not blame quakes if unable to raise the full amount he had promised. Later, other collectors were prosecuted when they failed to live up to their bids.[56]

While *heredados* were struggling to pay the *diezmo*, the Crown threatened to compound their problems. Faced with severe financial strains from prolonged European conflicts, the king ordered a full-scale review of colonial taxation during the late 1620s in hopes of finding new ways to increase revenues. Among many recommendations, the Council of the Indies proposed several imposts on the wine industry. One was an annual tax of 2 percent on each estate owner's production, a measure justified on the grounds that many *heredados* had put in vineyards without royal licenses. When a royal decree ordered its collection beginning in May 1631, Arequipans lobbied strenuously against it in Lima; they argued that they not only had had royal permission since the 1540s to set up vineyards, but that also they had complied with the government's additional requirement in the 1590s that they legalize holdings. Both conditions, they held, warranted a regional exemption from this tax. The viceroy backed down, postponed implementation, and passed the problem on to Spanish home authorities.[57] They, in turn, referred the matter to Lima's *audiencia*, but did advise a course of action. Recommending that one suit against the tax be selected and that judicial proceedings be carried out speedily, they wanted this case to serve as a precedent; *heredados* must not delay implementation for years by protracted litigation. The Crown hinted broadly at how judges should find in this suit by restressing its contention that most vineyards were illegal and must be taxed.[58] Despite such clear guidelines, the *audiencia*, aware of the tax's unpopularity, shelved the whole matter. The Crown subsequently pressed viceroys, but, like the Marqués de Mancera, they generally promised only to look into the matter. As in earlier instances, they did not ignore the king altogether, but compromised by enforcing another impost that they considered less inflammatory. This tax, a fifteen-year levy of two reales per *botija* shipped along the Peruvian coast, was applied in 1639. Arequipans accepted it, since the duty was temporary and few shipped wine by sea anyway.[59]

The wine industry's continuing difficulties meant that some *heredados* had to borrow further or renegotiate loans. Some could prevail on wealthier colonials or marry sons and daughters to those with funds, but most came to rely on the increasingly wealthy religious orders in the city. The church enjoyed a close relationship with the *heredado* community. As noted previously, during the better days of the late 1500s, estate-owning families had contributed generously to religious houses and Arequipa's cathedral; many had placed family members in city convents and monasteries. Although seventeenth-century Arequipans could not afford to be as generous as were their forebears, they did continue to establish chantries, to join the various religious orders, and even occasionally to donate land, including *heredades*, to the church.[60] The monies and land enabled several orders to emerge as important seventeenth-century rural proprietors. Whereas the religious houses had possessed only a few *chácaras* and vineyards in 1612, they had many more two generations later.[61] The Mercedarians and the nuns of the Convent of Santa Catalina de Sena came to own substantial land, but the Jesuits were the most prominent rural proprietors (see table 4).[62]

The Jesuits, like other religious groups, emerged as landowners as a result of several important bequests. The first came from Antonio de Llanos, a merchant in the early postconquest years who eventually became an *encomendero* and landowner. Shortly after his wife's death, he joined the order and gave it his properties. Although the donation included few landholdings (some *chácaras* in the Arequipa Valley), it contained a number of mortgages, which provided the Jesuits with enough capital to buy and

Table 4
Rural Property Management by Arequipa's Jesuits

Acquisition Date	Property	How Acquired	Disposition
ca. 1580	Arequipa Valley *chácara*	Purchased	Unknown
1586	Arequipa Valley *chácara*	Purchased	Retained
ca. 1590	Arequipa Valley *chácara*	Donated	Sold
ca. 1590	Vítor Valley land	Purchased	Rented
1598	Arequipa Valley *chácara*	Purchased	Unknown
1601	Highland *estancia*	Unknown	Retained
1601	Arequipa Valley *chácara*, San Gerónimo	Public auction	Retained
1601	Small Arequipa Valley *chácaras*, next to San Gerónimo	Purchased and traded	Retained

Table 4 (continued)
Rural Property Management by Arequipa's Jesuits

Acquisition Date	Property	How Acquired	Disposition
1605	Siguas Valley *estancia*	Unknown	Sold
1610	Moquegua Valley *heredad*	Donated	Sold
1612	Arequipa Valley land, Guasacache	Public auction	Retained
1615	Majes Valley *heredad*	Donated	Unknown
1624	Two small Arequipa Valley *chácaras*	Donated	Unknown
1625	Arequipa Valley *chácara*, Santa Marta	Purchased	Sold
1625	Lluta Valley and Islay hills olive groves	Donated	Retained
1625	Vitor Valley *heredad*, San Juan de la Vega	Donated	Retained
1630	Ica Valley *heredad*	Purchased	Unknown
1631	Vitor Valley land, next to San Juan de la Vega	Purchased	Retained
1639	Vitor Valley land, next to San Juan de la Vega	Purchased	Retained
ca. 1640	Small Arequipa Valley plot	Donated	Unknown
1651	Arequipa Valley *chácara*, next to San Gerónimo	Purchased	Retained
1652	Vitor Valley *heredad*, La Viña Nueva	Public auction	Retained
ca. 1650	Majes Valley *heredad*	Purchased (?)	Retained
1662	Vitor Valley *heredad*, next to San Juan de la Vega	Public auction	Retained
1665	Vitor Valley land, next to San Juan de la Vega	Public auction	Retained
1669	Majes Valley *heredad*	Donated	Sold

Sources: ADA, Aguilar, 19 April 1605, 22 April 1605, Muñoz, 29 November 1595, Tejada, 4 June 1615, Ufelde, 12 December 1616; ANP, Temporalidades, Títulos, Guasacachi (1767-1779), Matarani y Lluta, Pacaychacra, San Gerónimo, and San Javier de Vitor (1767-1770), Compañía, Títulos, leg. 1 (1539-1605), leg. 2 (1606-1628), leg. 3 (1628-1652), leg. 4 (1652-1675), Títulos, leg. 1, cuad. 24 (1595), leg. 2, cuad. 66 (1628), leg. 3, cuad. 72 (1601), cuad. 73 (1634), cuad. 74 (1651), leg. 4, cuad. 96 (1665), leg. 5, cuad. 150 (1662), leg. 6, cuad. 155 (1600), cuad. 171 (1643), leg. 7, cuad. 215 (1645), leg. 25, cuad. 662 (1612).

develop estates.[63] Juan Gómez Chacón and his wife, Juana Ramírez, two fixtures of Arequipa's agricultural elite, subsequently willed other lands to the order. Their legacy included two olive groves, houses in the city, and an estate with thirty-four thousand vines and twenty black slaves.[64]

The Jesuits efficiently managed these and other holdings without over-extending themselves. When they obtained potentially profitable land too expensive to develop initially, they rented it. They leased one such parcel, for example, for three generations. The leaseholder had to pay a moderate annual charge of 150 *botijas* of wine, but he was required to put in a vineyard, fruit garden, house, storage shed, and wheat mill.[65] In other instances, when the Jesuits inherited poor lands, they sold them. Their sale of an *heredad* in Moquegua given them by the poet Alonso de Estrada was artful. Estrada had previously tried to unload the estate for 30,000 pesos, but the deal fell through. Within six months of gaining possession, the Jesuits sold it for 43,077 pesos and 2 reales, 191 *botijas* of wine, a chasuble, and a maniple. Since the property was encumbered by debts, they did not realize much, but the sale was wise. The buyer soon discovered that the lands were barren; the Jesuits may have listened politely to his constant complaints about poor wheat and grape yields, but they held him to the bargain.[66]

Table 4 provides a compilation of all Jesuit properties and their disposition until the late seventeenth century. San Juan de la Vega and La Viña Nueva were the order's main estates during the mid-1600s. As the data suggest, its members strove to expand San Juan by adding adjacent tracts. Like other successful *heredados*, the Jesuits also succeeded in the wine industry by cultivating regional markets. Recognizing that wholesaling their goods to merchants reduced profits, the order operated two retail stores in the city of Arequipa and also tapped the increasingly lucrative wine market in the Southwest's Indian highlands.[67] This trade blossomed during the 1600s. Indian wine consumption, held in check previously by royal disapproval and limited Indian purchasing power, expanded as *corregidores* encouraged it while in office in order to make money.[68] No doubt, consumption also grew as *curacas* acquired coastal vineyards and sold their wine, and as colonists dragged other Indians into the wine economy by having them work in the Cailloma and Castrovirreyna mines and serve as transporters.

The new market was a godsend to some *heredados*, for here Arequipans enjoyed a practical monopoly in an area isolated from trade routes. Cutthroat competition, however, set in among them and persisted throughout the seventeenth century. In one instance, after the Jesuits acquired Pacaychacra (in 1677), an *heredad* in the Majes Valley, and began to sell to Indians and mestizos from Chuquibamba and surrounding small towns, several *heredados*, long-accustomed to being the major suppliers, became so enraged that they persuaded the local *corregidor* to stop these sales. In complying, he probably also protected himself, since the normal pattern was to sell wine through retail shops that *corregidores* established in various towns under their jurisdiction. The Jesuits appealed to the viceroy through their contacts in Lima, and he reprimanded the *corregidor* for interfering with free trade.[69]

Despite their careful exploitation of markets and land donations, the Jesuits had to find other ways to protect themselves against declining wine prices. They diversified, acquiring olive groves and *estancias* within the coastal belt in addition to wheat *chácaras* in the Arequipa Valley (San Gerónimo being the most important). Here they raised crops and livestock for various local and regional markets. Nor did they confine their holdings to rural property, but derived income from urban rentals, homesites, and shops, as well as from mortgages and chantries. The Jesuits consequently had substantial working capital: they retired seven mortgages prior to the 1640s on which they collected 24,000 pesos.[70]

Although the church possessed significant capital resources, it did not outdistance Arequipa's major *heredado* families in land holdings during the seventeenth century. The Jesuits may have commanded the largest *heredad* along the Vítor River by mid-century, but they still owned only a fraction of the valley's total land. Further, their estate is impressive only if compared with the holdings of one *heredado*; it becomes less so if laid beside the properties of many families.[71] Indeed, the heirs of the *encomendero* Don Baltasar de Cárdenas, a latecomer as a proprietor, owned dispersed vineyards along the Vítor River whose total value equaled that of the property held by the Jesuits. Of course, this order had lands elsewhere, but so did the Cárdenas family. Three children and five grandchildren of Don Baltasar owned two estates along the Majes River and three *chácaras* in the Arequipa Valley.[72] All their holdings, though less extensive than the total Jesuit holdings, fully equaled those of the Mercedarians. Pinpointing precisely the proportion of non-Indian lands held by the church is difficult now, but, roughly calculated, the orders probably controlled about as much rural property as a handful of Arequipa's major families.[73]

Several factors account for the church's not dominating Arequipa's countryside. Like others interested in rural property, the religious orders' desire for land was restrained by the scarcity of arable lands and the landowners' unwillingness to sell. Developed lands thus came their way only infrequently, usually when a proprietor died without heirs. Even with substantial income, few in the church besides the Jesuits could afford the expense and risk of purchasing barren lands and investing in irrigation works. In most instances when the orders opened up land, they concentrated on the Arequipa Valley, a tendency related to the difficulties in marketing wine and to the profitability of wheat grown close to the city.[74]

Consequently, as the church accumulated funds and found it onerous or undesirable to invest them in land acquisitions and development, it turned to lending. By doing so, its monies buttressed private landownership— ownership by a narrow faction within the community. Since most friars, nuns, and secular clergy were the sons and daughters of *heredados* and their relatives, loans could hardly help but be influenced by family ties. Not surprisingly, then, a survey of those extended credit by the Mercedarians from 1578 to 1643 reveals that eight out of twenty recipients were either close relatives of members of that order or had an affiliation with the brotherhood, generally that of having previously established a chantry with them; an additional seven had distant family connections.[75] Similarly, other orders lent to those their members knew well. It was surely not coincidental that the half-brother of Joseph de Paz y Sosa's wife happened to be the steward of Santa Catalina when Joseph received from the nuns a loan for his Vítor estate.[76]

Nonetheless, the orders regarded their loans as serious business arrangements and were not averse to seizing the lands of those who defaulted.[77] A determined *heredado*, however, could stymie such seizures. Properties along the western rivers lay within a different administrative district than the city of Arequipa. If debtors fled to their estates along the western rivers, urban-based creditors had to appeal their claims through two sets of officials. The proceedings were so complex and time-consuming that frustrated creditors tried to have the Vítor Valley incorporated into the city's district during the 1630s. They failed and evasion persisted. As late as the 1680s the Convent of Santa Catalina de Sena was still trying to resolve difficulties with delinquents by having the viceroy appoint a special judge. The best solution devised by creditors was to await the death of an owner and then sue before authorities formally awarded the estate to heirs.[78]

Land Fragmentation

Not all *heredados* fell into desperate straits and had to flee to their estates. A few did surprisingly well, since viticulture still offered opportunities for those blessed with capital, sagacity, influence, and a little luck. Good lands, after all, might be secured within the coastal belt as an occasional indebted owner sold off portions of his estate to pay bills or as officials auctioned properties. By being patient, one might establish a foothold and gradually expand as adjoining tracts became available. Successfully following this course could result in an occasional *heredad* of up to 500 acres. Since consolidating estates of this size required constancy, the advantage lay with institutions like religious houses rather than with individuals.

Yet men like Don Alvaro Laso de la Vega y Bedoya Mogrovejo managed to do extremely well as rural entrepreneurs. He began as a landowner when he inherited property along the Vítor River from his father in the late 1500s. The vineyard was so badly damaged by earthquakes and floods that from 1604 to 1614 he could not meet the interest on a loan from the Convent of Santa Catalina de Sena. He finally met the obligation by paying in wine and then, negotiating simultaneously with the Jesuits to take over one of their properties then in disrepair, he slowly improved the estate. By promising to revive their estate, he gained its use for his lifetime and two succeeding generations. With this sound base, two of his sons enjoyed impressive careers. One, Don Diego, rented various properties in the Vítor and Arequipa valleys from time to time and trafficked in mules; his brother, Licenciado Don Alonso, a parish priest in the city of Arequipa, also rented lands, supervised those he inherited, and became an active buyer of Indian lands near the city during the 1640s. Naturally, successful landowners like these joined the Jesuits in marketing wine through their own agents in the city and the highlands.[79]

But most *heredados* did struggle, especially during the early seventeenth century, as they paid off debts and survived on reduced profits. Although their difficulties stemmed from taxes, labor shortages, and glutted markets, the expansion of their families intensified those difficulties. Arequipa's important rural landowners reared large families: those who possessed *heredades* along the Vítor River during the late 1500s, for example, had an average of eight children apiece. (Naturally, wide variations existed: Diego de Peralta Cabeza de Vaca had eighteen children, but Diego de Porres had only one; yet almost all had at least four offspring.)[80] During the wine industry's better days, *heredados* had had little trouble supporting their households and had even been able to accommodate those children who remained in Arequipa as adults by purchasing land for each.[81] (Property was usually donated to a religious order if a child entered the church.)

As economic difficulties befell them during the early 1600s, curtailing family funds and preventing *heredados* from sending some offspring abroad, all sons, and daughters before they married, generally had to live off what their parents already possessed.[82] Some helped run the family enterprises or handled special business concerns of their parents and received regular allowances.[83] Only a few received a section of their father's *heredad* and a *chácara*, rented from their fathers, or bought the land and paid for it by carrying a mortgage.[84] Now when children entered a religious order, parents often mortgaged property, either promising a share of its proceeds for the sustenance of the son or daughter or earmarking a part of the yearly revenue for the religious house. Donations of land to a convent or monastery were infrequent and especially rare while the head of a household lived.[85] Now when parents arranged a son's marriage, they normally parted with a portion of their holdings to sustain the couple. Similarly, they sometimes transferred land to daughters, although a father and mother might occasionally prefer to borrow against their property for a cash dowry. Nevertheless, if a son-in-law insisted on land, he usually received it either through purchase (with a mortgage established to pay for the property) or as a gift.[86]

Given the costs of entailment, landowners rarely used this device from the late sixteenth through the mid-seventeenth centuries. Thus, properties fragmented further after landowners died. Heirs would bring in an outsider who estimated the cash value of the deceased's holdings and assigned equal shares to the survivors. In 1595, for example, two brothers, Hernando de Almonte and Gerónimo de Villalobos, had the estate they had inherited from their parents inventoried and divided. The partition went well when it came to the slaves, vineyard, garden, unworked lands, and tools, with each heir receiving half. But difficulties arose over the buildings, the owner's residence, the wine press, and the storage sheds. Hernando received all, though Gerónimo gained the use of the storage sheds and a specified number of the *tinajas*. The brothers also had to agree that, if one decided to develop his portion of the unused lands, they would share the costs of an irrigation canal and each would allow the other to run the ditch through his land.[87]

Although such fragmentation of *heredades* occurred frequently, coastal estates being the most valuable part of most inheritances, it was contained somewhat. Most second-generation heirs tended to divide estates into three or four sections; the third generation only rarely subdivided the estates further (see table 5). Several factors contributed to this development. Arequipans could occasionally create adequate shares for some offspring by assigning them the urban home, *chácaras*, and loans due the family. Also, by selling property to a son, daughter, or in-law, parents insured against excessive subdivisions when they died. Naturally, when arranging these sales fathers and mothers made sure that the other children had been provided for, generally by endowing the marriages of daughters with substantial cash, as well as by establishing annuities for other offspring from the proceeds of their holdings.[88]

The extreme indebtedness of some owners after the early 1600s further contributed to the survival of whole properties. When these debtors died,

Table 5

Disposition of Selected *Heredades*, ca. 1600-ca. 1640

Heredad Owner	No. of Sections	Section Owner			Acquisition by Nonfamily		
		Family	Church	Others	Auction	Sale	Donation
Hernando de Almonte							
2d generation	4	4					
3d generation	4	2		2	2		
Alonso Picado							
2d generation	2	2					
3d generation	4		1	3		3	1
Diego de Porres							
2d generation	1	1 (stepson)					
3d generation	1		1		1		
Juan de Quirós Vozmediano							
2d generation	2(?)	1(?)	1			1	
3d generation	2		1	1		2	
Miguel Navarro							
2d generation	2	2					
3d generation	3			3	2	1	
Rodrigo de Orihuela							
2d generation	3	3					
3d generation	3(?)						
Luis Cornejo							
2d generation	3	2	1			1	
3d generation	4	2		2		2	

Table 5 (continued)
Disposition of Selected *Heredades*, ca. 1600–ca. 1640

Heredad Owner	No. of Sections	Section Owner			Acquisition by Nonfamily		
		Family	Church	Others	Auction	Sale	Donation
Diego de Peralta							
2d generation	8	8					
3d generation	8	7		1		1	
Antonio de Valderrama							
2d generation	4	4					
3d generation	1	1		1	1		
Diego de Herrera							
2d generation	6	6					
3d generation	7	4(?)		3		3	
Alonso de Torres							
2d generation	3	1		2		2	
3d generation	3(?)						
Juan de Salazar							
2d generation	2	2					
3d generation	3	3					

Sources: *Almonte*—ANP, Títulos, leg. 9, cuad. 265 (1623), leg. 7, cuad. 215 (1645), Compañía, Títulos, leg. 1 (1539-1605), Compañía, Censos, leg. 2 (1636-1670); ADA, Ufelde, 7 August 1616, Muñoz, 16 July 1622, Francisco de Vera, 16 July 1622; AMA, leg. 5 (29 October 1597, 12 January 1598, 17 April 1623), leg. 6 (17 November 1620).

Picado—ADA, Tejada, 9 May 1615, Francisco de Vera, 13 March 1622, Muñoz, 3 November 1644, Gordejuela, 29 August 1636, Diego de Silva, 14 June 1644; ANP, Juicios de Residencia, leg. 17, cuad. 46 (1600); AMA, leg. 5 (23 August 1643).

Porres—ANP, Compañía, Títulos, leg. 3 (1628-1652); ADA, Muñoz, 23 June 1600, Tejada, 4 April 1614; AMA, leg. 6 (14 May 1611).

Quirós Vozmediano—ANP, Compañía, Títulos, leg. 1 (1539-1605), leg. 3 (1628-1652); ADA, Antonio de Silva, 4 June 1657.

Navarro—ADA, Diego de Aguilar, 18 November 1603, Tejada, 24 July 1612, 1 September 1612, 21 April 1616.

Orihuela—ADA, Aguilar, 11 March 1596, 21 June 1596, Tejada, 9 May 1615, Muñoz, 5 January 1622, 12 October 1622; BNP, ms. B1241 (1623); ANP, Títulos, leg. 7, cuad. 215 (1645).

Cornejo—ADA, Tejada, 9 May 1615, 7 January 1616, 13 March 1616, 21 April 1616, 25 June 1616, Ufelde, 7 January 1616, Francisco de Vera, 18 January 1622, Diego de Silva, 24 September 1653, Antonio de Silva, 9 May 1657, Diez, 20 August 1665: ANP, Compañia, Títulos, leg. 3 (1628-1652), Títulos, leg. 7, cuad. 215 (1645), Archivo de Temporalidades, Expedientes sobre Títulos, Tacar; AMA, leg. 1 (7 May 1661), leg. 5 (17 April 1623).

Peralta—ADA, Aguilar, 12 May 1603, 16 June 1603, Ufelde, 9 August 1616, Tejada, 4 April 1614, Diego de Silva, 22 June 1644, 8 November 1644, 24 September 1653; ANP, Compañia, Censos, leg. 1 (1567-1636), leg. 2 (1636-1670); AMA, leg. 5 (23 August 1643), leg. 7 (15 July 1658), BNP, ms. B428 (1645).

Valderrama—ADA, Aguilar, 28 November 1596, 9 January 1598, Tejada, 10 July 1612; AMA, leg. 7 (11 April 1623).

Herrera—ANP, Compañia, Títulos, leg. 1 (1539-1605), leg. 3 (1628-1652), Títulos, leg. 4, cuad. 96 (1665); ADA, Muñoz, 29 November 1594, Tejada, 1 September 1612, Ufelde, 13 March 1616, 14 September 1616, 12 December 1616, Laguna, 25 August 1648, Antonio de Silva, 6 October 1657; AMA, leg. 1 (7 May 1661).

Torres—ADA, Muñoz, 17 November 1600, 5 January 1622, Tejada, 6 July 1612; AMA, leg. 2 (18 July 1583).

Salazar—ANP, Compañia, Títulos, leg. 3 (1628-1652); BNP, ms. B1529 (1619); AMA, leg. 5 (16 January 1631); ADA, Aguilar, 12 January 1598, Tejada, 20 August 1612, Ufelde, 19 December 1616, Diego de Silva, 3 June 1644.

creditors expected heirs to assume the debts on the land, but if they refused, government officials rented or sold the property, thereby maintaining the estate as one entity. Interestingly, when these authorities disposed of the land through an auction, a family member of the previous owner sometimes successfully bid for it. Such was the case, for example, when Diego de Porres's estate was sold after his death.[89]

Some heirs may have preferred auctions by government officials rather than partitioning the land among themselves in order to avoid the dangers of subsequent disputes. All too often a partition later led to wranglings over the property division or the assignment of debts. Economic considerations no doubt played a role as well, particularly when the property was a small *heredad*, since operating a fraction of a vineyard during a period of high labor costs and low prices could be unprofitable. The widow of an *heredado* who had inherited a portion of his father's estate, for instance, reported that the property perennially ran in the red.[90] More than one descendant of a sixteenth-century proprietor failed to manage with a part of an estate and was forced to sell to meet debts.[91]

Auctions also occasionally enabled the family of a deceased owner, who had become heavily indebted and had mortgaged his *heredad*, to negotiate better terms with creditors than those the family would assume if it simply inherited the estate. When the property was put up for auction by authorities to pay off the creditors, a family member would bid below the total accumulated debts.[92] But a family could run into trouble if it chose this alternative, for there was no guarantee that an outsider who was also interested in the property would not bid higher. Thus, families that wanted to retain estates usually went through the motions of a partition among heirs and then arranged intrafamily sales. The sellers in these instances were invariably those who had chosen or planned a life in the church or brothers and sisters who had already acquired land either from their parents or through marriage. Frequently the buyers agreed to carry a mortgage on the land in their relative's name, or in the case of a seller who had joined the church, in that of an order.[93] These arrangements generally went smoothly, but sometimes someone, convinced that the deal had not been in his or her best interest, tried to renegotiate terms or get the land back.[94] These wrangles must have convinced sellers that they should have held on and rented the land, as some others had done,[95] thereby gaining the time to think the whole matter through.

In time, therefore, ownership of those estates created in the late 1500s, and occasionally of *estancias* and *chácaras* as well, became quite complicated. Table 6 traces ownership of two coastal *heredades* from 1583 to the early 1660s and illustrates some of the various patterns that emerged.

Table 6
Successive Owners of Sections of Two Vitor Valley *Heredades*, 1583-early 1660s

ESTATE OF JUAN DE SALAZAR

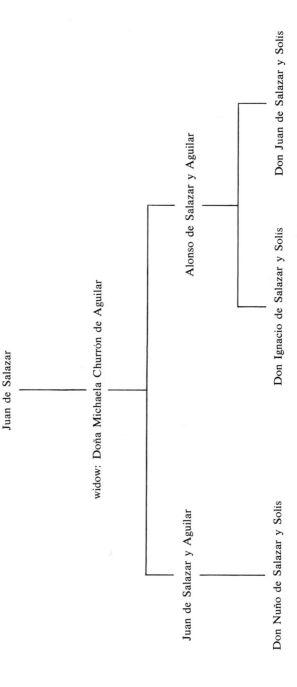

Juan de Salazar

widow: Doña Michaela Churrón de Aguilar

Juan de Salazar y Aguilar

Don Nuño de Salazar y Solis

Alonso de Salazar y Aguilar

Don Ignacio de Salazar y Solis

Don Juan de Salazar y Solis

Table 6 (continued)

ESTATE OF DIEGO DE HERRERA

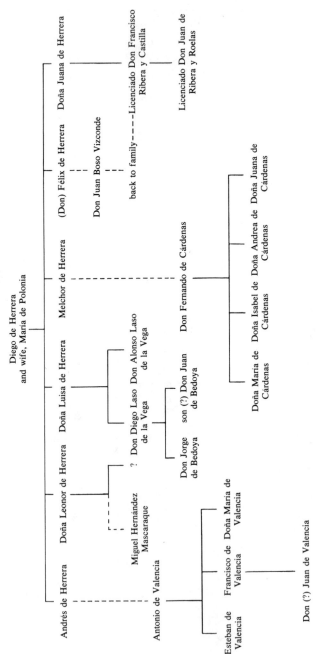

Sources: *SMC*, pp. 146-149; *SMA*, pp. 49, 55-56, 87, 113-114, 119-120, 128; *SMG*, p. 90; *SMF*, p. 425. Additional evidence for both families can be found in the sources for table 5.

Note: A solid line indicates inheritance by a family member, a slashed line, sale to nonfamily.

Juan de Salazar's property passed smoothly through some of his direct heirs, broken down into only three parts by 1660. Diego de Herrera's family, on the other hand, fragmented the estate as it was inherited by second-generation descendants, and as the Herreras sold to outsiders; however, the family later recovered a portion.

The contrasting experiences of the Salazars and Herreras should not suggest that the seventeenth century witnessed the onset of important economic differences among descendants of major sixteenth-century Arequipans. On the surface, Diego de Herrera's sons do appear to have had disastrous careers, yet the loss of inherited Vítor Valley lands was not catastrophic. Andrés and Félix actually enjoyed some success as landowners. During the 1590s, Andrés not only possessed a portion of his father's former vineyard, but also an olive grove and an *estancia* on the coastal hills and a *chácara* close to the city of Arequipa. After selling his portion of the Vítor *heredad* to pay off debts, he disposed of his other holdings, using the proceeds to buy another and larger coastal wine estate. He became a prominent *heredado* and a permanent councilor in the city.[96] Félix, too, reemerged as an important landowner after having sold his Vítor inheritance. He bought new lands near Moquegua, where property was cheaper, and soon established a wine estate with an impressive number of black slaves for the time. This *heredad* and other lands he owned closer to the city of Arequipa eventually enabled him to purchase a council seat as well.[97] Consequently, Arequipans came to regard him as Don Félix for much of his adult life.

Rather remarkably, in surveying the lives of each descendant of important *encomenderos* and major landowners of the sixteenth century, it is difficult to find an individual who went begging in the period from the late 1500s to the mid-1600s. The information in table 5 hints at this, for, despite the subdivision of twelve estates into at least thirty-seven sections after two generations (data are questionable on the Orihuela and Torres third generation sections), half of these sections remained with the descendants of the original owners. Some idea of the survival of families as landowners can also be gained by comparing Appendices B and C, which list proprietors along the Vítor River in 1583 and during the early 1660s. The new owners who appear in the later list, as the discussion below will indicate, were overwhelmingly immigrants who had married into estate-owning families. But such comparisons, as the case of the Herrera brothers suggests, are only of limited value, for descendants of landowners often remained important regional *heredados* even after selling inherited land. They would acquire other property, renegotiate loans, rent tracts, and thus survive.[98]

Admittedly, however, not all descendants of *heredados* endured as landowners. Over the course of the seventeenth century, some who joined the church parted with land. Those who became members of the regular clergy, of course, could not legally hold land and so some turned over their inheritance to the religious orders. A few exceptional secular churchmen, like Licenciado Don Alonso de Bedoya Mogrovejo, remained active landowners, holding on to an inheritance, renting property, and acquiring *chácaras*.[99] Some female offspring outside the church also retained no family land, but were supported by their husbands' holdings and their land-poor dowries. Other sons and daughters of landowners and their heirs who left the city after they married did not keep land. Thus, in the case of Juan de Salazar's family (as the data in table 6 indicate), only two sons became landowners like their father; of the six other children, three joined the church, one daughter married into a landowning family of a *corregidor*, and another child wed a *corregidor* and then apparently left the city. (I could find no information on Doña María, the remaining child.)[100]

In rare instances, all offspring parted with family property. The children of Alvaro Fernández de la Cuadra and Doña Teresa Almonte Laso de la Vega, for example, allowed the estate of their maternal grandfather to be auctioned to cover debts when their parents died. They did not suffer unduly for it, since each was well fixed by then. One son had already become a priest, two daughters had entered the Convent of Santa Catalina de Sena (one would become a prioress), another daughter had married a *corregidor* and settled in Moquegua, and the remaining daughters wed landholders (one the great-grandson of the *encomendero*-founder Miguel Cornejo).[101] Perhaps their parents' heavy borrowing against the land, which led to the sale, was due to efforts made to set up the children for life.

Recurrent fragmentation of estates in the old wine-producing area produced some negative effects. Among these, of course, was the emergence of smaller *heredades*, which yielded reduced profits. By the mid-seventeenth century, properties rarely exceeded 40 acres. Notably, fragmentation also diminished differences in the size of Arequipans' holdings. A survey of landowners in the Vítor Valley, prepared during the early 1660s, noted not only the names of proprietors, but also the tax assigned to each, a determination based on the size and value of the estate. Forty-nine owners had to pay annually from three to six *botijas*; only ten paid more than six, and eleven less than three (see Appendix C). The surveyors even judged that most owners who paid above six or under three *botijas* held parcels quite similar in value to those possessed by the others. (Their assessments were only slightly more or less than the three to six *botijas* assessed the forty-nine.) They assessed only one owner, the Compañía de Jesús, the unusually large contribution of twenty-four *botijas* of wine. In short, descendants of sixteenth-century *heredados* had come to own small properties, barely distinguishable in size and value.[102]

Conclusion

Despite the absence of a major administrative or mining center in the region, the southwestern colonial economy flourished during the sixteenth century after landowners geared their production to certain agricultural commodities in great demand elsewhere in the viceroyalty. Once established, the wine trade endured as the mover of the Arequipan economy.

But the Arequipan economy did not fare as well during the seventeenth century. The difficulties cannot be ascribed to changed conditions in colonial markets inasmuch as many indicators point to a robust Peruvian economy. As David Brading and Harry Cross have demonstrated, the mines at Potosí and other sites remained productive. Peter Bakewell's work confirms their finding that no major mining recession occurred in Peru before the late 1600s. Indeed, market conditions may even have improved, since a great deal of silver now stayed in the colony. María Encarnación Rodríguez Vicente has found that a large proportion of the Crown's share of mined silver and that collected for taxes went into the salaries of viceregal bureaucrats.[103]

Neither can Indian depopulation be isolated as a major factor in Arequipa's economic straits. *Heredados* needed only a small number of workers after vineyards had been put in. Their situation reinforces Bakewell's telling point that New Spain's mining recession of the early 1600s should not be attributed to Indian population losses, since miners employed only a few such workers and soon supplemented them with black slaves. Arequipans, too, turned to black laborers, as did others throughout the coastal strip of the southern viceroyalty, and their access to slaves suffered no major disruptions until the mid-1600s.[104]

Paradoxically, Arequipa's agriculturists suffered because of their initial success. When trade expanded to a level requiring merchants' expertise and connections, *heredados* lost control of the marketing of their goods, which cut into their profits. Simultaneously, other colonists, those in valleys to the north of Arequipa and in western Argentina, developed vineyards. These producers enjoyed greater proximity to the colony's best markets and became even stronger competitors when Southwesterners lost an important trade route because of a viceregal decision to divert silver and mercury away from Arequipa and to the port of Arica.

The position of Arequipans eroded even further as earthquakes and consequent flooding destroyed *heredades*. These, coming at the crucial moment when competition was stiffening, reveal vividly the delicate nature of parts of the Peruvian colonial economy. A region lacking sufficient local consumers for its products and dependent on colonial trade could be crippled swiftly if another supplier lay in the wings. This was especially true if an area's producers enjoyed no significant advantages with respect to credit, labor, and imperial laws and taxes. The Arequipan case also underscores the diverse economic fortunes of colonials. The region's difficulties had much in common with those of other areas, such as western Central America. But there was no wholesale economic depression. As a number of studies have suggested, colonials elsewhere found opportunities and succeeded admirably during the 1600s.[105]

Fortunately, local resources existed in Arequipa to cushion the negative consequences of lost colonial markets. The interrelationship that had developed between the church and the secular world proved particularly important: sons and daughters of the landed elite found refuge in religious orders; these orders often provided the necessary capital to sustain many an owner. A number of producers adjusted to diminished markets by expanding their sales in the one area where Arequipa had a commanding position—the Indian highlands to the east of the city. By these and other business arrangements, most landed families managed to cling to their holdings and parcel them out to descendants. Such doggedness meant survival, and later it enabled Arequipans to devise other alternatives to their economic plight.

6. Colonial Expansion into the Indian Southwest

*En la venta de tierras que hico el dicho Don Luis de Lozada . . .
[los] indios fueron notablem^{te} agraviados . . . despoxandoles de
sus tierras y posess^{on} que tenian que eran las mejores por tener las
experimentadas y encavezera de aguas . . .*
————Maestre de Campo Don Joseph de Bolívar,
Corregidor of Arequipa

*[Los indios están] quietos y pasificos y sin tener necessidad de mas
tierras de las que se les dexaron ellos y para sus comunidades.*
————Fray Tomás de Argüello

    Landowning families did not simply accept the fragmentation of their
properties when problems beset Arequipa's wine industry. Slowly at first
and then with increasing rapidity as opportunities presented themselves
during the 1640s, these families acquired lands in previously ignored
sections of the Southwest. They initially concentrated their acquisitions in
the coastal belt to the south of the valleys that had been exploited after 1557;
they turned afterward to the Arequipa Valley, the northern coastal valleys, and
the sierra. In expanding Arequipa's rural domain, colonials hoped to
accommodate their increasing numbers and to find the room to diversify agricultural production. Expansion posed a major problem in that it severely challenged many Indian landholders for the first time since the Spanish arrival.

Use and Ownership of Coastal Land during the Early Seventeenth Century

    Several early seventeenth-century travelers vividly described coastal southwestern Peru. Journeying south from Lima, most entered the Bishopric of Arequipa close to the Pacific at the Acarí River and then traversed the coastal belt as far south as the Loa River. As would be expected, they usually described the region's wine estates, particularly those of the Majes, Vítor, Siguas, and Tambo valleys. Invariably they stressed both the importance of viticulture to Arequipans and the economic reverses that followed the catastrophes of 1600 and 1604.[1]

Their writings, when supplemented by reports of government-appointed inspectors and royal officials, also provide a rich source of information on land use and land ownership outside the core area. The travelers noticed that those parts of the coastal belt neglected by Arequipa's major landowning families were farmed by a few *castas* and Spaniards living in small settlements. From the Acarí River to the Majes, most grew maize, wheat, beans, olives, and assorted fruits on modest farms; others grazed livestock on the coastal hills. Theirs was a subsistence economy, though in the north some managed a small surplus, which they sent to Nazca. Those farther south shipped olives and olive oil to Lima and some wine inland. Coastal *estancias* and olive groves were also found south of the Tambo River, where isolated farms, specializing in grains, pimientos, and chilies, dotted many valleys as well. Mule raising was particularly important to residents of the town of Arica, since carriers needed the livestock for transport inland to Potosí.[2]

More Indians lived north of the Majes River and south of the Tambo River during the early 1600s than in the core area of Arequipan viticulture.[3] These natives, as they had at the conquest, also practiced subsistence farming that emphasized Peruvian crops. They had altered their landholding patterns somewhat after the early 1570s because of royal insistence that natives consolidate villages and because colonials seized or bought Indian property.[4] Yet, if patterns within the northern quarter of the coastal belt were typical, Indians still held more than the bare minimum necessary to survive. A 1590s survey revealed, for example, that each of the eight male heads of household of one community based in the village of Santiago de Parcos de Acarí possessed not only a village house and usually a horse, but also an average of ten rural land plots; three of four single adult women owned at least seven plots. The parcels of many Indians were scattered over several valleys, which suggests that, as some had been forced to relocate, they kept farm plots while acquiring others.[5]

A number of *curacas* residing throughout the coastal belt had become major landowners and adopted Old World crops. Don Alonso Satuni, the principal *curaca* of Indians in northern valleys, for instance, owned almost 20 acres in Amato, around 16 in the Jaqui Valley, a plot in Parcos, another in Llangascanta, twenty-one parcels in the Acarí Valley, seven others devoted to maize in Guarato, one devoted to coca in Acarí, and another fifty nearby, to chilies. He also owned two hundred goats, five mares, one horse, and sixty cows.[6] To the south, Don Diego Catari, *curaca* of Indians in the Tacna region when the Spaniards founded Arequipa, gradually acquired rural property in various valleys, which he passed on to his son, Don Diego Caqui. The son, while *curaca*, added more landholdings and when he drew up a will in 1588, it recorded several *chácaras*, four vineyards (three with over thirty thousand vines each), a wine-storage shed, a wine press, one hundred llamas used to transport produce to inland Peru, and three ships that he no doubt used for trafficking wine along the coast.[7]

The Highlands during the Early Seventeenth Century

Few *castas* and Spaniards resided permanently or owned land in the highlands during the early seventeenth century. No doubt the isolation of the region, cut off as it was from the city of Arequipa by rugged mountains and bleak highland plains, discouraged their presence. Royal requirements that Indians live separately from Spaniards may also have played a role. The government's choices of highland officials—*corregidores* like Licenciado Juan Polo de Ondegardo—and the selection of Franciscans for pastoral care were excellent, and on the whole, up to the 1590s, such men seemed bent on improving the Indians' lot by introducing Christianity and innovations in the Indian economy.[8] Their exploitation of Indian labor, land, and livestock appears to have been kept to a minimum.

By the turn of the century, however, that had begun to change. Indians properly accused *corregidores* and their lieutenants of retailing wine in native villages at exorbitant prices. Officials and priests also forced Indians to sell them livestock cheaply. They grazed these llamas on community lands and then disposed of the animals at a profit. Some required Indians to weave textiles so that they too might be sold. And, they exploited Indian lands. Government officials apparently appropriated the plots of those who lived away from the villages or who had died. Natives complained that such practices violated custom and contended that each community should reassign the land to its members. But at least one *corregidor* countered that he had actually rented the land from Indians for himself. Other *corregidores* defended their use of Indian labor on these plots by claiming that they paid fair wages. Indians often rejoined that they received either no pay or paltry sums. They further charged that outsiders, often *yanaconas* whom *corregidores* introduced to the area, supervised the work.[9] Whatever the case, Indians apparently expended a fair amount of labor for some *corregidores* and their lieutenants. One royal official allegedly insisted that Indians tend from 2 to 5 acres on the outskirts of each village under his jurisdiction. If we accept the Indian testimony that about 4 acres under production required the labor of thirty Indians five days per year, the official tied up a considerable number of the natives.[10] Nevertheless, the exploitation by royal functionaries probably did not greatly affect highland ownership patterns until the mid-1600s. Each Indian community lost only a few acres to Spaniards, most perhaps only temporarily as the government rotated *corregidores*.

Some of these highland Indians, like those along the coast, were relocated beginning in the 1570s. Although historians have charted their movement to new towns, it is difficult to assess the effects on landholding.[11] Occasional seventeenth-century disputes between native communities suggest that some villagers had trouble retaining parcels as they moved away from their traditional lands and that they resorted to Spanish courts to preserve these tracts.[12]

But no matter what lands they possessed, most resettled Indians tried to maintain their landholding customs. Farmland remained divided between property assigned to individuals and that held communally. Each community decided how to apportion its lands; at the death of members, their parcels usually returned to the community for reassignment. Individual holdings remained scattered, as they had been in the past, and located at various elevations, apparently, so that the Indians could raise several crops. On the average, an adult male possessed from 2 to 4 acres.[13] Several highland farming villages retained outposts along the coast as well, trading with them for fish and guano. Those who did not have such outposts procured fertilizer from sierra llama herders, exchanges that likely involved barter.[14]

As they had at conquest, Indian farmers emphasized maize and potatoes on their individual holdings in the valleys, and quinoa and tubers at higher elevations. Most farming families worked their own plots, yet a few hired others, particularly groups, at planting and harvest. Whether this meant a corruption of former practices, with the proprietor paying for the work in cash rather than by exchanging labor, cannot be determined.[15] Community lands also served mainly for native crops. Indians at Viraco, for example, grew only maize on their town's highland tracts; however, they did plant wheat on their property in the Arequipa Valley. This conversion to an Old World crop may have been forced on them by *cabildo* regulations, but the Indians may have wanted to participate in the money economy, given their access to a major colonial market.[16]

The farms close to Arequipa owned by highlanders such as those from Viraco normally had been donated to them by *encomenderos*. Indians also received several vineyards. Located along the headwaters of coastal rivers, these properties originally had been developed during the mid-1500s when colonists first experimented with viticulture. As the lower elevations proved better for raising grapes, the Spaniards turned them over to their Indians, who continued to work the vineyards or leased them to colonials. Indians at Viraco possessed two such parcels, one with seven thousand vines, the other with nine thousand. The Andagua *hurinsaya* Indians possessed 4 acres, a wine-storage shed, and *tinajas*; the Andagua *hanansaya* Indians owned a vineyard in the Ayo Valley.[17]

Indian accommodation to Old World agriculture, however, was not simply a product of Spanish regulations and donations. Highlanders in the Condesuyos region enthusiastically raised European livestock, principally sheep. They owned them communally and grazed the animals alongside their llamas and alpacas. One town of around two thousand persons possessed over 1,000 sheep and almost 150 llamas for its own needs; another held around 620 sheep, 7 cows, and 50 llamas. Indians living away from the river valleys, at higher elevations where grass was scarce, could not introduce such livestock in large numbers. Thus, Indians at Tisco in Cailloma, a town with almost six hundred residents, continued to rely on native animals. Ninety-eight persons owned 1,479 llamas and alpacas: sixty residents possessed from 2 to 10 head apiece; the rest, up to 80. Interestingly, these Indians did not own herds communally, an apparent deviation from past practices.[18]

Differences also existed among highland Indians regarding the amount of land to which each had access. As within the coastal belt, native officials generally possessed more than others. Among the Yanque Collaguas, *curacas* held about 12 acres each; other Indians held less than 4 acres each. The smaller holdings of highland *curacas*, compared with coastal-belt *curacas*, probably resulted from the survival of more Indians there, thereby giving leaders less opportunity to appropriate land. Yet this does not seem to have been the only reason, for surplus land existed after a drop of around one-third in the adult male population over the last thirty years of the sixteenth century.[19] Such a surplus is apparent in the unexploited communal tracts that could be found in certain villages.[20] Highland *curacas* may have had trouble finding the labor to work vacant lands—a development linked to labor draft requirements at mines—or may not have wanted to add to the burdens of those under their control. They were, after all, concerned enough to complain of *corregidor* and Spanish exploitation on more than one occasion.[21]

Landholding in the Arequipa Valley to the Early Seventeenth Century

Although the rather difficult terrain of the desertic coastal belt and of the mountainous highlands helped the Indians survive as landholders throughout the sixteenth century, colonials' lack of interest in these areas was more important. Having decided to emphasize viticulture along the Vítor, Majes, Siguas, and Tambo rivers, the Spaniards concentrated resources there and turned their backs on much of the Southwest, save for demanding labor.[22] That lack of interest extended to landholding in the Arequipa Valley from the 1560s through the early seventeenth century.

Arequipans did not ignore lands around the city altogether, but they remained satisfied with modest properties that rarely exceeded 50 acres. Owners of the largest *chácaras*, normally *heredados*, religious orders, wealthy artisans, merchants, and government functionaries, used the land to supplement domestic needs by raising wheat (which flourished in the valley's cool climate), maize, vegetables, and alfalfa. Numerous impecunious Arequipans also possessed land by the early 1600s, generally no more than 3 or 4 acres.[23] Most gained these parcels after 1557, when pressures for land in the valley slackened slightly as wealthier residents turned to coastal viticulture. Not only did poorer colonists purchase land from founders, from Indians, and occasionally from the royal government, they also received it during the early years through *cabildo* grants and a few simply squatted on unclaimed parcels. Some proprietors worked their small holdings, yet most, like the larger owners, lived in the city and relied on drafted Indian laborers whom authorities parceled out weekly in the central plaza.[24]

Indians shared the Arequipa Valley with colonials following the conquest, despite their loss of some land when officials accommodated the founders or when settlers bought parcels. Until the 1570s, Indian crop choices and land use changed gradually, as *encomenderos* badgered them and insisted that the Indians plant wheat. Municipal authorities soon encouraged the trend by demanding an annual tax of one fanega of wheat from each adult male for the city's storehouse.[25] Most natives complied unenthusiastically, but a few seized on the opportunity to market Old World crops as well as indigenous foodstuffs in the city. The more successful, often *curacas*, built up impressive private landholdings. Don Sebastián Tito Gualpa, for example, owned several farms in the Tambo Valley, three *chácaras* in the Arequipa Valley, and livestock *estancias*.[26]

Indians not native to the region also held Arequipa Valley land near the city by the late sixteenth century. A few had probably immigrated as the personal servants of colonists and had initially worked on Spanish-owned *chácaras*. In return, the Spaniards sometimes gave them small plots, usually in their wills.[27] Other Indians, who may have been attracted by the opportunity to work, drifted in and bought lands. Their familiarity with the Hispanic world explains why they grew native as well as Old World crops and raised European livestock.[28] Still, most Indian immigrants had difficulty acquiring land. As a consequence, many survived as household servants or artisan helpers, insisting in contracts with Spaniards that they be fed. Most others hired themselves out to farm owners and normally received a small wage and the use of slivers of land on which to grow food.[29]

Landholding patterns of *originarios* (natives of the region) began to change more dramatically during the 1570s. While in the city, Viceroy Toledo ordered all Arequipa Valley Indians enumerated and consolidated into ten towns. His subordinates assigned farmland within a three-mile radius of their new homes to those uprooted from their scattered small villages and hamlets. In theory new plots had to be of the same quality as those given up. Land to accommodate those transferred came from formerly vacant tracts and from Spanish holdings within three miles of each native town. (The officials recompensed the Spaniards with lands taken from the Indians.)[30]

The relocation initially appeared to go well, at least in the eyes of royal authorities, but soon the hope that natives would live in neat, grid-patterned villages while farming surrounding lands was dashed. Many Indians built homes on their farms, others retained or acquired land beyond the three-mile limit, and some planted on their village house plots.[31] As important as this corruption of Toledo's plan was the tendency of some Indians to abandon native customs. The more Hispanized Indians began to consider their assigned tracts personal rather than communal property, a development common to natives elsewhere in the Americas. Over the years, they sold them with no compunction. Others, particularly *curacas*, drew up wills before notaries and passed their lands on to their heirs. Spanish officials generally accepted this treatment of property.[32]

Nevertheless, most *originarios* retained the land they received from Viceroy Toledo's subordinates through the early seventeenth century. It is difficult to spell out exactly the amount of land each Indian possessed at the end of the sixteenth century, but many seemingly had at least enough to survive on without having to supplement their incomes by working elsewhere. Several communities even enjoyed a surplus of land and occasionally rented out plots or left parcels fallow. The best evidence on individual Indian landholding close to the city of Arequipa dates from the 1590s. Unfortunately the documentation is for some groups that lived near Camaná, a Spanish town outside the Arequipa Valley. Their circumstances, however, were probably worse than those of Indians residing nearer the city, since their holdings lay within the coastal belt, an area where Southwesterners coveted land for vineyards. Whatever the case, the data reveal that one Indian group was quite well endowed with land: all married males (ages eighteen to fifty) held at least four farm plots apiece; a goodly number had ten. Each single or widowed woman possessed at least seven parcels of land.

In other communities, where officials measured holdings more precisely, married males held from 2 to 7 acres apiece; over 50 percent had 4 acres or more.[33]

Steady Indian depopulation partially explains why the natives still possessed so much land.[34] Municipal protection of Indian landholdings in the Arequipa Valley played a major role as well. In holding off colonial usurpers, authorities simply recognized the natives' crucial role in feeding the city. Those in the vicinity not only served as drafted laborers on Spanish *chácaras*, but also raised needed produce. The municipal requirement that Indians raise wheat along with native sales of foodstuffs supplemented colonials' output. Without Indian labor and crops, the city would have been in dire straits, a situation regularly made clear when epidemics laid low the natives or an early freeze damaged their crops.

Yet even in normal times, colonials suffered from food shortages. Local authorities consequently battled vigorously to insure supplies by rationing and curtailing exports whenever dangers loomed.[35] These measures generally proved unsuccessful, and the cost of most foodstuffs, save for wine and olives, remained high. Attempts to regulate prices rarely worked well. Not surprisingly, some royal officials claimed that they could not sustain themselves in Arequipa and sent detailed lists of household expenses to Spain in hopes of receiving raises.[36] Matters would have reached a critical stage for all colonists during the latter half of the sixteenth century if the city's non-Indian population growth had been less moderate.[37]

The Appropriation of Arequipa Valley Lands: 1604-1641

Control of communal Indian land came under increasing attack after the major earthquakes of the early seventeenth century. At first some colonists of mixed race forced their way into Indian villages and seized lands. Most of these depredations, however, succeeded only temporarily. Colonists were defeated in the end by the Indians themselves or by the Spanish authorities, either the Santa Hermandad (a rural constabulary) or *corregidores*.

The more significant early incursions were peaceful, the result of individual mestizos and mulattoes settling in Indian villages with native women. Although local officials should have routed them out or at the very least insisted on the couples' marrying as laws dictated, they generally did not. Municipal authorities simply had their hands full with matters they judged more important. Enforcement was deemed too costly: few on the city council wished to spend the community's meager public income in rounding up the unmarried poor.[38] Far better to use the revenue from the few properties the city possessed and from taxes to promote the wine industry. Bridges needed to be built and repaired to insure commerce; representatives had to be sent to Lima and Spain to protect Arequipans in matters relating to viticulture. Then, too, these officials probably recognized the unmanageability of the *casta* problem as their numbers grew.[39] If any controls were to be exercised, it was thought best to concentrate on threats to drafted Indian laborers or on brigands in the coastal hills and valleys and in the sierra who hampered commerce and stole from *estancias* and *heredades* owned by council members or their kind.[40]

Although some valley Indians no doubt found *casta* penetration disturbing, many more must have been distressed when powerful colonials took an interest in Arequipa Valley farming. That interest was born of the unusually high food prices that followed the earthquakes of 1600 and 1604. As local food shortages continued, keeping prices high, *heredados* turned to valley agriculture as a way to supplement their income. Nor were such landowners oblivious to the possibilities valley land offered in accommodating their children. Possession of *chácaras* could obviate the need to fragment some coastal estates and would make offspring more attractive marriage partners.

Others who did not have much property within the coastal belt but who were accumulating capital also regarded *chácara* ownership as a sound investment. Among these, the most obvious were religious groups like the Mercedarians and the Santa Catalina nuns. Probably the regularity with which *heredados* defaulted on loans encouraged the orders' desire for Arequipan lands that they might rent. A renter could be evicted summarily with only a year's loss of income; a defaulter meant costly and protracted litigation. *Chácaras* also attracted Arequipans because wheat and maize now had a surer market than wine in interior Peru. During the 1620s, that market improved when Spaniards discovered silver in highland Arequipa, and a mining center developed swiftly; the city council insured accessibility by ordering a trail laid there.[41]

The biggest problem for many colonists interested in farming the Arequipa Valley remained access to land. By the late 1570s the *cabildo* had been stripped of the right to apportion tracts unless empowered to do so by the royal government. Those who wanted land therefore requested that the city council petition for it or appealed directly to imperial officials. But both approaches proved cumbersome and slow. When the city solicited lands near the Indian village of Caima from the Crown, it took officials years to justify their plea: the award came a decade after the original request.[42] Colonists could acquire property more rapidly when the royal government carried out its sporadic reviews of land titles and auctioned illegally held or vacant lands. Unfortunately for Arequipans, the last such review had been held during the early 1590s, before their interest in the Arequipa Valley developed and, consequently, only a few had bought land from the royal officials.[43]

Hampered by royal control of land grants, Arequipans during the postearthquake days sought to purchase tracts. But as the records of three notaries indicate, they had little luck: only eight sales were made for the years 1603 through 1605 and 1612 through 1616, and of these, two involved the same property, two other sales transferred tiny parcels among Indians, and one involved a transaction between relatives.[44] These and other sales during the early seventeenth century generally occurred only if an owner was deeply in debt, if the property was inherited, or if the proprietor emigrated. Arequipans had some limited success obtaining land from Indians who possessed lots near the city but who resided elsewhere. Yet these Indians, such as those from the village of Pampacolca located in Condesuyos (who had received 110 acres in the Guasacache Valley from their *encomendero*), knew the value of arable lands and drove a hard bargain. Even the undeveloped Guasacache tract fetched 3,400 pesos in 1611 because of its location close to water.[45] Purchasers of developed properties near the city had to pay up to 176 pesos per acre in 1622. Land farther out sold for around 20 pesos per acre in 1616. Annual rental charges also reveal land's increased value: property close to the city of Arequipa fetched 6 pesos per acre during the early 1600s; owners received 7 pesos, 4 reales, to 11 pesos per acre by the 1630s.[46]

Frustrated by the limited prospects for purchasing farms, some Arequipans sought to develop the valley's unused stretches. But this alternative was costly: the land had to be prepared and irrigation canals put in. In one instance, the Jesuits spent almost 3,000 pesos to construct an irrigation canal for their San Gerónimo *chácara*. Only a few persons possessed that kind of capital. Not surprisingly, then, when the city finally received land without canals around Caima from the Crown in 1636 and tried to auction off plots, few bid on them. As late as 1642, the *cabildo* discussed the possibility of constructing a canal at public expense so that the land would be more attractive.[47]

Wheat cultivation by colonials until 1641 thus remained in the hands of a small group identified as *"personas poderosas"*—the lucky few who had the larger *chácaras*.[48] There was, however, another faction of powerful people who possessed little land in the Arequipa Valley, but sold wheat. These people, who included a few *encomenderos*, merchants, and *heredados*, gained access to wheat in two ways. The merchants and *heredados* generally bid for the wheat that the royal government collected from Indians it controlled after taking over the administration of certain *encomiendas*. Given the high local prices for foodstuffs, colonists competed fiercely for the auctioned wheat, and the winning bidders even tormented the Indians unmercifully to extract as much grain as they could. The *encomenderos*, who sold wheat alongside these merchants and *heredados*, had access to the grain because of an obligation that dated from the early 1570s. When Viceroy Toledo had ordered new tribute lists drawn up, the lists required that Indians in the Arequipa Valley turn over to each *encomendero* a specified amount of crops: the bulk was to be raised on native lands, the rest on the lands of the *encomendero* with seed he supplied. By 1600 most wheat delivered by the Indians to meet this requirement was raised only on communal land. (Perhaps the use of Indian lands exclusively to meet tribute obligations developed because communities had more land than they needed.)[49]

Although Arequipans who owned *chácaras* enjoyed an enviable position by the early seventeenth century, they faced several problems. Agriculture in the valley continued to be plagued by periodic floods or sporadic freezes early in the growing season. Another constant difficulty was labor. Landowners now depended on a mix of Indians and *castas* for voluntary wage workers. Indians' retention of land and the increasing *casta* appropriation of plots in the valley and in other regions of the Southwest made both an unsure labor source, which led employers to raise wages (see table 7).

Had farm owners not been able to avail themselves of drafted Indians as well, wage inflation would have been even more severe, akin to that on coastal estates. Local authorities increasingly preferred important *chácara* owners above all others in assigning drafted Indians, a development no doubt due to the vital role their produce now played in colonial trade and in feeding the city. Naturally that favoritism occasioned objections from many artisans, shopkeepers, mill owners, *estancieros*, and others in the city who wanted domestic help. To quell these complaints, local officials provided *chácaras* with the largest allotments only during planting and harvest, but this solution proved imperfect. The royal government dispatched special officials from Lima, but even their repeated efforts at dealing with the problem proved unsuccessful.[50]

An important underlying cause of these difficulties was the shortage of highland Indians. Arequipa's labor draft depended not only on Indians living in the valley around the city but also on the Collaguas based along the Colca River. Although their numbers declined in the seventeenth century, they would probably have been numerous enough to meet the city's needs had other factors not impinged. *Chácara* owners increasingly vied with others for the services of the Collaguas. The Indians had to assist carriers in the highlands after the 1580s; subsequently, they worked in the silver mines at Cailloma and in textile workshops near the mines. Aware that the Crown regarded work in the mines as most important, highland *corregidores* satisfied that labor draft first. The *cabildo* explained (unsuccessfully) to

Table 7
Sample Annual Wages Paid to *Chácara* Laborers, Arequipa Valley

Notary	Date	Wage Noted
Diego de Aguilar	10 July 1596	12 pesos, a land plot, medical care, and religious instruction
Diego de Aguilar	13 July 1604	16 pesos, 2 pieces of woolen clothing, one-half fanega of wheat per month, some salt and chilies, medical care, and religious instruction
García Muñoz	23 December 1610	12 pesos, 2 pieces of woolen clothing, one-half fanega of maize per month, medical care, and religious instruction
Benito Luis de Tejada	15 December 1614	12 pesos, 2 pieces of woolen clothing, one-half fanega of maize per month
Benito Luis de Tejada	16 March 1615	Tribute paid, 2 pieces of woolen clothing, one-half fanega of maize per month, and a land plot
García Muñoz	11 April 1622	12 pesos, 2 pieces of woolen clothing, a basket of maize or wheat per month, and 2 reales a week for meat
Juan Pérez de Gordejuela	7 July 1631	25 pesos, 2 pieces of woolen clothing, a basket of food per month, and 2 reales a week for meat
Juan Pérez de Gordejuela	4 September 1636	Tribute paid (7 pesos), 2 pieces of woolen clothing, 6 baskets of wheat or maize, 2 reales a week for meat, and a land plot
Diego de Silva	31 May 1644	12 pesos, 2 pieces of clothing, one-half fanega of wheat or maize per month, and 2 reales a week for meat
Alonso Laguna	4 September 1648	30 pesos, 2 pieces of woolen clothing, a basket of maize or wheat per month, 2 reales a week for meat, and bread

Note: All pesos are of 8 reales.

imperial authorities time and again that, as the oldest, the city's draft should be given preference.[51]

Demands on Indians by *corregidores* and *curacas* made the situation worse during the 1600s. These officials regularly insisted that Indians tend llamas for them; they also prevailed on Indians to serve as drivers when they leased the llamas to merchants who transported goods inland from Arequipa or the coastal belt. A few *curacas* with *heredades* in the coastal valleys required Indians to work there as well.[52]

Although these obligations hurt Arequipa's share of the draft, Indian absenteeism also interfered. Dislike for the required work—often unfamiliar chores to rural highlanders—no doubt accounted for the reluctance of many to serve. Most probably resented the disruptions and personal costs as well, since such labor took them at their own expense far from native villages and cut into their family life. Some Indians found the alternative of hiring replacements more palatable; *curacas* relieved an influential few from serving, a solution that increased the burden of others. Refusing to serve in the labor draft was particularly common when Indians faced emergencies in their own towns. The destruction by a flood of a major irrigation canal deemed vital by farmers of Pocsi, for example, kept these Indians from serving in Arequipa during the early 1620s. The city's *cabildo* quickly dispatched an official there to speed up repairs so that laborers could once again be sent to the valley.[53]

Despite the unreliability and inadequacy of drafted Indian labor for the community, most of the important *chácara* owners managed a fairly regular supply of workers. Beyond the favoritism they enjoyed from Arequipa's officials, some managed to secure a guaranteed allotment of drafted Indian laborers by petitioning authorities in Lima. Crown officials directed local officials to assign Indians to the petitioners first, no matter what municipal priorities had been set.[54] Wealthier farmers supplemented their share by hiring wage workers. And a few agriculturalists who had *yanaconas* in the sixteenth century retained them, even though the royal government decreed in the early 1600s that such Indians should be treated as voluntary wage laborers. The Jesuits, for example, continued to provide their former *yanaconas* with small parcels of land and a yearly sum to cover tribute. That these Cailloma Indians did not return to their native towns, where they retained plots of land, or hire themselves out for the higher wages now common in the valley resulted from the Jesuits wisely requiring only three days of work per week. The Mercedarians may have employed similar incentives to retain their *yanaconas* during the seventeenth century.[55]

The Seizure of Indian Lands in the Arequipa Valley after 1641

By husbanding their laborers, *chácara* owners with the largest farms in the Arequipa Valley could, if climatic conditions were particularly favorable, produce more than enough to lower bread prices in the city after 1620.[56] Yet with the more normal pattern of crop shortages and high prices for wheat at local and inland markets, Arequipans of whatever economic status continued to regard landholding as desirable, if not necessary.

Access to land remained difficult until 1641, when circumstances suddenly changed. For some years before then, the royal government had considered various measures to deal with its financial troubles. During the 1630s, the Crown decided that the solution was another review of all colonial landholding. It instructed officials who found deficient land titles to allow owners to rectify the error by paying a fine; those owners who refused were to have their property seized and auctioned. The government also empowered officials to sell vacant tracts and to check on the status of Indian holdings. If any native community had surplus land, these were to be auctioned.[57]

In 1641 officials were appointed to review the situation in the Southwest. The review, which in its initial stage lasted until 1648, proved disastrous for Indians native to the Arequipa Valley. Royal officials charged with evaluating their holdings defined Indian needs parsimoniously: each married adult male was provided with only 1.25 acres. On the grounds that Indians should be protected by having lands in consolidated blocks away from other colonists, they also regrouped many holdings. Each Indian whose old parcel was replaced by a new one was to receive land of the same quality, but most did not, suffering then the double penalty of less and inferior land. Significantly, many whose plots were exchanged for new ones had had farms in the valley core, within the very valuable stretch along the Chili River near the city. Other damages resulted from the inspectors' habit of not assigning any community land. As one *corregidor* observed, some surplus was needed to enable a community to accommodate not only Indians who had chosen to live elsewhere temporarily, but also additional members should there be population growth. In the meantime, any surplus land could be rented to pay tributes. The Indians, he concluded, had been treated shabbily.[58]

On the whole, the *corregidor*'s remarks accurately depicted the calamity. Indians had suffered a considerable reduction in their holdings; they now possessed some of the worst farmland in the valley. Complaints from throughout Peru of similar despoliation of other Indians led to a series of royal orders that *originarios* not be allowed to sell communal lands or private holdings without a license from the viceroy or the *audiencia*. Nor could that license be granted unless the Protector of Indians demonstrated the sale's benefit to the Indian. Even then, the purchaser would not be issued a royal title for ten years. But these regulations hardly improved the Indians' lot: they were misdirected and failed to address the loss of community lands and the quality of individual holdings that had been assigned. In 1648 the

Crown finally suspended the provisions for review and sale of Peruvian land. It appointed new inspectors to rectify all damages done to Indians who lived in native communities. Three men, all friars, were assigned by the royal government to the Arequipa Valley and served there at various intervals until 1660.[59] These friars were concerned principally with whether each *originario* had enough land, whether non-Indians had property too close to native villages, and whether each Indian community had sufficient land for rental and growth. They carefully examined the titles of Arequipans who had recently acquired Indian lands and occasionally revoked titles to property located near native plots. In this way, they accumulated enough land to expand communal reserves and raise each Indian's allotment. Apparently, they sought to increase each married adult male's share from 1.25 to 2 acres and to provide the *curaca* with 6 acres and all other villagers with at least .75 acre. They also assigned approximately 10 acres to each community for reserve lands.[60]

Several communities with which the friars worked expressed deep appreciation. One suspects that the sentiment may only have reflected the views of a narrow group, since it was always the *curacas'* satisfaction with the results that were recorded.[61] Whatever the case, the review did not turn back the clock to pre-1641. The friars had undone some damage, but they had not returned all former holdings, especially the better lands. Nor did Indians given property during the 1650s possess as much land as before: the majority now had 2 rather than the 4 acres or more held by some *originarios* during the early 1600s. And the review never covered the entire valley. The first royal inspector, Fray Pedro Altamirano, died shortly after he was appointed, and his replacement, Fray Francisco de Loyola, withdrew when he became ill. (Fray Francisco had already spent over a year reviewing Indian landholdings in the Condesuyos area, and such thoroughness may very well have exhausted him.) Fray Gonzalo Tenorio, his successor, worked very carefully and would likely have redressed many Indian grievances had he been given the chance. Still, increasing royal mistrust, brought on by the slow pace and escalating costs of the Peruvian review, hampered efforts, until the Crown finally ordered all its officials to close the matter in 1660. In the years that followed, Arequipans filed suits, with some success, to regain land taken by the friars to meet Indian needs.[62]

The royal government's land reviews between 1641 and 1660 enabled a number of people, including a few squatters and non-Indians who owned small *chácaras*, to acquire additional rural property in the Arequipa Valley. On the whole, however, as the examples in table 8 make clear, the established landed families benefited most, and the reviews intensified differences in the amount and quality of land held by this group compared with other non-Indians. The position of such landed families was probably enhanced not simply by greater wealth, but also by their access to credit and willing guarantors. The royal government did not demand immediate payment from buyers or from those who legalized their titles, but it did insist on guarantees that the money would be forthcoming.[63] These requirements worked against the poor and those unfamiliar with administrative details. The worst-off were *originarios*, many of whom still did not speak Spanish. *Curacas*, on the other hand, managed well, given their knowledge of the Hispanic world. Not only had they been involved in the colonial economy for years as *chácara* owners, but they had on occasion married family members to Spaniards, albeit not to the city's more prominent residents. They now moved aggressively and purchased lands. A group in the town of Pocsi, for example, bought around 100 acres near Yarabamba. In at least one other instance, a *curaca* in the region managed to regain land auctioned to a Spaniard by appealing to royal authorities outside the area on the grounds that the property had been an Indian holding.

Although there is no conclusive proof that such Indian officials also appropriated lands formerly belonging to native communities, they likely did. Within a few years after the reviews, Arequipans accused *curacas* of having excess property and of renting lands to Indians and Spaniards.[64] Other Indians, migrants to the valley and their descendants, did not gain much from the reviews. Royal officials felt no obligation to provide them with land, and so they had to bid alongside non-Indians for property. There are no indications that those who were former *yanaconas* acquired additional holdings in this way, and only occasionally did other migrants do so, no doubt hampered by modest funds. What did arise, however, were purchases by Indian migrants after 1641 of a few plots from *originarios*, persons who had received lands from the royal inspectors but probably were not farmers. The parcels generally were smaller than an acre. Indians not native to the valley thus remained in fairly much the same position vis-à-vis landholding as had nonnatives during the early seventeenth century.[65]

As *originarios* lost land and were consigned to small parcels of poor quality, their situation worsened. Owning plots that at best only met bare subsistence needs, the Indians were still required to fulfill labor draft obligations. Whether necessity forced them to use additional plots on non-Indian *chácaras* in order to survive, or whether farm owners found ways to attract them to such lands, drafted Indian laborers gradually began to work the properties of others year in and year out. Spanish rental and sale agreements for over two decades after 1660 reveal a propensity of these laborers to stay with certain lands. Mention is normally made of such Indian workers and of transferring the right to Indian labor when colonists sold or

Table 8
Sample Land Purchases and Title Confirmations, Arequipa Valley, 1640s

Landowner	Status	Transaction
Diego Llocsa	Indian from village of Yura	Confirmed title to .25 acre (with fig trees) he inherited. Title had been disputed by Spaniard
Juan Rafael Gualpa and Antonio Gualpa	Indians	Confirmed title to 2 acres near Tiabaya
Lucas Martínez Vegaso	Mestizo, descendant of *encomendero*'s brother	Purchased 8 acres of worked land whose title had been in dispute
Pedro de Quirós	Possibly of *heredado* family	Purchased 12 acres he had been renting from Indians
Juan Meléndez de la Cerda	Squatter	Confirmed title to ca. .5 acre
Gerónimo Ramírez	?	Purchased 15 acres of public land formerly worked by another
Doña Catalina Pizarro	Widow of *corregidor*'s son	Confirmed title to a tiny parcel
Don Pedro de Tapia y Padilla	*Heredado*, former *alcalde*, descendant of *encomendero*	Purchased 10 acres that had been Indian land
Don Juan Zegarra de Casaús y Peralta	Admiral, *heredado*, *alcalde*, descendant of *corregidor*	Confirmed various titles; one farm sold to him by Spaniard
Don Alonso Mogrovejo	Priest, *heredado*, descendant of *heredados*	Confirmed title to 2 acres he acquired from Indians and colonists
Don Juan Zúñiga Sobaco	Captain, immigrant, married into *heredado* family, former *alcalde*	Purchased land near Indian village of Caima
Don Juan Ramírez Zegarra	*Heredado*, former *alcalde*, descendant of *corregidor*	Confirmed title to 6 acres acquired before the 1640s
Don (?) Juan del Postigo Gálvez	Permanent councilor	Purchased 15 acres that had been Indian land

Sources: *SMA*, pp. 74, 79, 101-102, 112; *SMF*, pp. 58, 201-202; ADA, Laguna, 6 January 1638, Diego de Silva, 12 May 1644, Diego Ortiz, 2 August 1594; ANP, Compañía, Títulos, leg. 3 (1628-1652), Tribunal de Cuentas, Real Hacienda, Composiciones, Tierras y Indígenas, leg. 5, cuads. 5-8, 11-16, 21, 23; BNP, ms. B857 (1646), ms. B1787 (1673); AGI, Justicia, leg. 1189.

rented their *chácaras*. Apparently only a few *originarios* managed to secure greater independence, joining with some *castas* in becoming renters of non-Indian lands. Yet, because of their limited funds, most did not pay for the use of land with cash, but promised instead to perform certain services such as building mud walls around a field, putting in irrigation ditches, and leveling property. The trade-off was not a particularly good one, but it did relieve Indians of the labor draft and possibly from tribute.[66]

Arequipan Acquisitions in the Coastal Belt

The reviews from 1641 to 1660 altered not only landowning patterns within the Arequipa Valley, but also those in coastal areas outside the traditional *heredad* core. The changes were only of degree to the south of the Tambo River, because Arequipan colonists had migrated in significant numbers into the zone beginning in the late 1500s. Several factors, including the desire to prevent excessive fragmentation of existing estates, prompted this movement. The zone, especially the Moquegua Valley, which became the most popular settlement site, was climatically and geographically similar to the Arequipa or coastal valleys. Locating an estate there offered Arequipans the additional advantage of proximity to an important colonial trade route—that between Arica and Potosí. Land could also be acquired rather easily. Although prospective *heredados* could not turn to Arequipa's *cabildo* for a land grant, as they had during the westward drive after 1557, when they opened up the Vítor and Siguas valleys, property might be purchased from the steadily declining Indian communities.

Reports suggest that, during the late 1500s and early 1600s, the Indians' lot worsened considerably, because they lived close to an imperial trade route. Local officials commonly required Indians to serve as carriers or drivers of mule and llama trains traveling between Arica and the highlands. These business ventures were so profitable that the posts of *corregidor* and their lieutenants sold for impressive sums. The work load not only further weakened the Indians' health, but prevented their maintaining farms and led to extensive flight. Sales of Indian land and extensive squatting by colonists followed. To gain from the situation, royal officials rented former Indian lands; they no doubt sold others.[67]

Colonists' migration southward began slowly when several *encomenderos* like Hernán Bueno and Hernán Rodríguez de Huelva left the city of Arequipa during the mid-1500s to develop farms.[68] It grew considerably later in the century as property close to the city became scarce. When men like Don Félix de Herrera y Castilla demonstrated that Arequipan landowners could profit from a move, their relatives and others followed.

Don Félix's nephew, Don Apóstol Laso de la Vega, for example, chose to renounce his share of a Vítor estate and migrated south. There he wed Doña Jacinta de Alcázar y Padilla, a descendant of several migrants who had left the city of Arequipa years earlier.[69] The steady migration from Arequipa, along with the arrival of others, including relatives of *corregidores* assigned to the Moquegua area who often married locals, led in 1618 to the formal founding of the *villa* of Santa Catalina de Guadalcázar. When the Carmelite Padre Antonio Vázquez de Espinosa visited the settlement shortly after, he estimated the Spanish population at eighty householders. These colonists relied principally on lands devoted to viticulture and crops like those of the Arequipa Valley.[70]

The regional dispersion of heirs of Arequipa's sixteenth-century *encomenderos* and landowners also involved towns farther south. Descendants of Pedro Pizarro, for example, who had been assigned Indians along Peru's south coast by Francisco Pizarro, settled in Tacna; some of the Cáceres family moved to Arica. From these towns, such families came to dominate the surrounding countryside, as the Cáceres did the Putre Valley. A bishop reporting in 1618, after a lengthy visit south of Arequipa, reckoned that the non-Indian population had already reached one thousand (one-fourth the number of natives) and that, although most resided in the Moquegua Valley, many lived in Arica, a town with over one hundred householders.[71] When their numbers increased as a result of procreation and additional migration, the colonists spread their holdings into most coastal valleys south of the Tambo River. By the mid-1600s, for instance, the grandchildren of Don Luis de Alcázar y Padilla and their spouses held major properties along the southwest coast; Don Diego Pacheco Delgadillo possessed important estates in the Sama and Locumba valleys; Don Luis Yánez de Montenegro also had *heredades* and lands in the Sama Valley and Ycuy. Other familiar Arequipan names like Cornejo, Valderrama, and Herrera surfaced among the rural proprietors.[72]

Much of the activity of landowners in this southern region after the land reviews began in 1641 involved confirming titles to properties either they or their forebears had acquired through sales or by taking over idle lands. Don Francisco de Ribera, an estate owner in the Locumba Valley, for example, received legal title to a land plot, which he had held for years. Don Fernando de Peralta likewise confirmed his rights to lands purchased from an Indian.

In many ways, then, these people acted much like Arequipan *heredados* had during the review in the 1590s, when they formally secured royal titles to holdings in the Vítor Valley and areas close by. Nevertheless, a few colonists, predominantly established landowners, also acquired additional, vacant tracts, either adjacent to their estates or elsewhere. The amount bought by any one individual was impressive by southwestern standards. In one sale, an *heredado* paid 5,000 pesos for land, which, if we use the average auction price for the best parcels near the city of Arequipa (no doubt an excessive amount, since outlying lands went for less), would indicate that he acquired over 50 acres.[73] Many landowners in the southern valleys thus came to own properties larger than those held by Arequipans west of the city. Whereas many estates in the old core had been reduced by the mid-seventeenth century to around 40 acres, several Moqueguans possessed sizeable *heredades*, each of which had nearly forty thousand vines planted.[74] Not surprisingly, even before the last round of land acquisition during the 1640s, agricultural production in some valleys south of the Tambo River compared favorably with that in the Vítor Valley.

Table 9
Tithe on Agricultural Products, Southwestern Peru

Valley	Tithe Collected (pesos)	
	1629	1631
Sama	6,000	4,500
Moquegua	5,000	5,250
Siguas	2,266+	2,116
Locumba	1,000	1,000
Vitor	7,656+	4,109

Source: AGI, Lima, leg. 309.
Note: Map 1 locates valleys.

Whereas the southern coastal valleys attracted Arequipa's *heredad* families, this was not initially the case with the valleys to the north of the sixteenth-century estate core. Perhaps colonists judged the soils to be of poor quality; certainly the zone's isolation from colonial trade routes played an important role in discouraging migration. Thus, poorer Southwesterners moved in during the early 1600s. *Castas*, like the mulattoes Martín and Alonso de Naveda, managed to acquire, sometimes through royal sales, farms of up to 40 acres. The review in the 1640s allowed these *castas* and colonists of modest social stature but of Spanish blood (persons whom royal officials refused to regard as "dons") to acquire additional tracts.

But the pressures on land closer to Arequipa had by 1641 raised the interest of the better-placed as well. Captains, like Don Pedro de Montesdeoca Grimaldo and Juan Díaz de Urbina, who had purchased land from Indians and colonists shortly before the royal officers arrived to conduct the land review, confirmed their titles and acquired through auctions more property to round out holdings. Several bought additional tracts in other locations, which they also used for vineyards and *estancias*.

When, during the 1650s, friars inspected the way in which royal officials had conducted the land review, they uncovered several problems. Fray Francisco de Loyola, who began his work in the Acarí Valley and gradually moved south, found that Indians had received too little land and that colonists all too often possessed property close to native holdings. Like *visitadores* in the Arequipa Valley, he raised the allotment of each married adult Indian male—in this instance from 2 to 3 acres—and assigned 1.5 acres to each of the other community residents. In providing land for all of these Indians, he took away portions acquired by non-Indians, often justifying his actions on the grounds that the previous officials' measurements had been inaccurate and that landholders held more than they had paid for.[75]

Colonial Penetration of Arequipa's Sierra

Although there can be no denying the important effect of the royal reviews on Indian and colonial landholding along the coast and in the Arequipa Valley, their impact pales compared with those carried out in the highlands. Non-Indian landholding in Cailloma and Condesuyos, in the highlands, was barely discernible during the early 1600s, but was impressive by the late seventeenth century. This encroachment by non-Indians cannot be blamed solely on the willingness of royal officials to sell them "vacant" tracts after 1641. It began earlier, though very gradually, when a few landowners in valleys such as the Majes pushed inland and acquired highland tracts. By the early 1630s, at least one colonist held rural property near the Indian village of Pampacolca.[76] During the period when the royal inspector Don Luis de Losada y Quiñones worked in the highlands, colonial penetration became pronounced. Employing the standard small allotments of land for *originarios*, he found plenty of excess property, which he then sold off. There may indeed have been unused tracts in the sierra, yet Don Luis definitely sold lands being worked by Indians.[77]

Not surprisingly, when Fray Francisco de Loyola assessed Losada y Quiñones's land review after 1650, he discovered irregularities and made major changes. Upon arriving in Condesuyos, Fray Francisco consulted with Indian communities, heard complaints about the inadequacy of their new holdings, and raised their allotments (following the per capita assignments he had used in northern coastal valleys). In one year he increased communal lands in the Condesuyos region by 1,671.5 acres. In the case of the village of Chuquibamba, for example, a community assigned

606.9 acres by Losada, Fray Francisco added 422 acres. These he found among portions of the best parcels sold to colonists; their removal was excused on grounds that Losada had incorrectly measured the land. Nor did Fray Francisco hesitate to rule royal auctions illegal and take entire holdings: he annulled five because of insufficient public notice before the sale.[78]

As elsewhere, nevertheless, the new royal officials did not altogether exclude colonists from the highlands. Fray Francisco accepted many of his predecessor's sales of surplus lands and, in reviewing them, only checked whether the amounts charged the buyers had been just and whether the titles were in order. Finding a few charges too low and some deficient titles, he demanded additional payments. The post-1641 reviews in the highlands, then, ratified the more extensive presence of colonists as landowners in the area. Moreover, most new owners possessed holdings in the more fertile sections of the sierra, along the Colca River in Condesuyos, where it bends and heads toward the coast, as well as along tributaries that flow from Pampacolca, Machaguay, and Viraco. These properties ranged broadly in size, but, strikingly, some were large tracts: Licenciado Bartolomé de Escamilla Chacón, for example, possessed 570 acres near Chuquibamba. Such impressive holdings resulted no doubt from the very moderate auction price of around 10 pesos per acre.[79]

A diverse group of Southwesterners, including mestizos and American-born whites, purchased property in the highlands. The most significant in terms of total acquisitions were from landed Arequipan families. Some were the descendants of the early seventeenth-century royal treasurer Don Pedro Chacón de Luna, and a few others, the children and relatives of the *heredad*-owning Valencias. Most had not developed a sudden interest in sierra landholding because of the 1640s' reviews. A few had served in the area before the reviews took place or were living there when the Crown's inspectors arrived. Don Cristóbal de Valencia Altamirano, for example, was a priest in Andaray when he purchased lands in the Churunga Valley. Others, as the associates or relatives of royal officials assigned to the region, also knew it well. The Rodríguez de los Ríos family, a particularly active group in buying land, descended from a *corregidor* who had had jurisdiction over Camaná during the early 1600s. The Cabreras possibly were offspring of a Condesuyos *corregidor* of the 1620s, Don Antonio de Cabrera Acuña. Juan de Amézquita, who had survived in the early 1600s off a small *chácara* devoted to chilies on a destroyed *heredad* in the Majes Valley, managed to become a government official in Condesuyos during the 1630s, a contact that after 1641 led to his son Diego's buying land there. The Chacón de Luna family's interest in highland property apparently was sparked by its ownership of land in the Camaná Valley after 1600. A smaller group, men like Alonso de Benítez and the priest Licenciado Alonso Gutiérrez Trujillo, were descendants (some of them mestizos) of sixteenth-century Arequipans with ties to the coastal valleys near Condesuyos. The common associations these families had with the sierra resulted in some familial linkages before the 1640s: the Rodríguez de los Ríos family intermarried with the Chacón de Lunas and apparently with the Cabreras as well; Captain Gonzalo Rodríguez de Cabrera had become Juan de Amézquita's father-in-law. Many of these new proprietors, therefore, moved into the highlands together.[80]

Some of the sierra's *curacas* also acquired property. Don Pedro Chuqui Yanqui, governor of Yanaquigua, bought lands near his home, as did Don Gregorio Pomacallao, *curaca* of Pampacolca. For the first time since 1540 some highland *curacas* became large landholders in the region. This increased differentiation in landholding among Indians appears to have had some ill effects shortly thereafter. Don Gregorio, who became a major rural entrepreneur, the owner of vineyards, several *chácaras*, and livestock, allegedly soon appropriated communal landholdings and livestock. He even insisted, or so certain witnesses claimed, that Indians irrigate his properties during the day and forced others to spend nights at the irrigation canals. Yet, too much should not be made of this one case, for Don Gregorio's main accusers were other *curacas*, an indication that Indian officials had not altogether abandoned their people.[81]

Conclusion

At the beginning of the seventeenth century, Arequipa's colonists held a rather modest share of the region's arable land and pasturelands, especially if compared with settlers in places like Mexico's central valley, where over half of such land was in non-Indian hands by the 1620s.[82] The contrasting situations reflected differences in the size of their colonial populations. Central Mexico had attracted more Spaniards, some of whom were accommodated on Indian property. When Arequipa's colonial population expanded beginning in the early 1600s, colonists also appropriated more land. Because of their proximity to the major trade route between Lima and Potosí, the southern valleys became the most popular for prospective owners. A smaller faction pushed northward within the coastal belt. In both instances, colonists emphasized livestock raising and viticulture alongside subsistence agriculture. As in the case of other colonial areas, such as sixteenth-century Oaxaca, their land-use patterns resulted mainly from inadequate local markets for the region's agricultural products.[83]

By the 1620s, the market prospects for certain crops, like wheat, improved as the city of Arequipa grew modestly and as mining expanded regional markets. Local Indian production could not meet the demand, a development that encouraged colonial exploitation of the Arequipa Valley. But fearing the negative consequences of tampering with Indian agriculture, the city council only reluctantly supported the settlers in their attempts to take over land. Its main action involved the distribution of drafted Indian laborers to the owners of existing, important *chácaras*. To be sure, the *cabildo*'s hands were tied, particularly with regard to providing colonists with land, for the royal government had reserved land granting to itself during the late 1500s. Restrained by this stricture, as well as by the natural shortage of arable land in the Arequipa Valley, colonists had to await the Crown's land reviews of the 1640s before they made major gains at the expense of the Indian community. These reviews also made possible the acquisition of sierra lands. The decisions of the royal government, then, played a crucial role in modifying local landholding patterns, as they did in portions of Mexico and elsewhere in the Americas.[84]

The expansion of the Hispanic rural domain and the attendant emergence of new labor relations—a greater reliance on wage laborers and tenants— indicate that by the late 1600s Arequipa's countryside developed characteristics common to other New World areas. Yet, important variations in the local situations continued. In southwestern Peru, many Indians retained property. *Originarios* had less land than before, but most possessed at least a small parcel. *Curacas*, too, owned land; indeed, the evidence suggests that their properties, including those in the highlands, were now more extensive. *Casta* landownership persisted as well. In these respects, conditions in Arequipa were similar to conditions found in Oaxaca and along parts of the sixteenth-century central Peruvian coast.[85] A distinctive feature of southwestern landownership was the endurance of Spanish proprietorship in modest tracts: most adult colonists possessed some property. This situation was inextricably tied to the state of the region's economy, which inhibited anyone's accumulating the capital necessary to monopolize land. As will be noted in the next chapter, social habits also contributed to the phenomenon. Modest and balanced colonial landholding was and remains a distinctive feature of southwestern land tenure, particularly in the Arequipa Valley.

7. Land and Society in Seventeenth-Century Arequipa

> *. . . y siguen los Licenciados de padres a hijos; y luego se dice, que los arequipeños del tiempo de la colonia estuvieron en completa ignorancia y decadencia.*
>
> ———Monseñor Dr. Don Santiago Martínez

The difficulties that befell the Southwest's economy during the seventeenth century affected Arequipa's society. From the mid- to the late 1500s, social preeminence in the region had depended in part on birth. Anyone of noble origins belonged to the city's elite. Nevertheless, since most original Arequipans and later immigrants descended from commoners, their respective places in local society came to depend on acquired position, such as selection as *encomenderos* or service as royal officials. Wealth also played a crucial role in determining social status, for with it colonists might gain possessions commonly associated with the Hispanic aristocracy and indulge its habits.

Whereas *encomiendas* frequently enabled early Arequipans to acquire the possessions associated with wealth and to mimic elite practices, their declining value saw land emerge as the principal financial support of social position. When difficulties engulfed landowners after the 1590s, Arequipa's leading families altered their emulation of the Hispanic aristocracy and devised new ways to retain their social prominence. Two other social developments occurred during the seventeenth century: over the years the elite expanded, and it became close-knit through marriage.

Arequipa's Late Sixteenth-Century Elite

A number of families from varied backgrounds dominated Arequipa's society by 1600. Those who derived their position from holding *encomiendas* and land composed the elite's core. A select few of this core could trace their descent back to persons whom Francisco Pizarro and other early viceregal governors had granted Indians, but most had gained their tributaries later. Not all of Arequipa's *encomenderos* and their legitimate kin, however, were members of the city's elite, although most could have been had they so desired. A small segment, predominantly those with the largest grants, spent little time in Arequipa, but preferred to reside in Lima. Another important faction of the elite was composed of former royal functionaries and their immediate relatives. Such persons had settled in the Southwest principally because the area offered them rewards. A few married into *encomendero* families (some married the widows of grantees) and thus gained access to Indian tributes. More often, former royal officials and their relatives acquired land in the coastal valleys and enjoyed the benefits of a flourishing wine economy. Others, a distinct minority, managed to share the position of city leaders. These were a handful of venturers and their relatives who had achieved singular status by virtue of the accumulation of wealth during the late 1500s. Most owned estates along the coastal belt, from the Majes River to the Tambo River. But not all of their kind were as fortunate. To be regarded as important in Arequipa, such a colonist could not be a *casta* and had to have married into either the *encomendero* or functionary clique. The remaining venturers-landowners occupied a second rung in the community.

Arequipa's leading families borrowed heavily from the social practices of Hispanic contemporaries to confirm their prominent position. This led them to build substantial urban homes, which they furnished impressively with imported finery and Peruvian silver. A host of Indians and blacks served as their domestics.[1] Parents also saw to it that young children received a rudimentary education at home or in one of the small schools, staffed by Spanish and American-born instructors, that sprang up in Arequipa. Some even managed to expose their offspring to such social graces as dancing.[2] Those who enjoyed sufficient wealth sometimes sent sons and daughters off to Castile for further education, to be placed in the church, or to be married well.[3] A few Arequipans provided for their children by creating entailed estates, most of which consisted of property purchased and located in Spain. Nevertheless, the burdensome cost involved in establishing a *mayorazgo* either in the Old or the New World limited this option.[4]

The heads of Arequipa's "better" families also insured their prominence by securing public posts. Seldom did any hold positions in the royal bureaucracy, however, since the royal government generally reserved these for immigrants to Peru or for those of the most distinguished colonial families. Political confirmation of preeminence required contacts with Spaniards in high places. When a Southwesterner managed after the mid-

1500s to become a *corregidor* or to secure a post such as that of royal treasurer, it was almost invariably someone who had decided to live in Lima.[5]

The more common political expression of significant community status consequently came to be service as a *regidor* on the city's *cabildo* or as an *alcalde*. These positions always carried some weight in Arequipa, dominated as they had been during the early years by *encomenderos*. By the late sixteenth century others shared them, either descendants of early colonists, who also possessed important rural properties, or former bureaucrats and their relatives.[6]

Although throughout the 1500s political service conferred on Arequipans additional prestige because posts depended on election, during the late sixteenth century it became possible for a few to buy their way into office. The royal government, always trying to increase revenue, put up certain of these posts for sale. This allowed a few men of quite modest origins, men like Andrés and Félix de Herrera, whose father had managed to do well in the wine economy, to secure these local symbols of importance. But no wholesale change occurred in the city's political leadership; traditionally powerful families only modified the way in which they gained some posts. These families, after all, were in most cases the region's wealthiest residents and could outbid others for municipal positions.[7]

A person's relationship to the church also had social implications by 1600. Of course, it would do serious injustice to many colonists to suggest that the donating of money and property to the church or the placing of children in a religious order were the result solely of social considerations. Surely a goodly number were motivated by their fealty to and love of Catholicism. But leading Arequipans did vie with each other in supporting the church. No longer satisfied with the rather crude edifices raised in the immediate postfounding years for several orders, they encouraged, with their gifts of money and urban land, the building of new temples and residences. Some also lavished funds on the Jesuits and other orders that arrived in the city after the 1550s.[8] No doubt this interest in the community's religious life also prompted the municipal officers' active concern that the royal government aid in constructing a new church for the secular clergy after the earthquake of 1582. Although construction proceeded slowly and another round of earthquakes destroyed much of what had been completed, local pride must have been intense when authorities designated the Southwest a bishopric in 1609.[9]

The interrelationship between support of the church and the social practices of Arequipa is most evident in the founding of chantries. During the late 1500s, the establishment of chantries was by no means restricted to the city's aristocrats, with even a few Indians of modest wealth becoming involved, but elite Arequipans certainly predominated among the benefactors. Men such as Juan Ruiz de León not only followed the dictates in a wife's will when setting up a chantry in her name, but also added funds beyond those requested to increase the number of masses said. Others, like Diego Rodríguez Bautista, who became wealthier than his parents, provided support for chantries in the name of forbears and of a wife.

Of course, these were to be perpetual masses for their souls, sometimes said as often as forty times a year. The funds on which such masses normally relied came from the interest on mortgages. Members of the elite frequently purchased mortgages on rural land, a fairly easy thing to do during the late sixteenth century, when many *heredados* had some ready cash and others often secured loans in order to expand their operations. But if a person did not have the capital, he or she could simply sell off some property, as did Inés Pérez, and use the proceeds to acquire a mortgage. Others promised that they would support a chantry from the annual returns of a business. Social considerations very likely influenced the selection of a church, as churches enjoyed varying degrees of prestige. But sound judgments on this point are impossible to make, because a number of religious houses in Arequipa do not permit access to their records. What can be surmised is that families tended to continue their allegiance to a church over many generations, regularly burying their dead there and establishing chantries.[10]

Arequipans not only extended financial support to the church and endowed chantries but also became seculars or regulars. A small number of those who entered the church were widowers and widows. One of the most renowned was Antonio de Llanos, a mid-sixteenth-century venturer who had acquired an *encomienda* and land. Shortly before his death, he became a Jesuit and provided the local chapter with most of his considerable holdings.[11] As prominent was Doña María Guzmán, who generously endowed the Convent of Santa Catalina de Sena before entering the cloister. Pope Urban VII eventually made her a prioress for life, a decision in which the royal government concurred.[12] More commonly, parents encouraged their children to pursue a life in the church. At first, several heads of household sent offspring to Castile for this purpose, but as various orders established houses in the Viceroyalty of Peru, these gained in favor. Doña Isabel de Padilla, for example, entered Arequipa's Convent of Nuestra Señora de los Remedios, a house her parents had been instrumental in founding. A survey of ten families reveals that five had children in the church by the early 1600s. In a few instances the numbers involved were impressive: one family had seven of eighteen children enter the church; another placed three of nine offspring. There were even cases of a parent and child cloistered together. Not surprisingly, one involved Doña María

Guzmán and a daughter.[13]

Support for the church, the securing of political office, a particular lifestyle, and even the entailing of property helped to define who belonged to Arequipa's elite and the respective status enjoyed by each of the aristocracy's families, but the marriages of children probably proved most critical. Making use of their lineage, their ties to *encomenderos* and functionaries, as well as their wealth—generally in the form of endowments of rural land—parents tried to wed offspring well. As noted, the most desirable spouses for leading sixteenth-century Southwesterners included persons from Spanish noble families (most would have been more than happy to find someone of the lesser nobility willing to marry them) and from families of colonial officials. Others of the elite wed outsiders, persons from Peruvian *encomendero* families or associates of bureaucrats. This penchant for marrying non-Arequipans reflects on the social benefits that accrued to locals when they wed well and makes clear the broad contacts elite members enjoyed in colonial Peru because of Arequipa's extensive commerce.

One family, that of Hernando de la Torre, will serve here to highlight the various ways Arequipans of the upper ranks comported themselves socially around 1600. An *encomendero*, the son of an *encomendero*-founder, and a man regularly elected to municipal posts, Hernando fathered ten children. He provided extremely well for his two sons, passing on to them vineyards in the Pitay Valley and *estancias* on the coastal hills. With funds from their father, the sons bought additional land, including coastal *estancias* and a parcel to expand the family's *heredad*. Hernando also purchased for 8,000 pesos the position of *alférez real* (royal standard-bearer) in 1592 for his eldest son. As would be expected, the sons married well, the eldest into a prominent immigrant's family, the second, the daughter of an *encomendero*. Their sisters, too, wed impressively: four married outsiders (one, the founder of a town in Argentina), and two, the sons of *encomenderos*. These unions were possible because of the de la Torres's social stature and because the husbands were given family lands (at least one received *chácaras* in the Arequipa Valley and another, a share of a wine estate).Two other daughters were placed in a local convent.[14]

Seventeenth-Century Social Practices

Maintaining the social practices they had adopted became onerous to Arequipans after the end of the sixteenth century. The income of those families that still relied on *encomiendas* shrank as the royal government restricted tributes and as the Indian population declined. Grantees of Indians who lived within the coastal belt, where native numbers fell off sharply, suffered most, but even highland *encomenderos* faced financial troubles as officials increasingly required Indians to labor in new mines and *corregidor* exploitation of natives became more common.

Other *encomenderos*, who relied on both their Indians and landholdings, and elite families with no grants also suffered financial difficulties during this period. The value of their estates declined as colonial competition, governmental harassment, and high production costs adversely affected the local wine industry. Although able to sustain themselves, most elite Arequipans had to reduce expenses. Seldom did any now found *mayorazgos* or send children to Spain. It was this tendency to keep children in the Southwest, along with their inability to purchase and develop new lands, that forced landowners to fragment their estates among sons and daughters through the mid-1600s. Offspring had to be given the means to survive financially and each also had to be provided with land so that a decent marriage might be arranged. Only when Arequipans got back on their feet several generations after the earthquakes of 1600 and 1604 were some able to find alternate means of sustaining children, by appropriating lands in more remote sections of the coastal belt, in the Arequipa Valley, and in the highlands.

But although the solution of some problems through the expansion of the city's rural domain still lay in the future, Arequipans of the early 1600s by no means renounced all their social practices. Despite their worsening financial circumstances, they continued to encourage children to enter local convents and monasteries. Seven elite families, for example, had from one to three children each in the secular or regular clergy.[15] Although there may be some merit to one historian's contention that, by encouraging vocations parents relieved themselves of the expense of supporting "excess" daughters and sons, more was involved.[16] Notably, it was generally those families best off by local standards that had more children in the church. (Don Pedro de Peralta, for instance, had three of his eleven offspring enter the church.) Nor did having a child pursue a religious life probably save a family a great deal of money. Prospective seculars demanded some education; regulars often required the mortgaging of family property, either because a share of the proceeds were promised to an order for the member's sustenance or because a part of the yearly revenue was earmarked for the religious house. Families expected some of their children to take up a religious calling and derived considerable satisfaction and social prestige from their doing so.[17]

Seventeenth-century Arequipans also continued their interest in public office. That interest appears to have been due in some measure to the economic value of municipal posts. The *cabildo*, as noted earlier, remained quite active, concerning itself with such matters as securing additional lands in the Arequipa Valley for residents, lodging complaints against Crown and viceregal efforts to tax wine exports or curb the supply of drafted Indians, and protecting and developing trade routes. The council's activity does suggest that the oft-repeated assertions of *cabildo* moribundity during the 1600s are exaggerated,[18] but there was some reduction in the frequency of meetings and an increase in members' absenteeism. The cause of both absenteeism and infrequent meetings lay not in any significant decline of *cabildo* powers, but in the increasing regularity with which *heredados* personally tended to their business ventures. Very often officials reported that, when a councilor failed to attend *cabildo* meetings, he was residing in a coastal valley estate.[19] No doubt, in trying times *heredados* took to overseeing wine production more closely to insure that all went well and that their estates ran as profitably as possible. It may be that a few also managed their farms to avoid the cost of hiring stewards. There are indications that the expense of managers became onerous, and that some *heredados* fell behind in paying their salaries.[20]

Naturally, because of their financial travails, landowners also could no longer afford to pay as much for permanent city-government posts.[21] Even at reduced prices, some were reluctant to buy offices, a development that resulted in stiffer competition for elected positions. Thus, unlike the thirty-year stretch from 1545 to 1574, when seventeen men had served as city *alcalde* two or more times (one, seven times, another, four times, and four, three times), during the period from 1645 to 1674, only four Arequipans served more than once, and none more than twice. In all, fifty men held judgeships during the later period, compared with thirty-three during the earlier epoch. (As previously noted, the city lost many of the elite during the earlier period because they were either killed in battle or emigrated. No doubt, even fewer men would have served as *alcalde* had there not been such a loss, for it was the surviving early colonists who most frequently secured the post of judge more than once.)[22]

The more extensive political participation of Arequipans was but one aspect of an extremely important development in the seventeenth-century community: the broadening of the Southwest's elite. Another indication of its expansion can be found in notarial records of the period. Whereas locals had previously used the designations of "don" and "doña" sparingly, reserving them principally for the socially superior major *encomenderos* and royal officials, together with their immediate relatives, by the mid-1600s they applied these honorifics to most persons of landowning families. Only rarely did someone employ the standards of an earlier day and distinguish among important rural proprietors by limiting the use of these respectful terms. Notaries certainly were not sloppy or indiscriminate in recording such titles. In expanding their use to encompass almost all *heredados* and their kin, the notaries recognized that such persons had come to be accepted as members of the region's elite.[23]

Marriage Patterns in Arequipa during the Seventeenth Century

No better measure of the broadened definition of the elite exists than the marriage habits of Arequipan families. From the mid- to the late 1500s the Southwest's *encomendero* and major landowning families had wed persons from outside the community. Such unions had been sought after because they reinforced or improved the social position of the Arequipans. Even into the early 1600s, when financial troubles engulfed Southwesterners, colonists seemed anxious to continue this practice and others associated with social status. A few wealthy families, like the Peraltas, who enjoyed unusual standing in the colony by virtue of descent from distinguished *encomenderos* and their forebears' marriages to impressive colonial and Spanish families, could still find excellent spouses for children. Diego de Peralta Cabeza de Vaca's grandchild, Doña Isabel Zegarra Casaús y Peralta, for example, wed the outsider Captain Gonzalo Ibáñez Dávila, the son of a permanent councilor of a *villa* in the Spanish Bishopric of Córdoba. Her brother, Don Juan, the heir to an *encomienda*, married Doña Petronila Valverde y Mercado, the legitimate daughter of a man who served as a president of the Royal Audiencia in Panama.[24]

But others of the elite could no longer do as well. Given Arequipa's economic recession, only a few could canvass the colony for distinguished mates. Voyages to Spain to find appropriate partners for themselves or for family members were out of the question. With holdings that now consisted primarily of reduced *encomiendas*, *heredad* fragments, depleted *estancias*, and some *chácaras*, Southwesterners had to face the reality that with regard to matrimony they no longer were judged as favorably as before. Most lacked the means to raise dowries of 20,000 pesos, often necessary to wed their daughters to socially impressive outsiders.[25] Nor would Arequipan sons inherit enough to insure the daughters of prominent outsiders an adequate future by their parents' standards. That certainly appears to have been the judgment of most *corregidores* who served in the city between 1600 and 1670. Although their predecessors and their families had often wed locals, of the fourteen non-Arequipans who occupied the post during these seven decades, none married a Southwesterner, and only one had a brother and another, a child who did. (Two daughters of a *corregidor* who died before arriving in the city continued on to Arequipa and married landowners after the viceroy provided each with a dowry.)[26] To make matters worse, the descendants of some functionaries who had settled in Arequipa during the boom years of the late 1500s now apparently regarded their prospects in the region so bleak that they emigrated. Such was the case with Doctor Don Cosme Carrillo's children, who left for Lima and Chile and arranged to sell off the family's *heredad* on the Majes River.[27]

Nevertheless, marriages to outsiders did not cease altogether; in total numbers more elite Arequipans probably wed such persons during the seventeenth century than before. The decrease was proportional, with a qualitative change in the individuals selected. No longer did Southwesterners marry into the families of *corregidores* sent to the city of Arequipa or of prominent royal bureaucrats based in Lima and elsewhere; they now chose from among local treasury officials, *corregidores* assigned to less prestigious posts in the region, outsiders who emigrated to southwest Peru, and distinguished individuals in other secondary colonial cities. That was the case, for example, with Doña Ana Orihuela y la Torre, the granddaughter of an *encomendero* and the descendant of a royal accountant. She married Don Melchor Eguiluz y Herencia, a Spanish immigrant. Her half-sister Doña Isabel Núñez del Prado y la Torre wed José de Paz y Sosa, whose mother was the daughter of a *corregidor* and whose father was from Lisbon. The Arequipans Doña Lorenza Fernández de la Cuadra and Doña Luisa de Ribera Butrón y Barraza married *corregidores* from Spain, the former a man assigned to serve in the town of Moquegua. Two Arequipans wed daughters of Spanish royal treasurers, another married the daughter of an *alférez real* of Cochabamba. Other prominent women married men like Don Juan de Zúñiga, a Spanish-born captain; Don Juan Santiago Moscoso, another Spanish captain, who served in the colony as Protector of Indians; Don Sebastián de la Rocha, a Spanish immigrant who apparently was related to a *corregidor*; and a Spaniard who belonged to the Order of Santiago. A spouse with the credentials of knighthood was now exceedingly rare; most outsiders commanded less social status than persons earlier leading Arequipans had wed.[28]

With old habits proving difficult to break, Arequipa's parents encouraged their children's unions to outsiders by providing them with rural lands, a practice that enabled a few newcomers to build up rural holdings. For example, Don Diego de Benavides, a public trustee and possibly the son of a royal official, after securing Vítor land through his marriage to Doña Constanza Dávalos del Castillo y Peralta, invested in mortgages and rented various properties in coastal valleys and near the city of Arequipa. His son, Captain Don Diego de Benavides, who served in the Royal Treasury, used the proceeds of his inheritance to purchase *chácaras* near Socabaya and a major estate, La Magdalena, along the Vítor River. He emerged as one of Arequipa's largest landholders during the mid-seventeenth century.[29]

But such careers were atypical. More commonly, an outsider only acquired some land from his in-laws. This was the case, for instance, with three newcomers who married the daughters of Don Fernando de Cárdenas y la Torre; each gained a share of the family's *heredad*. In the past, such men would have expanded their holdings, generally by pooling their funds with those of in-laws to buy adjoining tracts and other rural property. Partnerships of this type now were only rarely possible, because Southwesterners lacked the capital. Even if the newcomers had funds of their own, it was difficult for them to purchase land before the 1640s, because, given the economic and social importance of land, Southwesterners retained the tracts they possessed.[30]

The shrinking opportunities for outsiders in the countryside until the time that the royal government began to auction vacant lands after 1641 probably explain why some left the region even after marrying locals.[31] Reduced opportunities also apparently discouraged many relations to follow those who came to Arequipa. Relatives of immigrants were less numerous in the mid-1600s than they had been in the late 1500s.[32] In short, immigrants could still parlay their social credentials into access to land, but since, like Arequipans, they could own only small parcels, their social standing was not quite what it had been.

Intermarriage among Arequipans

As the possibilities of alliances with prestigious outsiders diminished and as each generation increased the number of Southwesterners eligible for marriage, many Arequipans began to marry each other or to wed the relatives of locals who had settled in other Peruvian cities. These unions not only became more socially acceptable, they also offered Arequipans considerable financial benefits. Such spouses and their parents, of course, would understand that dowries had to be moderate.[33] Uniting the daughter of one Arequipan landowner to the son of another had the additional advantage of assuring the couple portions of two estates or other rural property. That parents sometimes had more than one child marry offspring of the same family suggests that they may have attempted to maintain consolidated holdings. A couple could retain a block of land of one family (the shares that would have gone to two children) while the other also got a double-sized property.[34]

The changing nature of marriages in Arequipa can be seen in table 10, which summarizes the marriage patterns of fourteen landowning families over approximately 120 years. During the first period (1540 to ca. 1600), the overwhelming majority of residents in Arequipa married outsiders. Marriages to outsiders declined in the next period (ca. 1600 to ca. 1630), with corresponding increases in unions to those of either Arequipan or mixed parentage. Unions of Arequipans after that reveal a continuity in the trend of fewer marriages to outsiders, but there was a decrease in marriages to those of mixed parentage as well. This analysis of the marital habits of certain Arequipans also suggests the continuing premium placed by colonials on their children's entering the church. Indeed, in each of the periods studied, over 80 percent of the unmarried joined orders or became secular priests. There was a rise during the third period among unmarrieds who did not enter the church, which may indicate that when land was in short supply fewer Arequipans wed. However, because the evidence documents the careers of only a few persons, I cannot make sound observations on this point.[35]

Table 10
Family Marriage Patterns

Period	Total No. Children	No. Married[a]			Unmarried[b]	No Data
		To Outsiders	To Arequipans	To Persons of Mixed Parentage		
First (1540-ca. 1600)	76	44 (84.6%)	3 (05.8%)	5 (09.6%)	16 (23.5%)	8
Second (ca. 1600-ca. 1630)	70	22 (51.2%)	7 (16.2%)	14 (32.6%)	13 (23.2%)	14
Third (ca. 1630-ca. 1660)	53	13 (41.9%)	12 (38.7%)	6 (19.4%)	14 (31.1%)	8

Sources: *SMA*, pp. 21, 30-31, 41, 57, 64-71, 94-95, 98, 140-141; *SMC*, pp. 146-151; *SMF*, pp. 19-60, 65-76, 85-94, 114, 124-126, 210-216, 221-232, 272-305, 308-317, 339-340, 342-348, 431-436; *SMG*, p. 57; ANP, Compañía, Títulos, leg. 3 (1628-1652); ADA, multiple references.

Note: Figures are for fourteen landowning families: de la Torre, Cáceres, Hernández de la Cuba, Peralta Cabeza de Vaca, Bueno, Alvarez de Carmona, Pizarro, Cornejo, de León, Salazar, Herrera, Cárdenas, Almonte, Ruiz de León.

[a] Figures in parentheses are percentage of total married.

[b] Figures in parentheses are percentage of total number of children.

When Southwesterners first began to marry among themselves in significant numbers (after 1600), they generally perpetuated the social divisions that had been apparent in the community since the mid-1500s. Those belonging to Arequipa's elite—the descendants of major *encomenderos* who had remained in the city, government functionaries and their relatives, and a few landowners of venturer and merchant origins—wed within their own circle. Those Arequipans who occupied a social position immediately below this elite—the heirs of minor *encomenderos*, illegitimate children of persons in the upper tier, landowning venturers, and relatives of minor royal officials—also intermarried. Doña María de la Cuba Maldonado, the daughter of an *encomendero*-landowner, accordingly wed the son of another *encomendero*-landowner; their son, Don Francisco Retamoso de la Cuba, married the daughter of an *encomendero*. On the other hand, Melchor de Luque, the mestizo son of a scribe, wed a mestiza, and Ana Madueño y Mendoza, the daughter of a venturer who had married a minor *encomendero*'s widow, selected the Spanish notary García Muñoz Jiménez.[36] During the remainder of the seventeenth century, some would continue to marry as had their forebears. Thus, to cite but one family, when the Peraltas wed, they generally chose others descended from sixteenth-century aristocrats. Two grandchildren of Diego de Peralta Cabeza de Vaca (children of his son Captain Don Pedro) wed grandchildren of the *encomendero* Miguel Cornejo, offspring of Miguel's daughter Doña Ana, who had married an *encomendero* outsider of some prominence in Cuzco; another of Don Pedro's daughters wed a grandson of Hernando de la Torre (by his daughter Doña Beatriz), who also had married a non-Arequipan, an accountant in the city's Royal Treasury.[37]

Members of the elite rarely wed Arequipans outside their circle before 1600, and their offspring also were prone to intermarry in the years thereafter, but some of their descendants turned to the children and grandchildren of persons who had not been sixteenth-century aristocrats. Such was the case, for example, in the marriage during the 1650s of Don Pedro de Peralta Valenzuela y Mejía (another of Diego de Peralta's grandsons) to Doña Antonia de Ribera Roelas. Doña Antonia descended from a minor *encomendero* and founder and from the illegitimate son of a *corregidor* who had married into the family of a landowning venturer. There certainly would have been quite a stir during the mid-1500s had any of these forebears of Doña Antonia wed the child of a major *encomendero*.

A marriage such as that of Doña Antonia de Ribera Roelas to Don Pedro de Peralta should not suggest that elite Arequipans of the mid-seventeenth century had become more open-minded. Instead, marriages like this one were the result of some colonials having gradually improved their social standing. Doña Antonia's predecessors' mobility began when her great-grandfather acquired an estate and with its proceeds endowed his daughter's marriage to Diego Martínez de Ribera, the illegitimate son of a *corregidor*. Although Diego's illegitimacy meant that the union did not raise the family into Arequipa's elite, the marriage was a step in that direction because it established an association with a royal official. Diego used part of the land he had gained through marriage to acquire other parcels and a permanent councilorship in the city. A son, Licenciado Don Francisco, Doña Antonia's father, afterward inched his way up the social ladder. Aided by his land inheritance, some land acquisitions, and the prestige of being a permanent councilor, he wed Doña María Zegarra de las Roelas y Salazar, the legitimate daughter of a *corregidor* and Doña Isabel de Salazar.[38]

Doña Antonia's maternal predecessors had also been socially mobile. The Salazars originated as a landowning family in the area when Juan de Salazar, a native of Burgos, arrived from Spain and in 1584 purchased an *heredad* along the Vítor River (once the estate of an *encomendero*). Two of Juan de Salazar's sons proved astute and eventually wed daughters of a *corregidor* from Spain, thereby improving their social status. One purchased a permanent council seat in Arequipa and, significantly, also inherited an entailed estate in Spain through his wife. Before they enjoyed that success, the brothers pooled their resources to raise a dowry sufficient to marry their sister, Doña Isabel, to a *corregidor*. Doña Antonia was born to the couple.[39]

Several other families in Arequipa also enjoyed some social mobility during the seventeenth century. They included the Gutiérrez de Mendozas. Diego Gutiérrez de Mendoza had been one of Arequipa's most prominent early merchants. In the social world of sixteenth-century Arequipa, his financial success was only good enough to enable him to marry the illegitimate daughter of an *encomendero*. His daughters, living at a time when land became the major source of wealth and could provide the means for greater social advancement, wed outsiders. One married Cristóbal de Cárcamo, who served as *corregidor* in Condesuyos. This branch of the family, as well as that of a son, Andrés Coronado, remained important landholders in the region, buying estates along the Siguas and Majes rivers, as well as renting others from hard-pressed *heredados*. Cristóbal de Cárcamo's and Doña Isabel Gutiérrez Coronado's children, as might be expected, married well. A son, for example, wed the daughter of a *corregidor*, who was related to a royal treasurer.[40]

Thus, over the course of the seventeenth century, the composition of Arequipa's elite gradually broadened as descendants of persons who had not been part of this circle were admitted. The acceptance of these Arequipans, along with the increase in unions between those descended from the sixteenth-century aristocracy, resulted in remarkable social cohesion. This cohesion can be charted by examining familial ties of Vítor Valley proprietors during the early 1660s. For example, Don Francisco Pacheco de Chaves y Orihuela, a landowner I chose at random from a list of proprietors (see Appendix C), was related to almost two-thirds of the valley's *heredados*. A fair number of landowners were his close relatives and included an uncle, two brothers, three nephews, the husbands of a niece and of a cousin, and a grandnephew. Many of his ties to other proprietors were through his wife. She had a dozen close relatives who owned *heredades*; another twelve were her distant relatives. The existence of such associations is in marked contrast with the situation that prevailed during the 1580s.[41]

If even more remote familial ties are included, as well as some probable ones, the links between *heredado* families during the early 1660s become even more extensive. Further, given the ongoing process of social integration, it is not surprising that several owners of Vítor Valley land who were unrelated when the list was drawn up soon established familial bonds. Juan Bautista Calderón, for example, who married into the Treviño family, subsequently became father-in-law of Don Alvaro Cornejo de la Cuadra and thus a common relative of the Calderón, Treviño, and Pacheco families. The Pachecos, in turn, drew closer to the Cabreras when a grandnephew of Don Francisco Pacheco de Chaves y Orihuela wed a daughter of Don Nicolás Rodríguez de Cabrera.[42]

Social Differentiation among Seventeenth-Century Southwesterners

The social advancement of some Arequipans and the creation of extensive familial ties should not be taken as a suggestion that social distinctions among the region's elite ended during the seventeenth century. Members of Arequipa's upper society continued to be positioned along a continuum from lesser to greater prominence. The fine lines that differentiated the group remained drawn in large measure on the basis of whether members descended from prestigious forebears. Having a wealth of *encomenderos* or important royal officials in one's family tree recommended one highly. But whereas nothing could be done about ancestry, it was possible to improve or to reinforce a family's position through marriage. Hence, Arequipans continued their attempts to wed spouses of superior lineage. Because the titles of "don" and "doña" had become common among people of Spanish ethnicity who had any claim to prominence at all and because most families had some involvement in the city's government, members of the elite now sought other ways to distinguish among themselves. A particularly important trend was their acquisition of military titles from the Crown. Rather rapidly various members of the elite commanded positions such as admiral, general, captain, sergeant major, and aide-de-camp.[43] Of course, no one could deny the preeminent stature that a general's family enjoyed or the additional prestige that a few families attained when sons were admitted to a Spanish military order. As might be expected, the likes of the Peraltas secured such honors: in 1671 Don Pedro de Peralta y de los Ríos, great-grandson of the *encomendero* Diego de Peralta (and a descendant of the Cornejos), became a knight. Significantly, other families were involved, including a few that had not been considered a part of the pre-1600 elite. When Don Juan de Salazar y Solís Enríquez was received into the Order of Calatrava in 1668, his admission capped the upward social climb of the Salazars, which had begun with his grandfather's arrival in Arequipa during the late 1500s.[44]

Naturally, the attainment of such preeminence required funds. A son's admission to a military order generally demanded that he be sent to Spain for an education and to develop some influence there. Substantial wealth was also needed to bring off the impressive marriages that a few Arequipans now managed to arrange for offspring in Spain and the colony. That proved to be the case when Aide-de-Camp Don Juan de Salazar y Osorio wed his daughter to a count, and when another Arequipan, of the Peralta family, married a knight. It was, of course, the availability of land after 1641 and the diversification of agricultural production by some Southwesterners that made much of this possible. Nevertheless, financial success and thus social advancement were restricted to a few families. Because Arequipa's rural economy did not improve markedly during the late seventeenth century, others of the elite were still limited in their attempts to emulate Hispanic social practices.[45]

To leave the impression that neither downward mobility nor social stagnation occurred among landowners would be to distort social trends of the seventeenth century. The Torres family, the Valderramas, and the Carvajals, for instance, failed to develop close ties with members of Arequipa's elite despite each having had as much land as the Salazars during the 1590s.[46] Their social problems stemmed partially from the loss of land and the decreasing value of the *heredades* they retained. The Torres clan, for example, had to sell Vitor Valley property following the major earthquake of 1600; their heirs eventually disposed of the remainder. In succeeding years the only income they received from their once-sizeable holding came through a mortgage.[47] The Carvajals managed to hold on to their Siguas River *heredad* into the late 1620s, but it was practically worthless, for damage reduced the estate's value from 30,000 pesos to between 100 and 200 pesos.[48] Antonio de Valderrama's descendants, too, may have been hurt by destructive earthquakes, for soon after the 1604 earthquake they sold off equipment from their *heredad*. Whatever the cause, the family's property eventually had to be auctioned because of debts and was purchased by an outsider during the 1620s.[49] Although other members of the elite suffered similar reverses, these families had fewer resources on which to draw to survive socially within Arequipa. Of venturer and merchant origins, they lacked the bloodlines of *encomenderos*' children and so could not marry well when financially crippled.

Thus, ancestry could preserve social position, as poor descendants of major *encomenderos* made clear when they wed. But, if someone was not of the right stock and possessed only slender financial resources, ancestry could hurt in the small social world of the Southwest. As a result, descendants of merchants and venturers who were not wealthy turned to others like themselves when they married. A Torres, for example, married into the family of a minor sixteenth-century landowning *encomendero* who had wed a mestiza. Others chose less prestigious immigrants, their offspring and relatives, venturers, notaries, or minor merchants, as well as the kin of priests.[50] Those living in the city of Arequipa and other regional Spanish centers strove to separate themselves from the *castas* and from the Indian community, thus becoming a distinct, landowning clique, albeit of small properties, and members of a second-rank aristocracy in the Southwest. Interestingly, many of their social practices resembled those of the region's major landed families: they also used lands for dowries and chantries, fragmented rural properties among heirs, and actively drew on their holdings to support children placed in the church.[51] Many, no doubt, hoped for better days, when they might acquire more extensive tracts and marry into the "better" families.

Some non-Indian families did expand their holdings during the mid-1600s, though they tended to be from Arequipa's social elite. They took advantage of the opportunities provided by the royal government's sale of "vacant" lands, and whereas these acquisitions in areas once considered remote by Spaniards meant an expansion of Arequipa's rural domain and, soon, a modification of the rural economy, they did not appear at first to have significant social repercussions. Indeed, many of the new owners of tracts in the coastal stretches to the north and south of the old viticulture core and in highland valleys chose to live in the city of Arequipa, as had their forebears. They shared with other residents those social practices, including intermarriage, that I discussed above. The importance of residence in Arequipa even appears to have resulted in a few descendants of landowners with property some distance from the city disposing of their parcels rather than managing them, because they did not want to live elsewhere.[52]

Nevertheless, it was natural in a time of poor internal communications for others to prefer permanent residence near their holdings. Such had been the case earlier when a few Arequipans pushed southward from the city and settled in towns like Moquegua. The tendency now intensified and, as the population in various centers grew and enriched urban life in formerly isolated outposts, and as distinct local concerns evolved, inhabitants developed some regional autonomy. By no means did those who settled beyond the immediate surroundings of Arequipa cease marrying residents of the city—examples of such unions have been cited above and the practice persists to the present—but there can be no denying the gradual emergence of subregional elites after the mid-1600s.

The character of those elites would differ from area to area, differences only just beginning to surface during the late seventeenth century. Along the coastal belt and in other places where the Indian population was sparse, the elites tended to be overwhelmingly American-born. They wed predominantly their own but, repeating the practices of Arequipans, when able gladly married peninsulars.[53] In the highland interior, especially in Condesuyos and Cailloma, some fusion occurred between colonials and Indians. For example, as the excellent genealogical work of Salvador Rodríguez Amézquita reveals, a number of colonials wed the children of Indian leaders like Don Diego Quillama of the town of Pampacolca. Don Diego's daughter, Doña Gregoria, wed an Amézquita whose family had acquired highland property during the royal land reviews after 1641; another daughter and son wed into the landowning Rodríguez de Cabreras. The Indian Pomacallao family, major landowners because of acquisitions from the royal government during the mid-1600s, engaged in similar unions.[54] The onset of such marriages and the development of regional autonomy marked important departures in the social practices of Southwesterners and closed a chapter in the region's history that had begun with Arequipa's founding in 1540.

Conclusion

A few outsiders familiar with important colonial settlements throughout the Americas considered Arequipa's seventeenth-century elite both decadent and somewhat ignorant.[55] These observers could point to the rather rude education Arequipans received, to their small farms with modest yields, to their unimpressive marriages, to the few nobles to be found in the city, and to the lack of Arequipan *mayorazgos*. Although such a characterization is not totally inaccurate, it does Southwesterners a disservice. Having confronted difficult economic problems largely not of their making, they had adjusted and survived. Intermarried and wedded to land, they remained—and no doubt with quite justifiable pride—the colonial aristocrats of various centers in a corner of Peru. Upper-rank Arequipans failed to meet the expectations of many contemporary travelers, and they clash with notions some still retain about elites in colonial Spanish America. Certainly, Arequipa's aristocrats hardly fit the description of powerful landowners who possessed extensive holdings.

Yet, in many ways, particularly in their social practices, the differences between colonial elites were more a matter of degree than of kind. Spaniards throughout the New World shared a deep concern for social position and naturally expressed that concern by seeking to comport themselves as did the Hispanic aristocracy. Their ability to indulge aristocratic habits depended on financial resources and influence. Because Arequipans had only limited amounts of each during the seventeenth century, they had to settle for less: smaller landholdings, fewer *mayorazgos*, less-pretentious lifestyles, less support for the church, fewer titles, and even less-prestigious marriages. Their situation resembled that of leading colonials scattered in the many secondary centers of the Spanish colonies.[56]

Another important aspect suggested by the Arequipan example is the remarkable endurance of American regional elites. Although some social mobility occurred among Arequipa's colonists during the seventeenth century, the more striking social development was the preservation by leading families of their position generation after generation. Such stability stemmed in large measure from the retention of rural properties followed by their expansion at mid-century. When Arequipans parted with land, they generally did so in order to acquire the necessary funds to establish themselves even more firmly in the rural economy. More often, there was only the appearance of land changing hands.[57] New owners were overwhelmingly persons who gained tracts by marrying into landed families. These families actively promoted such unions so that they might reinforce or improve their social standing in the community, if not in the Hispanic world. Seventeenth-century Arequipans, then, had a clear understanding of land's function: it served the important role of sustaining and meeting family financial needs, but rural property also was the vehicle through which those of the elite, and occasionally a few others, realized their social aspirations.

Conclusion

During the last few years, some historians have moved away from an interpretation of Spanish American colonial history that explains the emergence of large landed estates as a response to economic difficulties. In its place they claim that colonials acquired rural holdings principally to make money. Consolidation of land followed the success of certain producers. Monopolizing land provided these few with two advantages: multiple resources on which to draw so that their ventures might become more efficient; and the ability to manipulate market prices by restricting supply. A corollary of this interpretation states that the lack of haciendas in certain regions resulted primarily from the colonists' lack of resources and from their limited access to markets. Unfortunately, much of the documentation for this more recent interpretation has come from the eighteenth century.[1]

This study supports the new approach and reveals that many of the land ownership and land use patterns of earlier colonists foreshadowed those of eighteenth-century Spanish Americans. Later patterns were but a part of an ongoing process in colonial America that began shortly after the Spaniards' arrival. As early as the mid-sixteenth century, Arequipa's colonists took an active interest in land and acquired tracts within the Southwest's coastal belt so that they might practice viticulture. They responded to the colonial demand for wine: Spain's inability to satisfy consumers through exports provided the opportunity for a profitable colonial industry. What encouraged Arequipans further was their fortuitous location along the principal trade route connecting Lima and Potosí, the viceroyalty's major administrative and mining centers, as well as their region's favorable climate and geography. Through the late 1500s, Arequipans, by judiciously manipulating local resources, improved their properties and profited. Simultaneously, some colonists began to consolidate properties in the four main wine-producing valleys to the west of the city of Arequipa. They shunted aside the inefficient and those who possessed meager financial means and only limited access to labor. This development did not proceed as far as it would later in other regions of the New World, because no *heredado* had the capital or labor pool to overwhelm other estate owners. Moreover, during these early years, the colonial market for wine was large enough to insure profits for most producers. Regional landownership also remained dispersed, because those whom *heredados* dispossessed of property in the valleys to the west of the city or who could not acquire tracts there still could come by parcels elsewhere, particularly small plots in the Arequipa Valley.

The early 1600s marked a critical point in forestalling the consolidation of southwestern rural property. These years brought economic difficulties for most *heredados*. Their properties suffered earthquake damage, and *heredados* had to cope as well with the competition of recently established wine producers located in regions that enjoyed better access to Peru's most important markets. But rather than part with land, Arequipa's major landholding families clung to their estates so that they might survive financially. They also retained their *heredades*, because such holdings served vital social needs.

Only during the 1640s and the 1650s did their situation change as some acquired additional properties. Fairly cheap land became available when the Crown sold public and Indian lots. Yet even then, huge properties failed to emerge, for most Arequipans still lacked sufficient resources to consolidate land. The Southwest endured throughout the sixteenth and seventeenth centuries as a region where mid-sized and small rural holdings predominated.

The Arequipan experience provides details of the early economic adjustments of Spaniards to the New World. One aspect that bears emphasizing is the rapid separation of the colonists' major agricultural pursuit and the indigenous economy. To be sure, viticulture involved Indians in a number of ways—Indians lost land as estates grew, natives worked the fields, and they transported wine—but the industry was predominantly Spanish: Arequipans raised Old World crops and borrowed heavily estate design and methods of production from Spanish models; Spaniards dominated as landowners; and the markets were predominantly non-Indian. Among several important consequences of this separation was that the wine industry could function without Indians. This became clear as the native population of the coastal belt declined. Spaniards soon replaced Indians with black slaves and eventually with *castas*. In this respect, Arequipans enjoyed an advantage over colonists elsewhere who fashioned economies that rested on an indigenous base. When that base crumbled because of Indian depopulation (as in portions of colonial Central America), or because of factors such as Indian rebellions (a problem that surfaced in parts of highland South America), these colonists were stranded.[2]

Another consequence of the separation between the Indian and Spanish economies in the Southwest was that colonials practically ignored Indian landholders. The major changes in native land use and land ownership patterns resulted from imperial government measures, particularly the orders to reduce Indian settlements, and later, to sell Indian lands. The isolation of natives was especially pronounced in the highlands through the mid-1600s. Yet, the few coastal Indians who managed to survive the ravages of Old World diseases lived quite independently. Those who adopted European crops and landholding customs appear to have done so on their own. The colonists' concern for viticulture even allowed Indian agriculture to survive close to the city of Arequipa, a situation very different from that in areas such as Mexico's central valley.[3] Granted, Spaniards did require some alterations in the Indian economy close to the city: colonists acquired land from some communities until the 1570s, and the municipal council thereafter used taxation to force Indians to raise wheat. But it was only during the mid-seventeenth century that Indians lost much of their land. As viticulture suffered, colonists turned to wheat farming in the valley, a course that offered greater profits, given the increased demand of the now more-populous city of Arequipa.

By dwelling on the separation between the Indian and Spanish economies, an important dimension of Arequipan rural history could be lost, however, notably, that those colonists originally most dependent on the Indian community established many of the wine estates. These colonists, the *encomenderos*, had, soon after settlement, benefited from their control of Indian labor and their access to native goods. The returns from the sale of tribute products as well as the leasing of workers provided the *encomenderos* with capital, a luxury in early Arequipa. They soon channeled that capital and the native work force into agriculture. At first, the *encomenderos* tended to introduce Old World crops and livestock on their Indians' lands throughout the Southwest. But as viticulture proved more practical and profitable, they turned to coastal-belt lands. Unlike in regions such as Chile, where grantees also responded to colonial market demands but by employing their Indians' land and then subsequently becoming owners of their tributaries' property, few acquired their Indians' holdings in Arequipa.[4]

The connection between *encomienda* and viticulture does suggest that the aforementioned interpretations of colonial rural history can be reconciled somewhat. Whereas it is certainly correct that many *encomenderos* plunged into the wine industry because of its profitability, and that some did so well before their tributes had fallen drastically, a number waited for years, until the seventeenth century, in fact, before they became estate owners. Most of these *encomenderos* had highland grants and they hesitated, while they continued to benefit from the Indian economy, to become landowners. Their tributaries remained numerous and they continued to receive more and better tribute as saleable commodities. The long-lived economic importance of highland *encomiendas* in this and other parts of the Viceroyalty of Peru probably explains why colonists there maintained an interest in preserving the institution long after others in the New World.[5]

The strong position *encomenderos* and others achieved in the wine economy served them well. Once established, they persisted as rural proprietors, and their descendants too generally remained important landholders. This development accords with the popular notion of landowning elites preserving their position for generations in Latin America. Heretofore, though, there have been few systematic attempts to establish the endurance of elites in the early colonial period, or at least not in one area over a long span.[6] Several factors account for the remarkable stability of this group of Arequipans through the late 1600s. One was their ability to handle well those governments to which they, theoretically, were subservient. At times, the royal government threatened their livelihood, but Arequipans succeeded in turning back most such threats. They lobbied in Spain and Lima and explained their concerns to officials stationed in the Southwest. That royal representatives frequently acceded to Arequipan wishes reflected in part the limitations on Spanish enforcement of unpopular measures in the colonies. It has long been recognized that, without police power, Crown officials had to forego insistence on compliance with royal orders. Arequipans, however, possessed other strengths. Their familial ties stretched to former royal officials and relatives of those serving in Peru (this was especially true of *corregidores* assigned to the Southwest). Arequipans also married into powerful Lima families and had business associations with these relatives or others in that city. Such connections could be used effectively to temper threats of the royal government. The greater recurrence of such threats during the 1600s may have been due to Arequipa's weakened economy and the withering of familial and business contacts with important persons in Lima as the wine trade to that city declined. Such lessened power may have contributed to Arequipan resentment of central authorities, a major theme in the history of the Southwest after the mid-1700s.[7]

Encomendero and landowner control of Arequipa's municipal council proved beneficial, of course. Through the early 1570s, the councilors sometimes granted land to themselves and to their associates. Tax revenues paid for lobbyists and for such things as improving the wine trade through bridge construction and repair. In several crucial instances, the *cabildo*, through various measures, protected landowners. It suspended debts when *heredados* could not meet their payments during the early 1600s, for example.

Landowners, too, received preferential treatment in the allotment of drafted Indian workers, and city officials protected their properties and trade when brigands threatened them.

Governmental manipulation and control certainly should not be discounted when explaining the stable nature of landownership in Arequipa, but it would misrepresent the history of the area to overemphasize them. The endurance of landholding families rested principally on their doggedness. They functioned within a relatively uncontrolled economy in which individual decisions and actions proved critical. That Arequipan landowners survived the sixteenth-century must be attributed largely to their sagacious dealings with laborers, investments, production, and marketing. When circumstances deteriorated for wine producers during the 1600s, they adjusted mainly on their own, by employing expedients such as renting portions of their estates, renegotiating labor and loan agreements, searching out new consumers, and later, by acquiring new lands where more saleable crops could be grown.

Just as Arequipa's rural economy involved the transfer of a Spanish industry, viticulture, to an American setting, the region's societal development reflected an interplay between Old and New World ingredients. Hispanic social practices deeply influenced the Southwest's colonists in the years immediately following settlement.[8] The economically powerful citizens (the *encomenderos*) adopted many of the habits of the Castilian aristocracy: they lavished attention on the church, established *mayorazgos* when able, sought political offices, and practiced a particular lifestyle. They imitated the Spanish aristocracy in large part because of their familiarity with these habits: after all, they were Spaniards. The pursuance of Hispanic social practices continued beyond the first generation. Indeed, it endured through the late 1600s, a natural enough occurrence, since elite membership remained the preserve of descendants of the early *encomenderos*, who passed on their habits, along with their social positions and rural properties. Then, too, the persons the elite intimately associated with during these years—royal officials and Spanish immigrants—often comported themselves in precisely the manner Arequipans had chosen, thereby reinforcing local behavior.

The identification of Hispanic practices with elite status led others in the community to adopt them. These colonists, who accumulated wealth through land after the mid-1500s but who were not members of the elite, viewed imitation of these habits as a route to social preeminence. But emulation did not suffice. The key to a family's social mobility lay also in its ability to arrange impressive marriages. This course proved difficult for the ambitious during the sixteenth century, because the region's aristocracy preferred to wed outsiders. Less-well-regarded Arequipans thus sought unions first with outsiders whom the elite admired, by trading land for status. By the early 1600s, when established Southwesterners turned to local marriages, a few on the edges of respectable society managed unions with some of the elite families.

Possession of rural property, then, became immensely important socially to many Arequipans. It was not so much that the possession of land was a social attribute, but that rural property provided the financial means to marry well and to indulge in other respected social practices. Arequipans did not lose sight of this reality and therefore they strove to make their *heredades*, *chácaras*, and *estancias* efficient and profitable holdings.

In this regard, their exploitation of the countryside was much like that of the religious orders that owned land. The concern of religious orders that agriculture be profitable was by no means unique to Arequipa. As Herman Konrad and Nicholas Cushner have indicated, the profit motive determined Jesuit actions in Mexico and in central coastal Peru. In these regions and in many others, the efficient estate management of certain orders, along with their capital resources, influence among important colonials and administrators, and stable organizations, enabled them to become major landowners.[9] Nevertheless, it proved otherwise in Arequipa through the late 1600s. (Ownership by the church in the Southwest would remain modest in terms of the church's share of the total land held by colonials to the end of the eighteenth century.)[10] It was not that the church in Arequipa lacked influence and wealth—it possessed both—it simply found it difficult to acquire good lands. Most of the best tracts had been appropriated during the sixteenth century by those outside the church and, given land's economic and social value, seventeenth-century descendants rarely parted with those tracts.

Another aspect of Arequipa's societal development was the tendency of the elite to readily accept immigrants into its ranks. As might be presumed, Arequipans did not indiscriminately incorporate all newcomers to the region. But those who had claims on noble ancestry, were well educated, or who held important posts, as well as their close relatives, found it easy to become assimilated. During the mid-1500s, a few such immigrants managed to secure *encomiendas* in the Southwest through viceregal grants, a development that occurred in other parts of the Americas.[11] Afterwards, those who came to Arequipa overwhelmingly became landowners. Although Southwesterners accepted all such persons as preeminent citizens by virtue of their backgrounds, the outsiders generally confirmed their incorporation into the elite through marriage. It was only during the seventeenth century, when leading Arequipans could not find enough prestigious outsiders to wed, that some began to intermarry. Yet, if given the chance, a Southwesterner would still opt for an immigrant or look for a spouse in Spain.

Although the state of research makes it impossible to judge whether elite social patterns like those found in Arequipa were common throughout the Americas from the mid-1500s through the late 1600s, the Arequipan preference for partners from outside the community recalls practices of later American-born colonists. Jacques Barbier has established the preference of Chilean elites for colonial bureaucrats during the late 1700s. David Brading and Doris Ladd, in turn, have demonstrated that there was extensive outside marriage among eighteenth-century Mexicans. Analyzing developments during the 1700s, John Frederick Wibel found that a few Peruvians in the Southwest married outsiders. Nevertheless, because economic conditions had not improved markedly since the late 1600s, most elite Arequipans apparently could still not afford the costs involved in marrying immigrants. With regard to marriage habits, therefore, it appears likely that eighteenth-century elite practices were but a playing out, albeit under changed circumstances, of patterns set in motion early in the colonial era. Knowledge of the long-lived existence of such social relations between colonists and outsiders lends perspective to Ladd's and Wibel's other finding that many colonists found it extremely difficult to detach themselves politically from Spaniards during the late 1700s through the early 1800s.[12]

Another manifestation of Arequipa's social bonding to Spain was the penchant for residence in Spain or in a colonial center where Spanish influence was strong. As early as the 1540s, some important southwestern *encomenderos* moved to the viceregal capital or to Spain. Certain *encomenderos* would continue to do so well into the 1600s, an exodus not unique to this group, as James Lockhart and Fred Bronner have shown.[13] Yet, there is something striking about members of landowning families emigrating as well. Residence outside Arequipa, especially in Lima, provided such persons access to the powerful who might enhance business interests or other ambitions. By leaving the Southwest for Lima or Spain, a colonist or his child might also enter a prestigious religious house, acquire status symbols of immense import like a *mayorazgo* or a knighthood, or broaden marriage options. Naturally, these redounded to the advantage of those family members left behind. That a few Arequipans steadily continued to cross the Atlantic through the late 1600s, despite the onset of financial difficulties, suggests, as Magnus Mörner has noted, that we need to know a great deal more about this aspect of colonial history.[14]

This study, then, has examined the way in which some Spaniards and their descendants made a place for themselves in one region of the Vice-royalty of Peru. They fashioned in the Southwest a rural economy and society influenced by Spanish examples but that reflected the need to mold such examples to New World circumstances. One is struck not only by the colonists' dependence on their past, but also by how the formation of a New World economy and society set in motion trends that would persist in Latin America for centuries.

Appendices

Recipient	*Encomienda* of
Gonzalo de Aguilar, Lope de Alarcón	Ocoña, Arones
Pedro Barroso	Guayba and Colan (?)
Miguel de Bonfil, Hernando de Silva	Viraco, Camaná, Arequipa Valley
Alonso de Buelta	Pampacolca
Cristóbal de Burgos, Juan López de Ricalde	Caravelí, Atico, Molleguaca
Juan Cansino (?), Juan de la Torre	Machaguay and Camaná
Garcí Manuel de Carvajal	Camaná
Miguel Cornejo	Vítor, Quilca, Chimba de Arequipa, Socabaya, Porongoche, Quispillata
Juan Crespo	Chuquibamba
Juan Flores	Lari Collaguas (highlands and Arequipa Valley)
Pedro de Fuentes	Chuquibamba
Pedro Godínez	Characato
Gómez de León	Majes, Pampanico, Acamaná
Gómez de Tordoya Vargas	Carumas
Diego Hernández	Puquina, Chichas, Socabaya, Tilumbaya, Yumina, Copoata, Guasacache, part of Tambopalla and Chule
Andrés Jiménez	Guayba and Colan (?)
Luis de León	Mitimaes (Arequipa Valley)
Martín López de Carvajal	Omate
Lucas Martínez Vegasco	Tarapacá, Pica, Loa, Llute, Arica, Ilo, Ite, Hilabaya, Carumas, Guaypar Yuminas
Martín López de Carvajal	Omate
Lucas Martínez Vegaso	Tarapacá, Pica, Loa, Llute, Arica, Ilo, Ite, Hilabaya, Carumas, Guaypar Yuminas

Appendix A (continued)
Francisco Pizarro's Indian Grants in Southwestern Peru

Recipient	*Encomienda* of
Pedro de Mendoza	Acarí
Francisco Noguerol de Ulloa	Ubinas
Order of Santo Domingo	Paucarpata
Cristóbal Pérez, Juan de Arbes, Lope de Idiáquez	Cabaı.ⁿ *Hurinsaya* and *Hanansaya*
Francisco Pinto	Chiguatɑ
Gonzalo Pizarro	Yanque Coɩɩaguas (highlands and Arequipa Valley)
Pedro Pizarro	Tacna, Arequipa Valley
Quirós (?)	Atiquipa
Francisco Rodríguez de Villafuerte	Chachas and Ucuchachas
Alonso Rodríguez Picado	Lari Collaguas (highlands and Arequipa Valley)
Alonso Ruiz (?)	Pocsi, Tambo, Chule
Antón Ruiz de Guevara, Juan Ramírez (?)	Cabana *Hanansaya* and Majes
Juan de San Juan (?)	Ocoña, Arones
Hernando de Torres	Tacna, Arequipa Valley (Guayba and Colan?)

Sources: Rafael Loredo, *Los repartos* (Lima: D. Miranda, 1958), pp. 194-202; Alejandro Málaga Medina, "Consideraciones económicas sobre la visita de la provincia de Arequipa," in *Tasa de la visita general de Francisco de Toledo*, ed. Noble David Cook, pp. 300-304 (Lima: Imprenta de la Universidad Nacional de San Marcos, 1975); Eduardo L. Ugarte y Ugarte, ed., "Información de servicios del conquistador Pedro Pizarro" (unpublished transcription, Lima, 1951); *BDA*, 1:40-48, 100-104, 265-269, 2:78-86, 89-93, 108-109, 112-113, 123, 3:1-3, 12-22, 25-30, 190, 214-220; AGI, Contaduría, leg. 1786; ANP, Titulos, leg. 1 (1557), Derecho Indigena y Encomiendas, leg. 1, cuad. 10 (1568), cuad. 15 (1572); and ADA, Hernández, 19 June 1556, Muñoz, 28 May 1561, Valdecabras, 9 November 1551, Aguilar, 17 October 1573.

Appendix B
Mercedarian Assessments on Landowners in Vítor Valley
for Pastoral Care, 1583

Landowner	Annual Assessment (pesos)	Landowner	Annual Assessment (pesos)
Hernando de Almonte	60	Juan Verdugo	23
Don Francisco Zegarra	50	Leonor Méndez	20
Juan de Castro	40	Navarro y (Tormes?)[a]	20
Diego de Herrera	40[a]	Pedro de (Valencia?)	20
Baltasar de Torres	40	Diego Cornejo	18
Diego Martínez de Ribera	30	Gómez de Tapia[a]	18
Alonso Picado	30	Cristóbal de Torres	15
Juan de Quirós Vozmediano	30	Juan de Vera	15
Juan Ramírez Zegarra[a]	28	Cristóbal Hernández	10
Juan de Castro Tristán	26	Diego de Porres	10
Andrés de Argüello	25	Hernando de (Prado?)	10
Juan Antonio Corco	25	(García de Figueroa?)[a]	8
Luis Cornejo	25	Pedro Hernández	8
Antonio de Valderrama	25	Rodrigo de Orihuela	8
Francisco de Vargas	25[a]	Juan de Vera	2

Source: AMA, leg. 6 (2 January 1583).

[a] Disagrees with *MP*, 3:180-181.

Appendix C
Archbishop's Assessments on Landowners in Vítor Valley
for Pastoral Care, ca. 1660

Heredado	Annual Assessment (pesos)	Heredado	Annual Assessment (pesos)
Compañía de Jesús	24	Don Ignacio Hernani	4
Juan de Rivera	12	Don Plácido Pacheco	4
Don Cristóbal Barreda	8	Tovar	4
Doctor Cabello	8	Doña Ana de Valencia	4
Don Pedro Ovando	8	Don Juan de Amaya	3
Juan de Valencia for Roelas	8	Sister-in-law of Don Juan	
Don Manuel de Zagarra		de Amaya	3
and brothers	8	Chantre	3
Don Fernando de Ceballos	7	Don Francisco de Cáceres	3
Doña María Ibáñez	7	Don Juan de Cáceres	3
Don Juan de Prado with		Don Alonso Dávila	3
Torres	7	Antonio González	3
Don Juan de Bedoya	6	Don Augustín de Meneses	3
Don Diego de Benavides	6	Don Juan de Navarro	3
Don Agustín Butrón	6	Don Alonso de Olazábal	3
Juan Bautista Calderón	6	Don Antonio de Prado	3
Doña María de Cárdenas	6	Domingo Pacheco for	
Don Alvaro Cornejo	6	Román	3
Don Josef Dávila	6	Don Juan de Salazar	3
Antonio Madueño and		Don Cristóbal Santayana	3
brothers	6	Don Sebastián de Sosa	3
Doña Isabel de Prado	6	Doña Isabel Trevino	3
Esteban de Ripacho	6	Canónigo Esteban de	
Martín Sánchez	6	Valencia	3
Don Juan de Vargas	6	Francisco de Valencia	3
Juan de Adriasola	5	Don Francisco de Villalva	3
Don Nicolás de Cabrera	5	Don Fernando de Aedo	2
Don Juan Fernández		Don Jorge de Bedoya	2
Dávila	5	Don Alonso Mogrovejo	2
Don Melchor de Eguiluz	5	Nicolás and Antonio Ponce	2
Don Rodrigo de Orihuela	5	Lic. Don Fernando de	
Don Francisco Pacheco	5	Beamud	1
Don Pablo Pacheco	5	Padres Dominicos	1
Don Ignacio de Salazar	5	Don Diego de Herrera	1
Lorenzo de San Juan	5	Don Diego Moscoso	1
Don Bernardo de Tapia	5	Don Fabián de Tapia	1
Don Luis de Vizcarra	5	Don Nuño de Salazar	1

Appendix C (continued)
Archbishop's Assessments on Landowners in Vítor Valley
for Pastoral Care, ca. 1660

Heredado	Annual Assessment (pesos)	Heredado	Annual Assessment (pesos)
Juan de Angulo	4	Don Alonso de Vizcarra	1
Cárdenas	4	Don Fabián de Tapia	1
Don Francisco de Cárdenas for his mother	4	Don Alonso de Vizcarra	1

Source: ANP, Títulos, leg. 4, cuad. 95 (1665); and BNP, ms. B1687 (1673). Two versions are available. The first list is not dated, although it is likely from the early 1660s. The other, dated 1673, appears to have relied on the first, with slight changes made because of deaths and sales (information on Don Fabián de Tapia, who died before 1665, supports this contention; ANP, Títulos, leg. 4, cuad. 95 [1665]).

Notes

The following abbreviations are found in the notes:

ACA	Archivo de la Catedral de Arequipa
ADA	Archivo Departamental de Arequipa
AGI	Archivo General de Indias, Seville
AMA	Archivo Mercedario de Arequipa
AMuA, LAS	Archivo Municipal de Arequipa, Libros de Actas y Sesiones y Acuerdos del Cabildo
ANP	Archivo Nacional del Perú, Lima
BDA	Víctor M. Barriga, *Documentos para la historia de Arequipa*, 3 vols. (Arequipa: Editorial La Colmena, 1939-1955)
BMHA	Víctor M. Barriga, *Memorias para la historia de Arequipa*, 4 vols. (Arequipa: Editorial La Colmena and Imprenta Portugal, 1941-1952)
BNP	Biblioteca Nacional del Perú, Lima
CGC	Pedro Cieza de León, *Guerras civiles del Perú*, 2 vols. (Madrid: Librería de la Viuda de Rico, n.d.)
HAHR	*Hispanic American Historical Review*
HHG	Antonio de Herrera y Tordesillas, *Historia general de los hechos de los Castellanos en las Islas, y Tierra-Firme de el Mar Occeano*, 10 vols. (Buenos Aires: Editorial Guaranía, 1944-1947)
LARR	*Latin American Research Review*
MNH	Museo Nacional de Historia, Lima
MP	Víctor M. Barriga, *Los Mercedarios en el Perú en el siglo XVI*, 3 vols. (Rome and Arequipa: Madre de Dios and La Colmena, 1933, 1939, 1942)
SMA	Santiago Martínez, *Los alcaldes de Arequipa* (Arequipa: n.p., 1946)
SMC	Santiago Martínez, *La Catedral de Arequipa y sus capitulares* (Arequipa: Tipografía Cuadros, 1931)
SMF	Santiago Martínez, *Fundadores de Arequipa* (Arequipa: Tipografía La Luz, 1936)

SMG   Santiago Martínez, *Gobernadores de Arequipa colonial, 1539-1825* (Arequipa: Tipografía Cuadros, 1930)
Archival references in the notes are generally given as follows: archival abbreviation; where appropriate, archival classification or section, number of the *legajo* (leg.), the document (doc.), the *cuaderno* (cuad.), the *libro*, and the manuscript (ms.); and date. There are two exceptions: in citing documents of the Archivo de la Catedral de Arequipa (ACA) and of the Museo Nacional de Historia, Lima (MNH), a descriptive title and date are provided; references to notarial records in the ADA include the name of the notary and the date(s) of the entry. Only the notary's surname is provided unless this causes confusion. The following is a list of all notaries:

Diego de Aguilar
Diego Diez
Gaspar Hernández
Antonio de Herrera
Alonso Laguna
García Muñoz
Juan Pérez de Gordejuela
Diego Ortiz
Hernando Ortiz
Antonio de Silva
Diego de Silva
Benito Luis de Tejada
Juan de Torres
Adrián de Ufelde
Alonso de Valdecabras
Francisco de Vera
Juan de Vera

Introduction
1. *La multitud, la ciudad y el campo en la historia del Perú*, 2d ed. (Lima: Huascarán, 1947), pp. 217-223.
2. *South America: Observations and Impressions*, 2d ed. (New York: Macmillan Co., 1914), pp. 60-74.
3. Jorge Polar, *Arequipa: Descripción y estudio social*, 3d ed. (Lima: Lumen, 1958), p. 203.
4. Magnus Mörner, *Historia social latinoamericana (Nuevos enfoques)*, Colección Manoa of the Universidad Católica Andrés Bello (Caracas: Arte, 1979), pp. 116-117, 129-136, 150-154. Also see Robert G. Keith, *Haciendas and Plantations in Latin American History* (New York: Holmes & Meier, 1977), and idem, *La hacienda, la comunidad y el campesino en el Perú*, Colección Perú-Problema, no. 3 (Lima: Moncloa-Campodónico, 1970); Henry Favre, "Evolución y situación de las haciendas en la región de Huancavelica, Perú," *Revista del Museo Nacional* (Perú) 33 (1964):237-257; Enrique Florescano, ed., *Haciendas, latifundios y*

plantaciones en América Latina (Mexico City: Siglo Veintiuno, 1975); Emilio Romero, *Historia económica del Perú*, 2 vols. (Buenos Aires: Sud-Americana, 1949), pp. 2:29-60, 196-219.

5. Several articles provide information on work done on rural Spanish America: James Lockhart, "Encomienda and Hacienda: The Evolution of the Great Estate in the Spanish Indies," *HAHR* 49 (August 1969):411-429; Magnus Mörner, "The Spanish American Hacienda: A Survey of Recent Research and Debate," *HAHR* 53 (May 1973):183-216.

6. Major studies on Mexico include François Chevalier, *La formation des grands domaines au Mexique: Terre et société aux XVIIe-XVIIe siècles* (Paris: Institut d'Ethnologie, 1952) (English version: *Land and Society in Colonial Mexico: The Great Hacienda*, trans. Alvin Eustis, ed. Lesley Byrd Simpson [Berkeley & Los Angeles: University of California Press, 1966]); Charles Gibson, *The Aztecs under Spanish Rule: A History of the Indians of the Valley of Mexico, 1519-1810* (Stanford, Cal.: Stanford University Press, 1964).

7. Jean Borde and Mario Góngora, *Evolución de la propiedad rural en el valle del Puangue*, 2 vols. in 1 (Santiago de Chile: Editorial Universitaria, 1956); Manuel Burga, *De la encomienda a la hacienda capitalista: El valle del Jequetepeque del siglo XVI al XX*, Estudios de la sociedad rural, no. 4 (Lima: Instituto de Estudios Peruanos, 1976); Alberto Flores-Galindo, *Arequipa y el sur andino: Ensayo de historia regional (siglos XVIII-XX)* (Lima: Horizonte, 1977); Magnus Mörner, *Perfil de la sociedad rural del Cuzco a fines de la colonia* (Lima: Universidad del Pacifico, 1978); Germán Colmenares, *Las haciendas de los jesuitas en el Nuevo Reino de Granada, siglo XVIII* (Bogotá: Universidad Nacional de Colombia, 1969); Johanna S. R. Mendelson, "The Jesuit Haciendas of the College of Popayán: The Evolution of the Great Estate in the Cauca Valley" (Ph.D. diss., Washington University, 1978); Pablo Macera, ed. *Instrucciones para el manejo de las haciendas jesuitas del Perú (ss. XVII-XVIII)*, Nueva Corónica, vol. 2 (Lima: Universidad Nacional Mayor de San Marcos, 1966); idem, *Mapas coloniales de haciendas cuzqueñas* (Lima: Universidad Nacional Mayor de San Marcos, 1968); Nicholas P. Cushner, *Lords of the Land: Sugar, Wine, and Jesuit Estates of Coastal Peru, 1600-1767* (Albany: State University of New York Press, 1980).

8. Burga, *Valle del Jequetepeque*, pp. 103-141; Robert G. Keith, *Conquest and Agrarian Change: The Emergence of the Hacienda System on the Peruvian Coast*, Harvard Historical Studies, no. 93 (Cambridge, Mass.: Harvard University Press, 1976); David A. Brading, *Haciendas and Ranchos in the Mexican Bajío: León, 1700-1860* (Cambridge: At the University Press, 1978); Herman W. Konrad, *A Jesuit Hacienda in Colonial Mexico: Santa Lucía, 1576-1767* (Stanford, Cal.: Stanford University Press, 1980); Eric Van Young, *Hacienda and Market in Eighteenth-Century Mexico: The Rural Economy of the Guadalajara Region, 1675-1820* (Berkeley & Los Angeles: University of California Press, 1981).

9. On Indian areas in Peru, see John V. Murra, *Formaciones económicas y politicas del mundo andino*, Historia Andina, vol. 3 (Lima: Industrialgráfica for the Instituto

de Estudios Peruanos, 1975); Karen W. Spalding, "Indian Rural Society in Colonial Peru: The Example of Huarochirí" (Ph.D. diss., University of California at Berkeley, 1967); idem, "The Colonial Indian: Past and Future Research Perspectives," *LARR* 7 (Spring 1972):47-76; Heraclio Bonilla Mayta, *Las comunidades campesinas tradicionales del valle de Chancay*, Tesis Antropológicas, no. 1 (Lima: Instituto de Estudios Etnológicos del Museo Nacional de la Cultura Peruana, 1965); Franklin Pease G. Y., ed., *Collaguas I* (Lima: P. L. Villanueva for Pontificia Universidad Católica del Perú, 1977); Nicolás Sánchez-Albornoz, *El indio en el Alto Perú a fines del siglo XVII*, Seminario de Historia Rural Andina (Lima: Universidad Nacional Mayor de San Marcos, 1973); Magnus Mörner, *La corona española y los foráneos en los pueblos de América* (Stockholm: Almqvist and Wiksell, 1970); Brooke Larson, "Economic Decline and Social Change in an Agrarian Hinterland: Cochabamba (Bolivia) in the Late Colonial Period" (Ph.D. diss., Columbia University, 1978); Steve J. Stern, *Peru's Indian Peoples and the Challenge of Spanish Conquest: Huamanga to 1640* (Madison: University of Wisconsin Press, 1982).

10. Several essays in Ida Altman and James Lockhart, eds., *Provinces of Early Mexico: Variants of Spanish American Regional Evolution* (Los Angeles: UCLA Latin American Center, 1976), demonstrate varied Indian and non-Indian landholding patterns in Mexico. Also see William B. Taylor, *Landlord and Peasant in Colonial Oaxaca* (Stanford, Cal.: Stanford University Press, 1972).

11. For studies on the internal society that existed on estates: Chevalier, *Land and Society*, especially chap. 8; and Konrad, *A Jesuit Hacienda*, part 3.

12. Virgilio Roel, *Historia social y económica de la colonia* (Lima: Gráfica Labor, 1970); Henry F. Dobyns and Paul L. Doughty, *Peru: A Cultural History* (New York: Oxford University Press, 1976); François Bourricaud, *Poder y sociedad en el Perú contemporáneo*, trans. Roberto Bixio (Buenos Aires: Sur, 1967); Antonio García, *Dominación y reforma agraria en América Latina*, Colección América-Problema, no. 3 (Lima: Moncloa-Campodónico, 1970); José Carlos Mariátegui, *Seven Interpretative Essays on Peruvian Reality*, trans. Marjory Urquidi (Austin: University of Texas Press, 1971); François Bouricaud et al., *La oligarquía en el Perú*, Colección Perú-Problema, no. 2 (Lima: Moncloa-Campodónico, 1969).

13. David Weeks, "European Antecedents of Land Tenure and Agrarian Organization of Hispanic America," and idem, "The Agrarian System of the Spanish American Colonies," *Journal of Land and Public Utility Economics* 23 (1947):60-75, 153-168.

14. The issue of motivations is discussed in James Lockhart's introduction to Altman and Lockhart, *Provinces of Early Mexico*, especially, pp. 5-6; Mörner, *Historia social*, pp. 122-129.

15. *SMA, SMC, SMF,* and *SMG* provide countless examples of Arequipan marriage patterns after the 1600s. For additional details on post-seventeenth century southwestern history, see Kendall Walker Brown, "The Economic and Fiscal Structure of Eighteenth-Century Arequipa" (Ph.D. diss., Duke University, 1979);

Flores-Galindo, *Arequipa y el sur andino*; John Frederick Wibel, "The Evolution of a Regional Community within Spanish Empire and Peruvian Nation: Arequipa, 1780-1845" (Ph.D. diss., Stanford University, 1975); Guillermo Zegarra Meneses, *Arequipa, en el paso de la colonia a la república; visita de Bolívar* (Arequipa: Cuzzi y Cia. for Banco del Sur, 1971).

Chapter 1: Indians, *Encomenderos*, and Arequipa's Early Rural Economy
    1. I have tried to maintain the original spelling in all quotations.
    2. *BDA*, 1:79-83, 94, 125-127, 129, 2:302-314, 341-383, 3:204; AGI, Lima, leg. 199; Francisco Xavier Echeverría y Morales, "Memoria de la Santa Iglesia de Arequipa," in *BMHA*, 4:11-13; and *SMF*, pp. 77-86. There may have been some Spanish women in the group, since many of the men had been in Peru for several years. Ladislao Cabrera Valdés, ed., *Documentos primitivos del Cabildo* (Arequipa: Caritg y Rivera, 1924), pp. 119-121, lists women he considered non-Indian founders, but I could find none in documents of the period.
    3. *BDA*, 1:108, 121-124, 133-134, 145, 147, 157-158, 2:96, 107; AMuA, LAS, libro 2 (5 June 1546, 9 June 1546). An index of this libro has been published: Alejandro Málaga Medina, Eusebio Quiroz Paz Soldán, and Juan Alvarez Salas, eds., *Indice del libro segundo de actas de sesiones y acuerdos del Cabildo de la ciudad de Arequipa, 1546-1556* (Arequipa: El Sol, 1974).
    4. *BDA*, 1:38-39, 57-58, 63-65, 80-81, 100, 2:104-106, 3:12; and *SMF*, pp. 261, 338.
    5. James Lockhart, *The Men of Cajamarca: A Social and Biographical Study of the First Conquerors of Peru*, Latin American Monographs, no. 27 (Austin: University of Texas Press for the Institute of Latin American Studies, 1972); idem, *Spanish Peru, 1532-1560: A Colonial Society* (Madison: University of Wisconsin Press, 1968).
    6. If Southwestern Peru is defined by the early colonial boundaries, its southern border should be the Loa River in modern Chile. *Encomenderos*, who were required to reside in the city of Arequipa, were granted Indians as far south as the Loa. Later, when the bishopric of Arequipa was created, it also included the coastal belt that stretches to the Loa River (see plate 1). However, since the region between the settlement of Arica and the Loa River was not of major interest to most Spaniards living in Arequipa, there is only brief mention made of it in this study. For the geography of Southwestern Peru, see Jorge Polar, *Arequipa: Descripción y estudio social*, 3d ed. (Lima: Lumen, 1958), pp. 14-38; G. de Reparaz, "La zone aride du Pérou," *Geografiska Annaler* 40 (1958): esp. pp. 4-6; Antonio Raimondi, *El Perú*, 6 vols. in 5 (Lima: Imprenta del Estado, Gil, & Sanmartí, 1874-1913), pp. 1:166-172, 232-237; Antonio Vázquez de Espinosa, *Compendio y descripción de las Indias Occidentales*, Biblioteca de Autores Españoles, no. 231 (Madrid: Atlas, 1969), pp. 334-350; Reginaldo de Lizárraga, *Descripción breve de toda la tierra del Perú, Tucumán, Río de la Plata y Chile*, Biblioteca de Autores Españoles, no. 216 (Madrid: Atlas, 1968), pp. 47-51; *BMHA*, 1, passim; Isaiah Bowman, *The Andes of Southern Peru: Geographical Reconnaissance Along the Seventy-Third Meridian* (New York: Henry Holt for the American Geographical Society of New York, 1916).

7. "Relación fecha por el Corregidor de los Chunbibilcas Don Francisco de Acuña, por mandado de su Ex.ª del señor Don Fernando de Torres y Portugal, visorrey destos reynos, para la discrepción de las Indias que su majestad manda hacer," in *Relaciones geográficas de Indias—Perú*, ed. Marcos Jiménez de la Espada, 3 vols., Biblioteca de Autores Españoles, nos. 183-185 (Madrid: Atlas, 1965), pp. 1:310-325; "Relación de la provincia de los Collaguas para la discrepción de las Indias que su magestad manda hacer," in ibid., pp. 1:326-333; "Relación del obispado de Arequipa," in ibid., pp. 2:53-57; George R. Johnson, *Peru from the Air*, with text and notes by Raye R. Platt, American Geographical Society Special Publication, no. 12 (Worcester, Mass.: Commonwealth, 1930), pp. 7-13; Raimondi, *Perú*, pp. 1:235-237; Salvador Rodríguez Amézquita, *Monografía de la Villa de Pampacolca* (Arequipa: Miranda, 1971), pp. 13-22; *BMHA*, 3, passim.

8. I arrived at this figure by comparing the number of tributaries noted in several *encomiendas* granted by Francisco Pizarro with the number of tributaries that figure in enumerations of the 1570s (*BDA*, 1:40-48, 2:84-86; AGI, Contaduría, leg. 1786). The Indian tributary population declined between 30 and 50 percent along the coast; it hardly declined in the highlands. I therefore raised the 1570 total for coastal grants by a third but not that for highland grants. I multiplied the resulting figure by four to account for children, women, the aged and infirm, and Indian officials. Frankly, as Noble David Cook has made clear, estimates on the Indian population at conquest should be treated guardedly; see *The People of the Colca Valley: A Population Study*, Dellplain Latin American Studies, no. 9 (Boulder: Westview Press, 1982), p. 15.

9. *BDA*, 1:44-45; Army Map Service, Corps of Engineers, *Map of Chuquibamba, Departamento de Arequipa, Peru* (Washington, D.C.: 1967). For similar residence patterns in the Arequipa Valley and the coastal belt, see *BDA*, 1:40-43, 46-48, 199-200; 2:84-86; 3:1-3, 12-22. Also see *SMF*, p. 107; ADA, Acuerdos del Cabildo, October 1559; ANP, Juicios de Residencia, leg. 21, cuad. 55 (1610); AGI, Justicia, leg. 480. (The latter document is available, with an introduction by Juan Carlos Crespo, in *Collaguas I*, ed. Franklin Pease G. Y. [Lima: P. L. Villanueva for Pontificia Universidad Católica del Perú, 1977], pp. 53-91.)

10. For background on land tenure under the Incas, see Juan Polo de Ondegardo, *Informaciones acerca de la religión y gobierno de los Incas*, Colección de Libros y Documentos referentes a la Historia del Perú, vol. 3 (Lima: Sanmartí, 1916), pp. 68-96 (the work has been translated into English by A. Brunel, John Murra, and Sidney Muirden and is available in microtext from the Human Relations Area Files, 1965). See also John V. Murra, "Social Structural and Economic Themes in Andean Ethnohistory," *Anthropological Quarterly* 34 (April 1961):48-55; Louis Baudin, *A Socialist Empire: The Incas of Peru*, trans. Katherine Woods and ed. Arthur Goddard (Princeton, N.J.: Van Nostrand, 1961); Sally Falk Moore, *Power and Property in Inca Peru* (New York: Columbia University Press, 1958); Garcilaso de la Vega, El Inca, *Royal Commentaries of the Incas and General History of Peru*, trans. with intro. by Harold V. Livermore, 2 vols. (Austin: University of Texas Press, 1966), esp. pp. 1:241-261; essays by Wendell C. Bennett, Luis E. Valcárcel,

and John Howland Rowe in *Handbook of South American Indians*, vol. 2: *The Andean Civilizations*, ed. Julian H. Steward (New York: Cooper Square Publishers, 1963), pp. 1-330; Luis E. Valcárcel, *Historia del Perú antiguo*, 6 vols., 2d ed. (Lima: Juan Mejía Baca, 1971), pp. 2:393-430.

11. *BDA*, 1:66, 113, 264, 3:21, 246; "Relación de la provincia de los Collaguas," pp. 327, 331-332.

12. Reparaz, "Zone aride," pp. 28-45, 55-60.

13. ADA, Acuerdos del Cabildo, October 1559, Hernández, 7 September 1549, 6 July 1553; *BDA*, 2:84-86, 3:290-291; Franklin Pease G. Y., "Collaguas: Una etnía del siglo XVI. Problemas iniciales," in *Collaguas I*, pp. 131-167; Rafael Loredo, *Los repartos* (Lima: D. Miranda, 1958), pp. 200-204; ANP, Juicios de Residencia, leg. 5, cuad. 9 (1584); "Relación fecha por el Corregidor de los Chunbibilcas Don Francisco de Acuña," pp. 312-314; "Relación de la provincia de los Collaguas," pp. 322, 331-332; MNH, Visita de la Villa de Camaná, 1592.

14. "Relación de la provincia de los Collaguas," p. 331; *BDA*, 1:158; Artemio Peraltilla Díaz, *Origen del vocablo Arequipa y su real significado* (Arequipa: El Sol, 1970), p. 26; Juan Gualberto Valdivia, *Fragmentos para la historia de Arequipa: Extractados de varios autores y de manuscritos antiguos y modernos y de las narraciones de los contemporáneos* (Arequipa: n.p., 1847), p. 65.

15. Bernabé Cobo, *Obras*, 2 vols., Biblioteca de Autores Españoles, nos. 91-92 (Madrid: Atlas, 1956), pp. 1:68-69, 290, 299-300, 306; ADA, Acuerdos del Cabildo, October 1559; *BDA*, 1:47, 2:85-86; Máximo Neyra Avendaño, *Prehistoria de la provincia de Cailloma (Los Collaguas)* (Arequipa: Universidad Nacional de San Agustín, 1964), pp. 16-17.

16. AMA, leg. 6 (9 September 1595); Alejandro Málaga Medina, "Los Collaguas en la historia de Arequipa en el siglo XVI, " in *Collaguas I*, pp. 99, 112-115; Juan José Cuadros, "Informe etnográfico de Collaguas (1974-1975)," in ibid., pp. 35-52; BNP, ms. B415 (1603); *BDA*, 1:45.

17. The legend apparently originated with Garcilaso de la Vega (*Commentaries*, pp. 1:153, 161-163). It has been repeated often, as in Echeverría y Morales, "Memoria," pp. 9-10. No major Indian sites existed in the region before or after the Inca conquest (Dorothy Menzel, "The Inca Occupation of the South Coast of Peru," *Southwestern Journal of Anthropology* 15 [1959]:125-142; Edward P. Lanning, *Peru before the Incas* [Englewood Cliffs, N.J.: Prentice-Hall 1967], pp. 14, 127; Francisco Mostajo, "Aportes para la historia de Arequipa," in *Historiadores*, ed. Bermejo, pp. 54-58; Cabrera Valdés, *Documentos*, p. 27; Raimondi, *Perú*, p. 2:82; Peraltilla Díaz, *Origen*, pp. 83-89; José María Morante Maldonado, "Arqueología del departamento de Arequipa, Condesuyos y Camaná precolombinas" [Ph.D. diss., Universidad Nacional de San Agustín, Arequipa, 1939]).

18. AMA, leg. 6 (9 September 1595); *BDA* 3:299-301; John V. Murra, "An Aymara Kingdom in 1567," *Ethnohistory* 15 (Spring 1968):115-151, and idem, "Una apreciación etnológica de la visita," in *Visita hecha a la provincia de Chucuito por Garci Diez de San Miguel en el año 1567*, Documentos Regionales para la Etnología y Etnohistoria Andina, vol. 1 (Lima: Ediciones de la Casa de la

Cultura, 1964), pp. 421-444; Marie Helmer, "La vie économique au XVIe siècle sur le haut-plateau andin. Chucuito en 1569. D'après un document inédit des Archives des Indes," in *Travaux de l'Institut Français d'Etudes Andines*, vol. 4, volume unique (Paris: Pierre André, 1954), pp. 115-149.

19. On Francisco Pizarro and his expedition, see William H. Prescott, *History of the Conquest of Peru, with a Preliminary View of the Civilization of the Incas*, 2 vols. (New York: Harper & Brothers, 1847); Raúl Porras Barrenechea, *Pizarro* (Lima: Editorial Pizarro, 1978); Garcilaso de la Vega, *Commentaries*; John Hemming, *The Conquest of the Incas* (New York: Harcourt, Brace, Jovanovich, 1970).

20. *BDA*, 1:20, 27, 3:1-3, 12-15. For early Lima, see Ralph A. Gakenheimer, "The Peruvian City of the Sixteenth Century," in *The Urban Explosion in Latin America: A Continent in Process of Modernization*, ed. Glenn H. Beyer, pp. 33-56 (Ithaca, N.Y.: Cornell University Press, 1967); Pedro Cieza de León, "La crónica del Perú," in *Crónicas de la conquista del Perú*, ed. Julio Le Riverend Brusone, pp. 369-371 (Mexico City: Nueva España, n.d.); and Garcilaso de la Vega, *Commentaries*, pp 2:775-777.

21. *BDA*, 2:37-39; Raimondi, *Perú*, p. 2:82; *HHG*, 7:201-203.

22. Garcilaso de la Vega, *Commentaries*, pp. 2:862; *CGC*, 1:351-451; Pedro Pizarro, "Relación del descubrimiento y conquista de los reinos del Perú," in *Crónicas del Perú*, 5 vols., Biblioteca de Autores Españoles, nos. 164-168 (Madrid: Atlas, 1963-65), pp. 5:220-221; *HHG*, 7:337-338, 8:64; Cieza, "Crónica," pp. 414-417; Gakenheimer, "Peruvian City," pp. 38-39, 50.

23. Raimondi, *Perú*, pp. 2:29-115.

24. *CGC*, 2:3-5. Some historians later confused the establishment of this town in the Majes Valley with the founding of Arequipa some miles away. This resulted in a furious debate over the founding date of the city of Arequipa. For arguments, see Raimondi, *Perú*, pp. 2:112-115; *HHG*, 8:126-127; Cieza, "Crónica," pp. 384-385; Antonio de Alcedo, *Diccionario geográfico de las Indias Occidentales o América*, 4 vols., Biblioteca de Autores Españoles, nos. 205-208 (Madrid: Atlas, 1967), p. 1:100; Vázquez de Espinosa, *Compendio*, p. 337; Juan Domingo de Zamácola y Jáuregui, *Apuntes para la historia de Arequipa*, 2d ed. (Lima: Lumen, 1958), pp. 23-24; Echeverría y Morales, "Memoria," p. 7; Cabrera Valdés, *Documentos*, pp. 54-55. Víctor M. Barriga's work in Peruvian and Spanish archives (available in the various volumes of *BDA*) put this debate to rest by clearing up the date of Arequipa's founding. His research findings are summarized in "El fundador de Arequipa y el Licenciado La Gasca," in *Historiadores*, ed. Bermejo, pp. 48-49. For Pizarro's intentions, see *BDA*, 1:41; Gakenheimer, "Peruvian City," p. 41.

25. *BDA*, 1:59.

26. *BDA*, 1:55-56, 61-62, 66-67, 75-76, 79; José María Morante Maldonado, *Monografía de la provincia de Camaná* (Arequipa: Editorial de la Universidad Nacional de San Agustín, 1965).

27. *BDA*, 3:1-3, 8-13; Pedro Pizarro, "Relación," pp. 225-226.

28. For information on the men granted Indians by Francisco Pizarro, see Pedro Pizarro, "Relación," pp. 211, 216; *CGC*, 1:189; *SMF*, pp. 6-18, 61-75, 140, 159-

164, 172-175, 179-190, 194-206, 217-225, 249-250, 258-259, 320-321, 357-358, 366; *SMG*, pp. 5-15, 22; *BDA*, 1:33-34, 39, 63-64, 78, 84-86, 171-176, 2:50-52, 90, 94-95, 269, 309, 321, 346, 352, 357, 360, 371, 3:12-13, 17-20, 25-27, 89-90, 102, 115-117, 217, 269, 327, 336, 344; Lockhart, *Cajamarca*, pp. 300-307, 327-328, 343-346, 469; Raúl Porras Barrenechea, *Cedulario del Perú, siglos XVI, XVII y XVIII*, 2 vols. (Lima: Torres Aguirre, 1944 and 1948), p. 1:57; Raúl Rivera Serna, *Libro primero de cabildos de la ciudad del Cuzco* (Lima: Universidad Nacional Mayor de San Marcos, 1965), p. 34; ANP, Compañía, Títulos, leg. 1 (1539-1605).

29. *SMF*, p. 355; Pedro Pizarro, "Relación," p. 220; *CGC*, 1:181.

30. Pedro Pizarro, "Relación," pp. 225-226; *SMF*, pp. 151-153, 236-237.

31. *BDA*, 1:42-43, 2:84-86; Lockhart, *Cajamarca*, pp. 300-305.

32. Loredo, *Repartos*, pp. 200, 204; Lockhart, *Cajamarca*, pp. 305-307, 327-328.

33. For *hidalgos*, see *SMF*, pp. 137-146, 154-158, 354-356; *SMG*, p. 2; *BDA*, 1:56, 2:17-33, 39, 54-76, 82, 3:14, 197-199. Some would claim to be *hidalgos*, claims that a few historians accepted and embellished. For example, contrast *SMF*, pp. 159, 249-250, and Lockhart's excellent appraisal in *Cajamarca*, pp. 327-332, 343-346.

34. Lockhart, *Cajamarca*, pp. 287, 300-307; *SMF*, pp. 176-181, 194-206; *SMG*, p. 22; *BDA*, 1:33, 3:25, 217, 269, 283; BNP, ms. Z:1264 (1562).

35. Porras Barrenechea, *Cedulario del Perú*, pp. 2:38, 74.

36. *SMF*, pp. 258-259, 264, 338-341; Lockhart, *Spanish Peru*, p. 79; *SMG*, pp. 37-38; *BDA*, 1:35, 2:351.

37. Charles Gibson, *The Aztecs under Spanish Rule: A History of the Indians of the Valley of Mexico, 1519-1810* (Stanford, Cal.: Stanford University Press, 1964), pp. 58-97.

38. For Inca political subdivisions and a general discussion of imperial administration, see John H. Rowe, "Inca Culture at the Time of the Spanish Conquest," in *Handbook of South American Indians*, pp. 2:185-192, 257-264, 273-274; and Nathan Wachtel, *The Vision of the Vanished: The Spanish Conquest of Peru through Indian Eyes, 1530-1570*, trans. Ben Reynolds and Siân Reynolds (New York: Barnes & Noble, 1977), pp. 61-84.

39. "Relación de la provincia de los Collaguas," esp. pp. 327-330; *BDA*, 1:42, 46, 3:31; and Loredo, *Repartos*, pp. 194-204.

40. *BDA*, 2:211, 3:21; Guillermo Cock C., "Los kurakas de los Collaguas: Poder político y poder económico," *Historia y Cultura* 10 (1976-77):95-118; ANP, Juicios de Residencia, leg. 5, cuad. 9 (1584); John V. Murra, *Formaciones económicas y políticas del mundo andino*, Historia Andina, vol. 3 (Lima: Industrialgráfica for the Instituto de Estudios Peruanos, 1975), p. 295.

41. ANP, Juicios de Residencia, leg. 5, cuad. 9 (1584), leg. 17, cuad. 46 (1600).

42. *BDA*, 3:14-16; ANP, Juicios de Residencia, leg. 9, cuad. 22 (1591).

43. Numerous grants are reproduced in the three volumes of *BDA*. On coastal grants, see Loredo, *Repartos*, pp. 194-199; *BDA*, 1:156, 199-200, 2:84-86, 3:299-

301; MNH, Visita de la Villa de Camaná, 1592.

44. *BDA*, 1:40-42, 2:113, 3:290-299; and Loredo, *Repartos*, p. 195.

45. *BDA*, 2:84-86; Pedro Pizarro, "Relación," pp. 221-222; Cobo, *Obras*, 2:131-132.

46. AGI, Contaduría, leg. 1786.

47. *BDA*, 1:46-48; Loredo, *Repartos*, pp. 195-198, 201-202, 204; AGI, Contaduría, leg. 1786.

48. Loredo, *Repartos*, pp. 194, 201-202; Alejandro Málaga Medina, "Consideraciones económicas sobre la visita de la provincia de Arequipa," in *Tasa de la visita general de Francisco de Toledo*, ed. Noble David Cook, pp. 301-302 (Lima: Imprenta de la Universidad Nacional de San Marcos, 1975); Málaga Medina, "Los Collaguas," pp. 111-112; Pedro Pizarro, "Relación," p. 210; *SMF*, p. 138.

49. *BDA*, 3:12-13, 21-22; Loredo, *Repartos*, pp. 194-204.

50. Eduardo L. Ugarte y Ugarte, ed., "Compilación de las ordenanzas de Arequipa, 1540-1575" (unpublished, Arequipa, n.d.), pp. 2-12; Manuel Belaúnde Guinassi, *La encomienda en el Perú* (Lima: Mercurio Peruano, 1945), pp. 40-42; *BDA*, 3:4-11.

51. ADA, Muñoz, 9 November 1557; AGI, Patronato, leg. 231, doc. 7, ramo 14; and *BDA*, 1:69, 100, 110-111, 2:89-92, 108-109, 112, 3:192.

52. Carmen Cornejo de Balbuena, "El comercio en Arequipa, 1549-1560" (unpublished, Arequipa, 1976), pp. 10-11; *BDA*, 1:68-69, 72-73, 2:124-125; and AMuA, LAS, libro 2 (11 September and 20 September 1546).

53. *BDA*, 1:52, 112, 128, 173-174, 2:89-93, 101-103, 105-106; Pedro Pizarro, "Relación," pp. 221-222; and Lockhart, *Cajamarca*, p. 301.

54. *BDA*, 1:110-111, 2:108-109.

55. Lockhart, *Spanish Peru*, pp. 4-5.

56. AMuA, LAS, libro 2 (esp. 21 March and 26 December 1546).

57. AMuA, LAS, libro 2 (20 May 1546, 5 June 1546, 2 November 1546); *BDA*, 2:112, 164, 167, 175, 360-361, 3:127, 131, 243; and Juan Polo de Ondegardo, "Relación de las cosas del Perú desde 1543 hasta la muerte de Gonzalo Pizarro," in *Crónicas del Perú*, p. 5:292.

58. Loredo, *Repartos*, pp. 358-359.

59. *BDA*, 2:268-269.

60. John Lynch, *Spain under the Hapsburgs*, 2 vols. (New York: Oxford University Press, 1969), pp. 2:214-215; Peter J. Bakewell, "Registered Silver Production in the Potosí District, 1550-1735," and idem, "Technological Change in Potosí: The Silver Boom of the 1570s," in *Jahrbuch für Geschichte von Staat, Wirtschaft und Gesellschaft Lateinamerikas*, 30 vols. (Cologne: Böhlau Verlag, 1964-1979), pp. 12:67-103, and 14:57-77, respectively; David A. Brading and Harry E. Cross, "Colonial Silver Mining: Mexico and Peru," *HAHR* 52 (November 1972):545-579; Gakenheimer, "Peruvian City," pp. 46-49; Robert G. Keith, *Conquest and Agrarian Change: The Emergence of the Hacienda System on the Peruvian Coast*, Harvard Historical Studies, no. 93 (Cambridge, Mass.: Harvard University Press, 1976), pp. 103-166.

61. Gwendolin B. Cobb, "Supply and Transportation for the Potosí Mines, 1545-1640," *HAHR* 29 (1949):25-45; Raimondi, *Perú*, pp. 2:141-142; Roberto Levillier, ed., *Gobernantes del Perú: Cartas y papeles. Siglo XVI. Documentos del Archivo de Indias*, 14 vols., Colección de Publicaciones Históricas de la Biblioteca del Congreso Argentino (Madrid: Sucesores de Rivadeneyra and Imprenta de Juan Pueyo, 1921-1926), pp. 3:542-619; Cieza, "Crónica," pp. 46-56; *BDA*, 1:364-365; and AMuA, LAS, libro 2 (6 January 1549).

62. Cornejo de Balbuena, "Comercio," pp. 5-15.

63. ADA, Registro de almoneda de los tributos de yndios vacos que pertenecen a S.M. 1555+; ADA, Hernández, 3 June 1549, 1 July 1549, 2 July 1549, 3 July 1549, 13 July 1549, 12 April 1550, 26 April 1550, 3 June 1550, 30 September 1550, 23 October 1550, 24 October 1550, 10 June 1553, 3 July 1553, 10 July 1553, 17 July 1553, Valdecabras, 9 November 1551; and BNP, ms. A510 (1557).

64. *BDA*, 3:314; AMuA, LAS, libro 2 (15 January 1546, 13 September 1546, 11 December 1546, 5 October 1549) detail use of Indians to transport goods. For efforts made by city officials to regulate trade, see AMuA, LAS, libro 2 (1546 passim, 16 January 1555, 18 February 1556). There were efforts made to maintain Inca trade routes by preserving inns, but most products came to the city by sea: see, for example, AMuA, LAS, libro 2 (22 June 1549, 14 March 1550, 1 August 1550, 4 August 1550, 3 April 1552, 3 October 1552). On interior trade routes, see AMuA, LAS, libro 2 (26 January 1551). Figure N.1 is a profile of prices paid for goods that some Indians delivered as tribute.

65. *BDA*, 1:42-43, 2:203-207, 3:37-40, 220, 305, 366-369; ADA, Muñoz, 9 November 1557; ANP, Derecho Indígena y Encomiendas, leg. 1, cuad. 10 (1568); *SMF*, p. 234.

66. *BDA*, 2:203-207. For similar lists, see ANP, Derecho Indígena y Encomiendas, leg. 2, cuad. 15 (1572).

67. AMuA, LAS, libro 2 (13 February 1551, 20 March 1551, 22 May 1551, 21 January 1555, 2 September 1555, 13 September 1555, 13 December 1555).

68. Woodrow Borah, *New Spain's Century of Depression*, Ibero-Americana Series, no. 35 (Berkeley & Los Angeles: University of California Press, 1951); Keith, *Conquest*, esp. conclusion.

69. ANP, Compañía, Títulos, leg. 1 (1539-1605); Títulos, leg. 1, cuad. 14 (1583).

70. On preconquest and postconquest Indian population, see Henry F. Dobyns, "An Outline of Andean Epidemic History to 1720," *Bulletin of the History of Medicine* 37 (November-December 1963):493-515; C. T. Smith, "Depopulation of the Central Andes in the 16th Century," *Current Anthropology* 11 (October-December 1970):453-464; José T. Polo, "Apuntes sobre las epidemias en el Perú," *Revista Histórica* 5 (1913):50-109. Several estimates on Indian population are available in Steward, *Handbook*, pp. 2:6-8, 184-185, 334-340; Angel Rosenblat, *La población indígena y el mestizaje en América*, 2 vols. (Buenos Aires: Nova, 1954); Nicolás Sánchez-Albornoz, *The Population of Latin America: A History*, trans. W. A. R. Richardson (Berkeley & Los Angeles: University of California Press, 1974); and especially, Noble David Cook, "The Indian Population of Peru, 1570-1620"

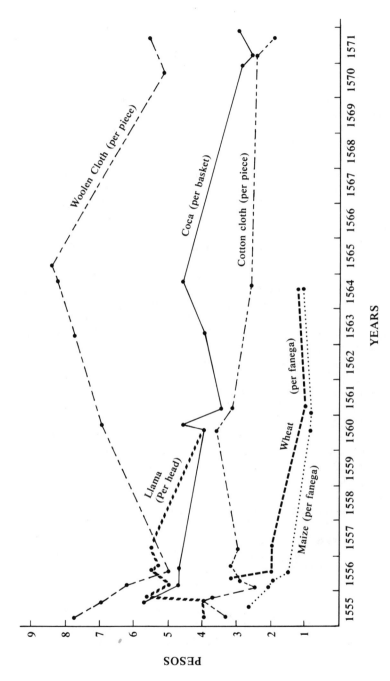

Fig. N.1. Prices of Goods Auctioned by Royal Officials in Arequipa

Sources: *ADA*, Registro de almoneda de los tributos de yndios vacos q'pertenecen a S.M., 1555+

(Ph.D. diss., University of Texas at Austin, 1973). Cook discusses the south coast on pp. 244-247. My estimate is based on comparisons of tributaries in 1540 and the early 1570s. For example, Lucas Martínez Vegaso's Indian tributaries at Tarapacá, Lluta, and Arica totaled 1,340 in 1540; in the 1570s, 957 (*BDA*, 3:85; AGI, Contaduría, leg. 1786).

71. AMA, leg. 6 (30 January 1597); ADA, Hernández, 17 January 1570; ADA, Acuerdos del Cabildo, October 1559; *BDA*, 1:392-400.

72. ANP, Títulos, leg. 25, cuad. 662 (1612); ADA, Hernández, 26 February 1570, 3 April 1570, 9 April 1570, 28 July 1570, Aguilar, 17 October 1573, Herrera, 5 August 1575; AMA, leg. 6 (7 January 1571); BNP, ms. A136 (1570); Juan Domingo de Zamácola y Jáuregui, *Historia de la fundación del nuevo pueblo de San Fernando de Socabaya*, prologue and notes Víctor M. Barriga, 2d ed. (Arequipa: n.p., 1954), pp. 8-9; Guillermo Lohmann Villena, *Juan de Matienzo, autor del "Gobierno del Perú" (su personalidad y su obra)* (Seville: Escuela de Estudios Hispano-Americanos, 1966).

73. ADA, Hernández, 17 January 1570, 9 April 1570, Juan de Vera, 29 October 1571.

74. For land sales, see ADA, Aguilar, 5 January 1575, Herrera, 5 January 1575; ANP, Compañía, Títulos, leg. 1 (1539-1605). Indian work to fulfill obligations is noted in ANP, Juicios de Residencia, leg. 1, cuad. 2 (1580).

75. For the condition of Indians and some *curacas'* opinions, see AGI, Contaduría, leg. 1785; Belaúnde Guinassi, *Encomienda*, pp. 120, 209, 213; Felipe Guaman Poma de Ayala, *Nueva corónica y buen gobierno*, Travaux et mémoires de l'Institut d'Ethnologie, Université de Paris, vol. 23 (Paris: Institut d'Ethnologie, 1936), p. 524; *BDA*, 3:290-298.

76. ADA, Hernández, 19 June 1556, 19 October 1557, 1 February 1570, 21 February 1570, 2 May 1570, 15 July 1570; and AMuA, LAS, libro 2 (17 October 1552, 26 March 1555).

77. AGI, Contaduría, leg. 1786; ADA, Muñoz, 10 September 1561, 16 September 1561, 18 September 1561, 10 March 1562; Belaúnde Guinassi, *Encomienda*, pp. 132-172; Eduardo L. Ugarte y Ugarte, "Los caciques de Arequipa contra la perpetuidad de la encomienda," *Hombre y Mundo*, Segunda Epoca, 1 (1966):41-50.

78. ADA, Hernández, 10 May 1570; AGI, Contaduría, leg. 1786; AGI, Justicia, leg. 499B.

79. Belaúnde Guinassi, *Encomienda*, pp. 174-181. Also see table N.1.

80. *BDA*, 2:203-207; ADA, Gaspar Hernández, 29 December 1570. Similarly, see ADA, Registro de almoneda de los tributos de yndios vacos que pertenecen a S.M., 1555+; ANP, Juicios de Residencia, leg. 5, cuad. 9 (1584).

81. See chap. 2.

82. *La función económica del encomendero en los orígenes del régimen colonial. (Nueva España. 1525-1531)*, 2d ed., Instituto de Investigaciones Históricas de la Universidad Autónoma de México, Historical Series, no. 12 (Mexico City: Imprenta Universitaria, 1965).

83. For example, see Keith, *Conquest*, chap. 2; idem, "Encomienda, Hacienda and Corregimiento in Spanish America: A Structural Analysis," *HAHR* 51 (August 1971):431-446.

84. Mario Góngora, *Encomenderos y estancieros: Estudios acerca de la constitución social aristocrática de Chile después de la conquista, 1580-1660* (Santiago de Chile: Editorial Universitaria, 1970); also, Borah, *Depression*; and Keith, *Conquest*.

Chapter 2. *Chácaras* and *Estancias* in Early Arequipa

1. Jorge Polar, *Arequipa: Descripción y estudio social*, 3d ed. (Lima: Lumen, 1958), pp. 12-43; Ventura Travada y Córdova, *El suelo de Arequipa convertido en cielo*, (Lima: Lumen, 1958), pp. 74-82; Antonio Vázquez de Espinosa, *Compendio y descripción de las Indias Occidentales*, Biblioteca de Autores Españoles, no. 231 (Madrid: Atlas, 1969), pp. 337-338; George R. Johnson, *Peru from the Air*, with text and notes by Raye R. Platt, American Geographical Society Special Publication, no. 12 (Worcester, Mass.: Commonwealth, 1930), pp. 17-31, 119-142; Army Map Service, Corps of Engineers, *Maps of Arequipa and Characato, Departamento de Arequipa, Peru* (Washington, D.C.: 1962); and personal observation.

2. I compared figures on tributaries noted in Francisco Pizarro's 1540 *encomienda* grant to Diego Hernández (*BDA*, 1:46-48) to those from the 1570s (AGI, Contaduría, leg. 1786). I assumed their 25 percent decline to be typical for other groups in the valley, and so I raised the total from the 1570s accordingly. I multiplied the latter by 4 (see note 8, chap. 1).

3. Sources cited in note 1; and, *BDA*, 1:40, 366-369, 2:84-85; Polar, *Arequipa*, p. 56.

4. Polar, *Arequipa*, pp. 17-19.

5. *BDA*, 1:66-67, 113-115, 119-120, 135-137, 3:246.

6. *SMF*, pp. 95-101, 251-252, 266, 326-327; *BDA*, 1:31, 265, 3:79, 346; ADA, Hernández, 13 July 1549, 5 October 1550.

7. *BDA*, 1:110-111, 3:245-250. The word "*chácara*" comes from the Quechua "*chacra*," or small farm. I use the former here because notaries preferred it. Not all people would agree with this decision: see Germán Leguía y Martínez, *Historia de Arequipa*, 2 vols. (Lima: Moderna, 1912; and El Lucero, 1914), p. 2:183, note 2.

8. ADA, Aguilar, 1 April 1548, Herrera, 2 November 1575, 22 November 1575, 24 December 1575, Muñoz, 19 April 1600, 23 December 1610, 19 January 1611, Juan de Vera, 27 June 1571; Eduardo L. Ugarte y Ugarte, ed., "Información de servicios del conquistador Pedro Pizarro" (unpublished transcription, Lima, 1951); and *BDA*, 3:245-250.

9. ADA, Hernández, April 1568, 24 May 1568, 4 June 1568, January 1569, 12 February 1570, 25 February 1570, Herrera, 14 October 1575, 29 October 1575, Juan de Vera, 29 December 1575; and Manuel Belaúnde Guinassi, *La encomienda en el Perú* (Lima: Mercurio Peruano, 1945), pp. 120-122, 130-131.

10. John V. Murra, "Current Research and Prospects in Andean Ethnohistory,"

LARR 5 (Spring 1970):15-16; idem, "New Data on Retainer and Servile Populations in Tawantinsuyu," *Actas y memorias del XXXVI Congreso Internacional de Americanistas*, 4 vols. (Seville: Editorial Católica Española, 1966), pp. 2:35-45; BNP, ms. A171 (1555), ms. A438 (1569), ms A595 (1559), ms. Z1264 (1562), ms. A136 (1570); and ADA, Hernández, 19 June 1556.

11. *BDA*, 1:119-120, 135-137; ADA, Hernández, 5 October 1550, 12 September 1551, 29 December 1551, 14 October 1552; BNP, ms. A510 (1557), ms. A595 (1559); AMuA, LAS, libro 2 (5 June 1546, 9 June 1546). Later descriptions of *chácaras* are more detailed: ADA, Aguilar, 16 August 1604, Muñoz, 3 November 1622, Laguna, 12 May 1648, 10 July 1648, Antonio de Silva, 18 December 1656, Diego de Silva, 22 February 1644, 29 May 1644, 31 May 1653, 9 July 1653, 22 September 1653, Tejada, 16 March 1615, Ufelde, 9 April 1616.

12. ADA, Hernández, 12 September 1551, 21 February 1553; BNP, ms. A512 (1557), ms. A595 (1559), ms. Z1264 (1562); *BDA* 1:159; AGI, Lima, leg. 309; and Vázquez de Espinosa, *Compendio*, pp. 337-339.

13. *BDA*, 1:119-126, 129-130, 133-137; ADA, Hernández, 30 July 1550. For contrasting patterns, see William H. Dusenberry, *The Mexican Mesta: The Administration of Ranching in Colonial Mexico* (Urbana: University of Illinois Press, 1963); François Chevalier, *Land and Society in Colonial Mexico: The Great Hacienda*, trans. Alvin Eustis, ed. Lesley Byrd Simpson (Berkeley & Los Angeles: University of California Press, 1966), pp. 84-114; and Mario Góngora, *Encomenderos y estancieros: Estudios acerca de la constitución social aristocrática de Chile después de la conquista, 1580-1660* (Santiago de Chile: Editorial Universitaria, 1970), pp. 4-8.

14. Eduardo L. Ugarte y Ugarte, ed., "Compilación de las ordenanzas de Arequipa, 1540-1575" (unpublished, Arequipa, n.d.), pp. 19-20; *BDA*, 1:110-111, 2:108-109; Leguía y Martínez, *Historia*, p. 2:190; Manuel de Mendiburu, *Diccionario histórico-biográfico del Perú*, 11 vols. (Lima: Enrique Palacios and Gil, 1931-1934), p. 1:176; Garcilaso de la Vega, El Inca, *Royal Commentaries of the Incas and General History of Peru*, trans. with intro. by Harold V. Livermore, 2 vols. (Austin: University of Texas Press, 1966), pp. 1:581-582.

15. AMuA, LAS, libro 2 (esp. 21 March 1546, 26 December 1546).

16. Guillermo Lohmann Villena, "Apuntaciones sobre el curso de los precios de los artículos de primera necesidad en Lima durante el siglo XVI," *Revista Histórica* 29 (1966):79-104.

17. ADA, Hernández, May 1549, 23 December 1549, 12 April 1550, 26 April 1550, 21 January 1551, 10 June 1551, 18 September 1551, 23 September 1551, 26 September 1551, 17 August 1552, 15 October 1552, 2 February 1560, Muñoz, 11 November 1557; BNP, ms. A512 (1557), ms. A485 (1575).

18. ADA, Hernández, 26 April 1550, 27 September 1552, 9 February 1560, Muñoz, 7 August 1561, Herrera, 16 November 1575.

19. Ugarte y Ugarte, "Compilación," pp. 19-22, 28-35; AMuA, LAS, libro 2 (5 January 1551, 25 September 1551, 27 May 1552).

20. AMuA, LAS, libro 2 (16 January 1555); Ugarte y Ugarte, "Compilación," p. 52.

21. *BDA*, 1:119-120, 2:130-132.

22. ADA, Hernández, 2 July 1549, 7 August 1549, 19 August 1550, 27 August 1550, 20 September 1550, 5 October 1550.

23. ADA, Hernández, 7 August 1549, 30 July 1550, 29 April 1552; AMuA, LAS, libro 2 (1 August 1550, 11 November 1550, 15 December 1550, 19 January 1551, 20 February 1551, 16 November 1551, 30 September 1552, 7 July 1553); BNP, ms. A171 (1555); *BDA*, 1:236-237.

24. ADA, Hernández, 30 January 1553, 31 July 1553. For continued use of coastal hills and valleys by ranchers, see ADA, Muñoz, 20 May 1595; AMA, leg. 1 (24 April 1548), leg. 6 (9 May 1589); Martín de Morúa, *Historia de los Incas: Reyes del Perú*, Colección de Libros y Documentos referentes a la Historia del Perú, Series 2, vol. 5 (Lima: Sanmartí, 1925), pp. 38-39; Vázquez de Espinosa, *Compendio*, pp. 334-335; ANP, Compañía, Títulos, leg. 3 (1628-1652), Títulos, leg. 5, cuad 150 (1662).

25. *BDA*, 1:46 reports that in 1540 the Indians of the valley *curaca* Caya totaled 359 and those of *curaca* Ate in the province of Puquina, 234. When visited in 1549 there were 319 and circa 200 under these officials (ANP, Derecho Indígena y Encomiendas, leg. 1, cuad. 10 [1568]). I estimated the drop from 1549 to the 1570s by comparing figures I found for the same *encomienda* in AGI, Contaduría, leg. 1786; and ANP, Compañía, Títulos, leg. 1 (1539-1605).

26. *BDA*, 1:264, 3:245-250.

27. Ugarte y Ugarte, "Información de Pedro Pizarro"; BNP, ms. A171 (1555). The office of Protector of Indians was established in Arequipa in 1539 (*BDA*, 1:23-24).

28. Ugarte y Ugarte, "Compilación," pp. 20-21; ANP, Compañía, Títulos, leg. 1 (1539-1605); Echeverría y Morales, "Memoria," p. 14.

29. From 1549 to 1554 two notaries recorded the sale of only eleven *chácaras* (several involved the same property, which indicates speculation).

30. AMuA, LAS, libro 2 (14 August 1550, 27 October 1551); *BDA*, 1:405-406.

31. Ugarte y Ugarte, "Compilación," pp. 16-17, 20-21; AMuA, LAS, libro 2 (14 August 1550).

32. *BDA*, 1:405-406, 2:264-265; ANP, Títulos, leg. 1, cuad. 4 (1557); AMuA, LAS, libro 2 (27 September 1550), libro 3 (17 April 1556).

33. ADA, Muñoz, February 1557, 3 July 1557, 9 July 1557, 7 October 1557, 8 October 1557, 19 October 1557, 25 October 1557, 26 October 1557, 8 November 1557, 27 November 1557, 29 November 1557, Hernández, 19 August 1550, 14 October 1552, 31 January 1558, 24 May 1560, Juan de Vera, February 1571; *BDA*, 2:145.

34. ANP, Compañía, Títulos, leg. 3 (1628-1652), Títulos, leg. 1, cuad. 4 (1557); *BDA*, 1:157, 2:302-313, 3:352; *SMF*, pp. 77-87; *SMA*, pp. 6-7, 9-11, 14-15.

35. ADA, Muñoz, 7 October 1557, 8 October 1557, 25 October 1557, 27 November 1557.

36. ADA, Muñoz, 30 July 1557, 19 October 1557, 27 November 1557, 29 November 1557.

37. ADA, Hernández, 31 January 1558, 24 January 1560.

38. The people I call "venturers" were much like the previously mentioned "men of affairs"; however, they tended to restrict their economic interests to land. Venturers also appear to have been more willing than men of affairs to take risks. Specific cases illustrating the type are discussed later.

39. ADA, Hernández, 30 July 1550, Valdecabras, 8 November 1552.

40. ADA, Hernández, 27 April 1549, 26 April 1550, 11 January 1551, 22 October 1551, 21 January 1552, 22 January 1552, 20 September 1552, 27 September 1552, Valdecabras, 8 August 1551; BNP, ms. A512 (1557).

41. ADA, Hernández, 8 August 1552, Muñoz, 11 November 1557.

42. ADA, Hernández, 28 April 1552, August 1552, 21 May 1556, Muñoz, 11 November 1557; Ugarte y Ugarte, "Compilación," and idem, ed., "Ordenanzas reales hechas para Arequipa y sus provincias por el señor dn. Francisco de Toledo en 2 de noviembre de 1575" (unpublished, Arequipa, n.d.), Título 14; BNP, ms. A136 (1570).

43. *BDA*, 1:397-398.

44. ADA, Hernández, 9 August 1549, 24 September 1550, 11 March 1552, 14 August 1552, 7 June 1553, 16 November 1553; BNP, ms. A512 (1557); Frederick P. Bowser, *The African Slave in Colonial Peru 1524-1650* (Stanford, Cal.: Stanford University Press, 1974), and idem, "The African in Colonial Spanish America: Reflections on Research Achievements and Priorities," *LARR* 7 (Spring 1972):77-94.

45. ADA, Hernández, 2 July 1549, Valdecabras, 12 September 1551; *BDA*, 1:119; AMA, leg. 6 (7 January 1571).

46. ADA, Hernández, 19 August 1550, 26 August 1550, 5 October 1550, 16 July 1551, 14 October 1552, Valdecabras, 12 September 1551.

47. ANP, Títulos, leg. 1, cuad. 14 (1583); AMA, leg. 6 (9 May 1589).

48. ANP, Juicios de Residencia, leg. 5, cuad. 9 (1584), Títulos, leg. 1, cuad. 14 (1583), Real Audiencia, Procedimientos Civiles, leg. 32 (1593); BNP, ms. A485 (1575); ADA, Hernández, 3 May 1570; *BDA*, 1:398-400; "Relación de la provincia de los Collaguas para la discrepción de las Indias que su magestad manda hacer," in *Relaciones geográficas de Indias-Perú*, ed. Marcos Jiménez de la Espada, 3 vols., Biblioteca de Autores Españoles, nos. 183-185 (Madrid: Atlas, 1965), p. 1:332.

49. *BDA*, 1:119-120, 3:245-250, AMuA, LAS, libro 2 (7 November 1550, 17 November 1550).

50. ADA, Hernández, 2 July 1549, 14 October 1552, 15 June 1553, October 1558; BNP, ms. A136 (1570).

51. AMA, leg. 6 (7 January 1571); BNP, ms. A485 (1575).

52. ANP, Compañía, Títulos, leg. 1 (1539-1605); ADA, Muñoz, June 1561, Herrera, 5 January 1575.

53. ADA, Muñoz, 31 July 1557.

54. Only four properties were resold by *encomenderos*, according to the records of

four notaries between 1549 and 1558 (ADA, Hernández, 2 July 1549, 26 August 1550, 14 October 1552, Valdecabras, 27 September 1552).

55. ADA, Hernández, 1 July 1549, 7 August 1549, 19 August 1550, 26 August 1550, 27 August 1550, 5 October 1550, 12 September 1551, Valdecabras, 8 November 1552.

56. AMA, leg. 4 (12 November 1555); ADA, Hernández, 19 August 1550, 16 July 1551, 15 June 1553, Valdecabras, 14 October 1552, 8 November 1552, Torres, 21 February 1556; BNP, ms. A512 (1557), ms. A136 (1570).

57. BNP, ms. A510 (1557); ADA, Hernández, 7 August 1549; James Lockhart, *Spanish Peru, 1532-1560: A Colonial Society* (Madison: University of Wisconsin Press, 1968), pp. 80-81; Carmen Cornejo de Balbuena, "El comercio en Arequipa, 1549-1560" (unpublished, Arequipa, 1976), pp. 11-12.

58. For example, see Juan de Quirós and Antón de Castro in ADA, Hernández, 1 July 1549, 3 July 1549, 26 April 1550, 19 August 1550, 16 July 1551, 23 September 1551, 10 August 1552, 30 January 1553, 13 February 1553, Valdecabras, 8 November 1552, Torres, 20 February 1556, 21 February 1556.

59. I discuss marriage patterns of Arequipans in chapter 4. On Diego Bravo, see AMuA, LAS, libro 2 (16 November 1551); ADA, Hernández, 21 August 1549, 30 July 1550, 26 August 1550, 16 July 1551, 15 October 1552, 15 June 1553, 30 April 1556, Valdecabras, 14 October 1552; BNP, ms. A595 (1559), ms. A285 (1569).

60. For example, Francisco Madueño and Antón de Castro owned various *chácaras* and livestock (ADA, Hernández, 19 August 1550, 4 May 1556, 15 June 1556, 24 May 1560, Valdecabras, 12 September 1551, 18 September 1551, 8 November 1552; BNP, ms. A510 [1557]).

61. Ida Altman and James Lockhart, eds., *Provinces of Early Mexico: Variants of Spanish American Regional Evolution* (Los Angeles: UCLA Latin American Center, 1976), Lockhart's introduction, esp. pp. 5-10.

62. Wayne S. Osborn, "Indian Land Retention in Colonial Metztitlán," *HAHR* 53 (May 1973):217-238; William B. Taylor, *Landlord and Peasant in Colonial Oaxaca* (Stanford, Cal.: Stanford University Press, 1972), esp. pp. 35-110.

63. Richard M. Morse, "A Prolegomenon to Latin American History," *HAHR* 52 (August 1972):359-394.

Chapter 3. Wine Estates and Landowners

1. Antonio Vázquez de Espinosa, *Compendio y descripción de las Indias Occidentales*, Biblioteca de Autores Españoles, no. 231 (Madrid: Atlas, 1969), p. 345.

2. Ibid., pp. 335-350; Reginaldo de Lizárraga, *Descripción breve de toda la tierra del Perú, Tucumán, Río de la Plata y Chile*, Biblioteca de Autores Españoles, no. 216 (Madrid: Atlas, 1968), pp. 47-50; Luis Urzúa Urzúa, *Arica, puerta nueva: Historia y folklore*, 2d ed. (Santiago de Chile: Editorial Andrés Bello, 1964), pp. 70-76; AGI, Lima, leg. 116.

3. AGI, Lima, leg. 111, Patronato, leg. 191, doc. 23; BNP, ms. B415 (1603); Vázquez de Espinosa, *Compendio*, pp. 336-337.

4. Guillermo Lohmann Villena, "Apuntaciones sobre el curso de los precios de los artículos de primera necesidad en Lima durante el siglo XVI," *Revista Histórica* 29 (1966):79-104.

5. Pedro Cieza de León, "La crónica del Perú," in *Crónicas de la conquista del Perú*, ed. Julio Le Riverend Brusone, pp. 465-467 (Mexico City: Nueva España, n.d.).

6. ADA, Hernández, 3 June 1549, 4 June 1549, 20 February 1550, 30 September 1550, 23 October 1550, 24 October 1550, 18 July 1551, 9 January 1552, 19 January 1552, 4 February 1552, 7 August 1552, 10 June 1553, 3 July 1553, 10 July 1553, 17 July 1553, 29 April 1556, Muñoz, 20 February 1557, 6 March 1557, 18 July 1557, 4 January 1561, 8 January 1561, 5 September 1561; BNP, ms. A285 (1569); Lohmann Villena, "Apuntaciones," pp. 79-104.

7. ADA, Hernández, 19 January 1551, 16 January 1552.

8. *BDA*, 1:163.

9. ANP, Compañía, Títulos, leg. 1 (1539-1605); ADA, Hernández, 21 February 1553, 15 July 1570; Edward Hyams, *Dionysus: A Social History of the Wine Vine* (New York: Macmillan Co., 1965), p. 294; Manuel de Mendiburu, *Diccionario histórico-biográfico del Perú*, 11 vols. (Lima: Enrique Palacios and Gil, 1931-1934), pp. 4:294-295; Bernabé Cobo, *Obras*, 2 vols., Biblioteca de Autores Españoles, nos. 91-92 (Madrid: Atlas, 1956), pp. 1:391-392.

10. ANP, Juicios de Residencia, leg. 9, cuad. 22 (1591), Títulos, leg. 1, cuad. 10 (1568); AGI, Lima, leg. 309; ADA, Aguilar, 7 March 1584; Rómulo Cúneo-Vidal, "El cacicazgo de Tacna," *Revista Histórica* 6 (1919):315-316.

11. AGI, Lima, leg. 111, Patronato, leg. 191, doc. 23; BNP, ms. B478 (1633); Eduardo L. Ugarte y Ugarte, ed., "Memoria y cuentas de Da. Juana Muñiz, vecina de Arequipa, sobre sus nietos hijos de Miguel Cornejo, 1570-1571" (unpublished, Arequipa, n.d.).

12. Vázquez de Espinosa, *Compendio*, pp. 336-337; ADA, Juan de Vera, 1 August 1571, Herrera, 16 November 1575.

13. AMA, leg. 1 (24 April 1584).

14. ADA, Hernández, 24 May 1570; ANP, Derecho Indígena y Encomiendas, leg. 1, cuad. 10 (1568).

15. ADA, Hernández, 17 January 1570, Aguilar, 5 February 1573, Herrera, 10 November 1575, 10 February 1576; ANP, Juicios de Residencia, leg. 1, cuad. 2 (1580), leg. 33, cuad. 93 (1646); AGI, Contaduría, leg. 1775, leg. 1786, Lima, leg. 32, leg. 199, leg. 274.

16. AMuA, LAS, libro 3 (2 October 1562), libro 4 (25 June 1573, February 1575); ADA, Aguilar, 2 May 1596; AMA, leg. 3 (10 June 1665); ANP, Títulos, leg. 1, cuad. 14 (1583); AGI, Lima, leg. 28B.

17. ADA, Herrera, 5 January 1575; ANP, Juicios de Residencia, leg. 1, cuad. 2 (1580); Alejandro Málaga Medina, "Las reducciones en el Perú (1532-1600)," *Historia y Cultura* 8 (1974):141-172; idem, "Las reducciones en Arequipa" (unpublished, Arequipa, 1971); AGI, Lima, leg. 572; ANP, Derecho Indígena y Encomiendas, leg. 23, cuad. 625 (1606); BNP, ms. B1832 (1624); Karen W.

Spalding, "Indian Rural Society in Colonial Peru: The Example of Huarochirí" (Ph.D. diss., University of California at Berkeley, 1967), pp. 79-89.

18. ADA, Ufelde, 15 October 1595; AMA, leg. 5 (26 January 1589); ANP, Titulos, leg. 1, cuad. 14 (1583), Juicios de Residencia, leg. 1, cuad. 2 (1580), Tribunal de Cuentas, Real Hacienda, Composiciones, Tierras y Indígenas, leg. 5, cuad. 2 (1643).

19. ADA, Herrera, 16 November 1575; AMA, leg. 6 (25 September 1599).

20. Franklin Pease G. Y., ed., *Collaguas I* (Lima: P. L. Villanueva for Pontificia Universidad Católica del Perú, 1977), pp. 191-452; ANP, Juicios de Residencia, leg. 5, cuad. 9 (1584); AGI, Indiferente General, leg. 1660.

21. See table N.1.

22. Although some historians believed that an *encomienda* grant conferred land rights, this point had been laid to rest by legal specialists (Silvio Zavala, *De encomiendas y propiedad territorial en algunas regiones de la América española* [Mexico City: Antigua Librería Robredo de José Porrúa e Hijos, 1940]). James Lockhart, "Encomienda and Hacienda: The Evolution of the Great Estate in the Spanish Indies," *HAHR* 49 (August 1969):411-429, has argued that the practices of *encomenderos* and landowners were remarkably similar. Evidence from Arequipa, as the later discussion attests, supports his observation. The Cornejo *encomienda* was in the Vítor Valley; Gómez de León and his son had a grant that encompassed the Indians in the Majes and Siguas valleys; Diego de Cáceres's included natives in the Tambo Valley (AGI, Contaduría, leg. 1786; on their acquisition of land, ADA, Aguilar, 11 March 1575, 18 January 1603, Hernández, 5 June 1560, Herrera, 11 August 1575; AMA, leg. 1 [17 September 1624, 6 March 1625]; Ugarte y Ugarte, "Memoria y cuentas").

23. Rafael Loredo, *Los repartos* (Lima: D. Miranda, 1958), pp. 195, 201; AGI, Contaduría, leg. 1786.

24. James Lockhart, *The Men of Cajamarca: A Social and Biographical Study of the first Conquerors of Peru*, Latin American Monographs, no. 27 (Austin: University of Texas Press for the Institute of Latin American Studies, 1972), pp. 318-320.

25. Ugarte y Ugarte, "Memoria y cuentas"; AGI, Contaduría, leg. 1786. In ANP, Derecho Indígena y Encomiendas, leg. 1, cuad. 10 (1568), the estimated value of each tributary's annual worth during the 1560s is given at 15 pesos.

26. *SMF*, pp. 172-175; ADA, Hernández, 7 August 1549, 30 July 1550, 26 August 1550, Valdecabras, 8 November 1552, Muñoz, 30 May 1561, 17 April 1562, Registro de almoneda de los tributos de yndios vacos que pertenecen a S. M. 1555+; *BDA*, 1:201.

27. Alejandro Málaga Medina, *Visita general del Perú por el Virrey D. Francisco de Toledo, 1570-1575* (Arequipa: El Sol, 1974), pp. 19-49; idem, "Consideraciones económicas sobre la visita de la provincia de Arequipa," in *Tasa de la visita general de Francisco de Toledo*, ed. Noble David Cook, pp. 299, 304-311 (Lima: Imprenta de la Universidad Nacional de San Marcos, 1975); AGI, Contaduría, leg. 1785, leg. 1786; ADA, Aguilar, 17 October 1573.

Table N.1
Rural Property Ownership, 1570

Encomendero	Owner of *Estancia* or *Chácara*	Owner of *Heredad*
Hernando Alvarez de Carmona	Yes	Possibly
Francisco Boso	Yes	Possibly
Hernán Bueno	Yes	Yes
Diego de Cáceres	Yes	Yes (2)
Don Fernando de Cárdenas	No	Yes
Juan de Castro	Yes	Yes
Hernando de Castro Figueroa	Yes	No
Luis Cornejo	Yes	Yes
Doña María Dávalos	Yes	No
Juan Dávila	Yes	Yes
García de Castro	No data	Yes
Antonio Gómez de Butrón	Yes	Yes
Francisco de Grado	Yes	No
Diego Hernández de la Cuba	Yes	Yes
Francisco Hernández Retamoso	Yes	Yes
Francisco Hernández Tarifeño	No data	No data
Don Francisco de Hinojosa	No	No
Fabián de León	No	No
Alonso de Luque	Yes	Possibly
Antonio de Llanos	Yes	No
Diego Marín	Yes	No data
María de Mendoza	Possibly	Yes
Gerónimo Pacheco	Yes	Yes
Alonso Picado	Yes	Yes
Pedro Pizarro	Yes	Yes
Diego de Porres	Yes	Yes
Juan Ramírez	Yes	Yes
Francisco Retamoso	Yes	Possibly
Hernando de la Torre	Yes	Yes
Doña Isabel Vaca	No data	No data

Sources: AGI, Contaduría, leg. 1786; ADA, Aguilar, 8 July 1575, 29 August 1583, 9 March 1584, 10 March 1584, 1 April 1584, 5 May 1584, 30 July 1591, 19 September 1591, 8 January 1596, 26 April 1596, 30 November 1596, 12 January 1598, 1 September 1603, 23 January 1604, Hernández, 7 August 1549, October 1558, 5 June 1560, 6 February 1570, 16 August 1570, Herrera, 11 August 1575, Diego Ortiz, 8 January 1584, 12 January 1594, 27

April 1594, 18 May 1594, 20 June 1594, 28 July 1595, Muñoz, 1 February 1557, 24 May 1557, 27 November 1557, 28 February 1560, 12 March 1560, 5 November 1561, 16 February 1600, Francisco de Vera, 18 January 1622, Juan de Vera, February 1571, 20 June 1571, Ufelde, 25 October 1595; AMA, leg. 1 (16 August 1578, 17 September 1624), leg. 2 (18 February 1581), leg. 3 (28 January 1568), leg. 5 (3 February 1589), leg. 6 (28 August 1566); ANP, Compañia, Titulos, leg. 1, cuad. 4 (1557), leg. 3, cuad. 72 (1601), Archivo de Temporalidades, Expedientes sobre Titulos de Propiedad, Hacienda Matarani y Lluta; BNP, ms. A171 (1555), ms. A595 (1559), ms. B1528 (1619); *BDA*, 2:245; Vázquez de Espinosa, *Compendio*, p. 346; Francisco Mostajo, "Aportes para la historia de Arequipa," in *Historiadores y prosistas*, ed. Vladimiro Bermejo, pp. 59-60 (Lima: Lumen, 1958); Francisco Xavier Echeverría y Morales, "Memoria de la Santa Iglesia de Arequipa," in *BMHA*, 4:11-12.

28. AGI, Contaduría, leg. 1786. The tribute of the Arones of Gerónimo Pacheco was set at 1,488 pesos of gold (quintado y marcado of 21.5 quilates), 496 pesos of silver (ensayada y marcada), 80 llamas (at 2.5 pesos each), 60 pieces of woolen clothing (at 2 pesos each), 176 chickens (at a tomin each).

29. The difference between previous allotments and those of Viceroy Toledo can be seen by comparing the 1549 tribute list of the Indians at Hilavaya (chap. 1) with the following: 295 tributaries, after the early 1570s, were to pay 1,327 pesos and 4 tomines of silver (ensayada y marcada), 80 pieces of cotton clothing (at 2 pesos each), 8 fanegas of wheat (at 6 tomines each), 20 baskets of chilies (at 6 tomines each), 120 chickens (at a tomin each). Each tributary thus paid 5.5 pesos yearly (AGI, Contaduría, leg. 1786).

30. Henry F. Dobyns, "An Outline of Andean Epidemic History to 1720," *Bulletin of the History of Medicine* 37 (November-December 1963):501-508; José T. Polo, "Apuntes sobre las epidemias en el Perú," *Revista Histórica* 5 (1913):62-68; Noble David Cook, "The Indian Population of Peru, 1570-1620" (Ph.D. diss., University of Texas at Austin, 1973), pp. 296-297; ANP, Compañia, Titulos, leg. 1 (1539-1605), Titulos, leg. 1, cuad. 14 (1583), Juicios de Residencia, leg. 1, cuad. 2 (1580).

31. AGI, Contaduría, leg. 1786, leg. 1822. The effect of disease on tributes is noted in AGI, Lima, leg. 32, leg. 199, leg. 274.

32. ADA, Ufelde, 2 June 1610, Tejada, 6 March 1616, 1 April 1616, 9 May 1616, Francisco de Vera, 13 March 1622.

33. ANP, Juicios de Residencia, leg. 4, cuad. 8 (1583-1598), leg. 5, cuad. 9 (1584), leg. 9, cuad. 22 (1591), leg. 10, cuad. 25 (1593), leg. 33, cuad. 93 (1646); AGI, Contaduría, leg. 1786; ADA, Hernández, 17 January 1570.

34. ANP, Derecho Indígena y Encomiendas, leg. 2, cuad. 15 (1572); ADA, Juan de Vera, 20 October 1571, Herrera, 5 August 1575, 2 November 1575, 9 December 1575, 24 December 1575, 5 January 1576, 8 January 1576, Aguilar, 5 January 1575, 8 July 1575, 30 March 1584, 1 April 1584, 29 August 1584.

35. Cook, "The Indian Population," pp. 249-250, estimates the annual rate of decline in this region between the 1570s and 1600 at approximately −1.2 percent.

Also see table N.2. ANP, Juicios de Residencia, leg. 9, cuad. 22 (1591), provides an example of changes in tributes as a result of a new list. According to the tribute list of the 1570s, 309 tributaries of the community of Machaguay were required to pay annually as follows: each Indian 4 pesos in silver and gold as well as a chicken; each 2 Indians one piece of woolen clothing; from the community lands 15 fanegas of wheat and 15 of maize. According to that of the 1580s, 202 Indians living at Machaguay paid as follows: each Indian 3 pesos and 5 tomines as well as a chicken; each 2 Indians one piece of woolen clothing; and from communal lands 13.5 fanegas of wheat and the same amount of maize.

Table N.2
Highland Tributary Population

Location of Tributaries	Year and Population Count					
	1570s	1580s	1599	1624	1640s	1656
Viraco	558	423	368	193	89	
						273
Machaguay	309	202	174	—	—	
Pampacolca	819	581	530	—	276	—

Sources: Cook, "The Indian Population," p. 366; ANP, Juicios de Residencia, leg. 9, cuad. 22 (1591); AGI, Contaduría, leg. 1786, leg. 1822, Lima, leg. 199, Indiferente General, leg. 1660.

36. Lizárraga, *Descripción*, p. 58; Cobo, *Obras*, pp. 1:74-76; Boleslao Lewin, ed., *Descripción del virreinato del Perú: Crónica inédita de comienzos del siglo XVII*, Colección de Textos y Documentos, series B, no. 1 (Rosario: Instituto de Investigaciones Históricas, 1958), pp. 84-86; Francisco Xavier Echeverría y Morales, "Memoria de la Santa Iglesia de Arequipa," in *BMHA*, 4:92.

37. ANP, Juicios de Residencia, leg. 33, cuad. 93 (1646); AGI, Lima, leg. 35, leg. 95, leg. 111, leg. 571, leg. 572, Indiferente General, leg. 1660; BNP, ms. A377 (1594).

38. ANP, Juicios de Residencia, leg. 10, cuad. 25 (1593), leg. 21, cuad. 53, cuad. 55 (1610), Derecho Indígena y Encomienda, leg. 6, cuad. 121 (1648); BNP, ms. A54 (1591), ms. B1351 (1600), ms. B1109 (1601); and table N.3 for drop in highland tributes.

39. BNP, ms. A54 (1591); ACA, Información y pesquisa secreta contra el P. Luis Velarde, cura coadjutor de Lluta, 7 September 1644, and Don Juan Condorpussa, cacique principal y gobernador del Pueblo de San Juan Baptista de la Chimba contra P. Fray Ignacio Torrejón, 4 September 1669; AGI, Lima, leg. 95, leg. 571, discuss Indian work in illegal textile shops; ANP, Juicios de Residencia, leg. 21, cuad. 53 (1610).

40. ANP, Juicios de Residencia, leg. 21, cuad. 54 (1610); AGI, Justicia, leg. 1187, leg. 1190.

41. ANP, Juicios de Residencia, leg. 17, cuad. 46 (1600), leg. 23, cuad. 61 (1617).

Table N.3
Tribute Lists for *Hanansaya* Indians, Chuquibamba

1570s (585 tributaries)	1636 (103 tributaries)
1,450 ps. (de plata ensayada y marcada)	231 ps. 6 tom. (ps. ensayados, 12.5 reales
1,160 ps. (de oro, 22.5 quilates)	206 ps. (de oro, 22.5 quilates)
40 llamas (at 2.5 ps. each)	6.75 llamas (at 2.5 ps. each)
40 pieces of woolen clothing (at 2.5 ps. each)	6.75 pieces of woolen clothing (at 2.5 ps. each)
50 fanegas of maize (at 6 tom. each)	8 fanegas, 6 almudes of maize (at 6 tom. each)
30 fanegas of wheat (at 1 ps. each)	6 fanegas, 1 almud of wheat (at 1 ps. each)
180 chickens (at 1 tom. each)	31 chickens (at 1 tom. each)
TOTAL: 3,190 ps. (de plata ensayada y marcada)	TOTAL: 538 ps. 4 tom. 8 gr (ensayados, 12.5 reales)

Sources: ANP, Juicios de Residencia, leg. 33, cuad. 93 (1646); AGI, Contaduría, leg. 1786.

42. See Lucas Martínez Vegaso's grant to Hilavaya and the division of the Carumas (BDA, 2:84-89, 203-207, 211-214, 3:28-30; Loredo, *Repartos*, pp. 194-204).

43. AGI, Contaduría, leg. 1786.

44. AGI, Contaduría, leg. 1786, leg. 1822, Lima, leg. 35, leg. 116, leg. 119, legs. 200-201, leg. 275, leg. 1061, Justicia, leg. 498A; ANP, Juicios de Residencia, leg. 9, cuad. 22 (1591).

45. ANP, Derecho Indígena y Encomiendas, leg. 1, cuad. 10 (1568); *SMF*, p. 424; ADA, Hernández, 17 April 1556, 25 June 1556, Torres, 20 February 1556, 9 February 1560, Juan de Vera, February 1571, Aguilar 20 April 1596, 26 April 1596; ANP, Compañía, Títulos, leg. 3 (1628-1652), Compañía, Censos, leg. 1 (1567-1636); AMA, leg. 1 (24 April 1584).

46. James Lockhart, *Spanish Peru, 1532-1560: A Colonial Society* (Madison: University of Wisconsin Press, 1968), p. 80.

47. *SMF*, p. 124; BNP, ms. A512 (1557), ms. Z1264 (1562), ms. A285 (1569); ADA, Hernández, 1 July 1549, 3 July 1549, 26 April 1550, 16 July 1551, August 1552, 30 January 1553, 10 June 1553, 3 July 1553, 10 July 1553, 12 May 1556, 15 July 1570, Valdecabras, 8 November 1552, Torres, 20 February 1556, 21 February 1556, Juan de Vera, 27 June 1571, Ufelde, October 1595; *BDA* 1:352; ANP, Títulos, leg. 1, cuad. 4 (1557), Compañía, Títulos, leg. 3 (1628-1652).

48. ADA, Aguilar, 10 March 1584, 19 May 1584.

49. ADA, Hernández, 27 January 1570, Aguilar, 17 January 1584, 7 March

1584, 10 March 1584, 20 March 1584, 19 May 1584, 10 June 1584, Muñoz, 13 January 1592, Diego Ortiz, 31 January 1594.

50. BNP, ms. A485 (1575); ANP, Compañia, Titulos, leg. 1 (1539-1605). The *encomendero* Juan de Castro, for example, had houses for *yanaconas* in Porongoche, a vineyard in Guasacache, four Arequipa Valley *chácaras*, property in the Cochuna Valley, slaves, and goats (BNP, ms. A595 [1559]; ADA, Muñoz, 31 July 1557, 29 October 1561, 30 October 1561, 13 January 1562, 22 January 1562, Herrera, 5 January 1576; *BDA*, 1:336, 3:308).

51. ADA, Muñoz, 25 October 1557, 26 October 1557, 8 November 1557, 24 May 1560; Ugarte y Ugarte, "Memoria y cuentas."

52. ADA, Muñoz, 19 October 1557.

53. Cobo, *Obras*, pp. 1:391-392.

54. ADA, Hernández, 7 October 1549.

55. ADA, Muñoz, 8 October 1557, Hernández, 16 August 1570, Aguilar, 6 September 1575.

56. ADA, Muñoz, 19 October 1557.

57. ADA, Aguilar, 3 February 1584, 10 March 1584, 19 May 1584.

58. ADA, Aguilar, 17 June 1575, 4 July 1575, Herrera, 23 November 1575.

59. ANP, Compañia, Titulos, leg. 3 (1628-1652), Titulos, leg. 2, cuad. 65 (1625).

60. Olivier Dollfus, *Le Pérou: Introduction géographique a l étude du développement* (Paris: Institut des Hautes Etudes de l'Amérique Latine, 1968), p. 165.

61. AGI, Contaduria, leg. 1822; ANP, Titulos, leg. 5, cuad. 150 (1662); AMA, leg. 6 (30 January 1597); ADA, Aguilar, 2 May 1596.

62. During the early sixteenth century, Spaniards in Peru used "*heredad*" in a broad sense to denote a person's possessions. By the last quarter of the century, Arequipan notaries employed the term in referring to a coastal estate and refrained from using it in its former sense. They also usually referred to an owner of such a property as an "*heredado*." For example, see ADA, Aguilar, 17 January 1584, 15 April 1584, 9 May 1584, 19 May 1584, 10 June 1584, Diego Ortiz, 20 June 1594, Ufelde, 5 October 1595, 23 October 1595. Such specific usage endured through the late 1600s.

63. Vázquez de Espinosa, *Compendio*, p. 337; ADA, Ufelde, October 1595, 25 June 1616.

64. ANP, Compañía, Titulos, leg. 2 (1606-1628); ADA, Aguilar, 21 August 1591, 9 March 1596, 19 April 1596, Ufelde, 23 October 1595; Vázquez de Espinosa, *Compendio*, p. 337.

65. ADA, Ufelde, 23 October 1595; Vázquez de Espinosa, *Compendio*, p. 336.

66. ADA, Hernández, 16 August 1570, Ufelde, 5 October 1595, 25 June 1616, Tejada, 21 January 1614, 16 July 1615; ANP, Compañia, Titulos, leg. 3 (1628-1652), Temporalidades, Expedientes sobre Titulos, Haciendas Matarani y Lluta.

67. ADA, Ufelde, 15 October 1595, 23 October 1595; ANP, Compañia, Titulos, leg. 2 (1606-1628).

68. The migration of *heredados* is noted in AGI, Lima, leg. 111, Patronato, leg. 191, doc. 23; BNP, ms. B478 (1633). For Don Francisco Zegarra's belongings, see

ADA, Aguilar, 3 February 1584.

69. ANP, Títulos, leg. 1, cuad. 24 (1595).

70. ADA, Muñoz, 8 July 1561, Hernández, 8 June 1570, 16 August 1570, 6 November 1570, Herrera, 23 November 1575, Aguilar, 9 March 1584, 1 April 1587, Ufelde, 25 October 1595, 29 August 1616, Laguna, 7 July 1648, 30 October 1648.

71. Ugarte y Ugarte, "Memoria y cuentas"; ADA, Aguilar, 9 March 1584, 6 January 1603.

72. BNP, ms. B415 (1603); Donald L. Wiedner, "Forced Labor in Colonial Peru," *The Americas* 16 (1960):364; AGI, Lima, leg. 32, leg. 571.

73. BNP, ms. B415 (1603).

74. AGI, Lima, leg. 169.

75. AGI, Lima, leg. 111; BNP, ms. B415 (1603); ANP, Juicios de Residencia, leg. 21, cuad. 54 (1610); ADA, Tejada, 26 December 1615.

76. ANP, Compañía, Censos, leg. 1 (1567-1636).

77. ADA, Hernández, 18 March 1568, 26 April 1568, Aguilar, 23 June 1575, 29 December 1575; and table N.4, chapter 5 notes.

78. Ugarte y Ugarte, "Memoria y cuentas"; ADA, Herrera, 13 October 1575, Aguilar, 1 February 1585, 10 June 1585, 19 April 1595, Ufelde, 23 October 1595, Muñoz, 14 March 1595, 26 January 1600.

79. Ugarte y Ugarte, "Memoria y cuentas"; ADA, Aguilar, 13 February 1584, 14 May 1584, 30 July 1584, 3 August 1591, 12 August 1591, 30 July 1596, 17 August 1596.

80. ANP, Compañía, Títulos, leg. 2 (1606-1628), leg. 3 (1628-1652); AMA, leg. 5 (27 April 1627). For prices, see figure 2.

81. *Encomenderos y estancieros: Estudios acerca de la constitución social aristocrática de Chile después de la conquista, 1580-1660* (Santiago de Chile: Editorial Universitaria, 1970), pp. 3-37.

82. Lockhart, "Encomienda and Hacienda," p. 424-426; Herman W. Konrad, *A Jesuit Hacienda in Colonial Mexico: Santa Lucía, 1576-1767* (Stanford, Cal.: Stanford University Press, 1980), pp. 175-214.

Chapter 4. *Encomenderos*, Landowners, and Society in Sixteenth-Century Arequipa

1. *Historia social latinoamericana (Nuevos enfoques)*, Colección Manoa of the Universidad Católica Andrés Bello (Caracas: Arte, 1979), pp. 115-136.

2. *Spanish Peru, 1532-1560: A Colonial Society* (Madison: University of Wisconsin Press, 1968), pp. 34-35. For *hidalgos*, see chap. 1, note 33.

3. The group also included men from New Castile, León, Navarre, and Vizcaya. On regional origins, see *SMF*, pp. 61-75, 159-164, 172-178, 182-190, 251-252, 258-259, 320-321, 330-332, 338-341, 366; *SMG*, pp. 2, 5-15; *BDA*, 1:63-64, 78, 105, 2:85, 92, 357, 3:283.

4. Mörner, *Historia social*, pp. 39-41. For Arequipa, see note 2, chap. 1.

5. *BDA*, 1:43, 55, 79, 90, 2:81, 83, 89, 3:19; *SMA*, pp. 3-14; *SMG*, pp. 7, 9-11.

6. In no document after 1540 were Luis de León and Nicolás de Almazán referred to as merchants. Almazán, like some other Arequipans, sought to insure his new social stature by requesting a coat of arms from the Crown (*BDA*, 1:160-161; also see James Lockhart, *The Men of Cajamarca: A Social and Biographical Study of the First Conquerors of Peru*, Latin American Monographs, no. 27 [Austin: University of Texas Press for the Institute of Latin American Studies, 1972], pp. 300-301).

7. *SMF*, pp. 8, 64, 86-87, 99, 100-101, 168, 241; Lockhart, *Cajamarca*, pp. 302-303. One *encomendero* later married his Indian mistress (*SMF*, pp. 233-235). For continued concubinage with Indians, see BNP, ms. Z1264 (1562); Magnus Mörner, *Race Mixture in the History of Latin America* (Boston: Little, Brown, 1967), pp. 21-41.

8. *SMF*, p. 152; *SMG*, pp. 15-17; *BDA*, 1:138-140; Lockhart, *Cajamarca*, p. 345. In his introduction to Pedro Pizarro's "Relación del descubrimiento y conquista de los reinos del Perú," in *Crónicas del Perú*, 5 vols., Biblioteca de Autores Españoles, nos. 164-168 (Madrid: Atlas, 1963-1965), p. 5:164, Juan Pérez de Tudela Bueso claims that Pedro Pizarro married Miguel Cornejo's daughter. He did not, but may have wed Cornejo's sister (see *SMF*, pp. 65-67, 77).

9. *SMF*, pp. 84-87, 255-256; ADA, Aguilar, 10 July 1584.

10. *SMG*, pp. 15-17; *BDA*, 1:138-140; Pedro Pizarro, "Relación," p. 228.

11. For two exceptions, see *BDA*, 2:230; Pedro Pizarro, "Relación," p. 228.

12. "Letter from the municipality of Arequipa to the Emperor Charles the Fifth, MS: Dated at San Juan de la Frontera, Sept. 24, 1542," in William H. Prescott, *History of the Conquest of Peru, with a Preliminary View of the Civilization of the Incas*, 2 vols. (New York: Harper & Brothers, 1847), pp. 2:514-517 (reproduced in *BDA* 1:167-170).

13. For Vaca de Castro's assignments, see Rafael Loredo, *Los repartos* (Lima: D. Miranda, 1958), pp. 194-204 (a Quirós, a man who already held an *encomienda* in the region, is included, but no other data on the man were found). The activities of these Spaniards are noted in Lockhart, *Cajamarca*, pp. 327-328; *BDA*, 3:28-36, 48-49, 58, 62-63, 163.

14. ANP, Títulos, leg. 6, cuad. 171 (1643); ADA, Valdecabras, 27 September 1552, Hernández, October 1558; BNP, ms. A590 (1575); *BDA*, 2:211-214, 3:119; *SMF*, pp. 342-343, 400, 430-431; *SMG*, pp. 17-19; *CGC*, 2:276.

15. Among the numerous sources that discuss the Gonzalo Pizarro rebellion, see Prescott, *History*, pp. 2:244-271; Garcilaso de la Vega, El Inca, *Royal Commentaries of the Incas and General History of Peru*, trans. with intro. by Harold V. Livermore, 2 vols (Austin: University of Texas Press, 1966), pp. 2:931-1225; Agustín de Zárate, *Histoire de la découverte et de la conquête du Pérou*, 2 vols. (Paris: Chez Cailleau, 1775), vol. 2; Diego Fernández, "Historia del Perú," in *Crónicas del Perú*, vols. 1-2; *HHG*, vols. 9 and 10; Rubén Vargas Ugarte, *Historia del Perú: Virreinato (1551-1600)* (Lima: A Baiocco, 1949), pp. 41-64. On Arequipa, see *HHG*, 9:149-150; *BDA*, 2:358, 3:49; Manuel Belaúnde Guinassi, *La encomienda en el Perú* (Lima: Mercurio Peruano, 1945), p. 71.

16. Pedro Pizarro, "Relación," pp. 233-234; *BDA*, 3:243-246; Juan Calvete de Estrella, "Vida de Don Pedro Gasca," and Juan Polo de Ondegardo, "Relación de las cosas del Perú desde 1543 hasta la muerte de Gonzalo Pizarro," in *Crónicas del Perú*, vols. 4 and 5, respectively.

17. Pedro Pizarro, "Relación," p. 235.

18. *BDA*, 1:220-229, 2:364, 368, 3:50-51, 114; Ondegardo, "Relación," pp. 292-293.

19. Calvete de Estrella, "Vida"; Prescott, *History*, vol. 2, esp. book 5; Ondegardo, "Relación," p. 313; *BDA*, 2:157-162, 3:53, 70-72, 107.

20. Ondegardo, "Relación," p. 327; ADA, Hernández, 14 July 1553; *BDA*, 2:231, 344, 354, 3:72, 79, 179, 216-217, 222, 254, 263, 280, 284, 329, 333-334, 340, 357; *SMF*, p. 343.

21. *BDA*, 2:359, 364, 3:65-66.

22. *SMF*, p. 319.

23. *BDA*, 2:368-369, 373, 3:100, 342.

24. *BDA*, 1:264, 267, 2:176, 213, 231, 243, 311, 350, 354-355, 359, 361, 369, 377, 3:74, 81, 97, 100-101, 222, 287, 329, 333, 345.

25. Appendix A; Loredo, *Repartos*, pp. 194-204; Alejandro Málaga Medina, "Consideraciones económicas sobre la visita de la provincia de Arequipa," in *Tasa de la visita general de Francisco de Toledo*, ed. Noble David Cook, pp. 300-304 (Lima: Imprenta de la Universidad Nacional de San Marcos, 1975); AGI, Contaduría, leg. 1786.

26. In addition to the nine killed at Huarina, Hernán Bueno, Lope Martín, and Luis de León died (*SMF*, pp. 248, 343; and sources for note 20).

27. Lockhart, *Cajamarca*, p. 302; *SMF*, pp. 145-146, 152-153, 244-246; *BDA*, 3:140-145.

28. Loredo, *Repartos*, pp. 194-204, 301-361; Enrique Torres Saldamando, *Apuntes históricos sobre las encomiendas en el Perú* (Lima: Universidad Nacional Mayor de San Marcos, 1967), chap. 5; Belaúnde Guinassi, *Encomienda*, esp. pp. 88-113.

29. AGI, Contaduría, leg. 1786; Málaga Medina, "Consideraciones," p. 301; *BDA*, 1:265-269, 2:165, 346-355, 360-362, 3:37-40, 97, 342; *SMF*, pp. 330-332.

30. *BDA*, 2:203-207, 239-247. For others, like Juan de Vergara and Hernando de Rivera, see Loredo, *Repartos*, pp. 358-359; *BDA*, 3:173-222, 280; also *SMF*, pp. 374-379.

31. *BDA*, 3:136-139, 173-175, 200-213, 219-232; *SMF*, pp. 306-307.

32. *SMA*, pp. 28, 32; *SMF*, pp. 9, 12-13, 176-177, 196-197, 331, 410-428; *SMG*, pp. 37-38; ADA, Hernández, 12 April 1550; Lockhart, *Cajamarca*, pp. 302-303, 319.

33. *SMF*, pp. 114-116, 189, 340, 343, 375; ANP, Derecho Indígena y Encomiendas, leg. 1, cuad. 10 (1568); ADA, Muñoz, 7 August 1561.

34. *SMF*, pp. 151-153; *BDA*, 2:295-297.

35. *SMF*, pp. 196-197, 256-257; Lockhart, *Cajamarca*, p. 302; ADA, Aguilar, 28 June 1596; ANP, Derecho Indígena y Encomiendas, leg. 2, cuad. 15 (1572).

36. *SMF*, pp. 267-272; *SMG*, p. 40; BNP, ms. A510 (1557); ANP, Compañía, Títulos, leg. 1 (1539-1605).

37. *SMF*, pp. 165-171; BNP, ms. A510 (1557), ms. A136 (1570); ANP, Títulos, leg. 1, cuad. 4 (1557); ADA, Muñoz, 21 July 1561.

38. *SMG*, pp. 63-66; *BDA*, 3:361-362; ADA, Aguilar, 21 June 1596; Guillermo Lohmann Villena, *Los americanos en las órdenes nobiliarias (1529-1900)*, 2 vols. (Madrid: Artes Gráficas, 1947), p. 2:88.

39. *BDA*, 2:386-392.

40. *SMG*, pp. 44-79.

41. *BDA*, 2:215, 3:352; ADA, Hernández, 4 February 1552, 13 November 1553, 17 April 1556, 12 May 1556, 11 November 1570, Muñoz, 9 November 1557, 5 November 1561, Aguilar, 5 February 1573, Diego Ortiz, 8 January 1594; AMA, leg. 1 (16 August 1578), leg. 4 (15 September 1585), leg. 6 (14 May 1611); BNP, ms. A391 (1594); ANP, Títulos, leg. 6, cuad. 155 (1600), cuad. 171 (1643), Compañía, Títulos, leg. 3 (1628-1652).

42. BNP, ms. A510 (1557), ms. A595 (1559); ANP, Títulos, leg. 1, cuad. 4 (1557), Derecho Indígena y Encomiendas, leg. 1, cuad. 10 (1568), Compañía, Títulos, leg. 3 (1628-1652); ADA, Hernández, 19 June 1556, 24 May 1560, Valdecabras, 12 September 1551, 8 November 1552, Acuerdos del Cabildo, October 1559, Muñoz, 1 September 1561, Aguilar, 30 January 1584; *BDA*, 1:348-349, 2:112.

43. *SMF*, pp. 423-425; ADA, Hernández, 2 July 1549, 9 June 1551, 22 October 1551, 15 June 1553, 17 April 1556, 25 June 1556, 9 February 1560, 5 June 1560, Torres, 20 February 1556, Muñoz, 1 February 1557, June 1561, Juan de Vera, February 1571, Aguilar, 2 September 1583; BNP, ms. A595 (1559); AMA, leg. 1 (24 April 1584, 25 September 1590, 5 June 1610), leg. 6 (20 April 1627); ANP, Derecho Indígena y Encomiendas, leg. 1, cuad. 10 (1568), Compañía, Censos, leg. 1 (1567-1636), Compañía, Títulos, leg. 3 (1628-1652), Títulos, leg. 1, cuad. 24 (1595); *BDA*, 3:332-335.

44. *SMF*, p. 321.

45. Men like Luis Miranda, Juan de Olivares, Bartolomé de Otazu, Alonso de Moya, and Francisco de Arciniega surface only briefly in the notarial records of 1540-1551 and then appear to have left Arequipa. For a broad discussion of this tendency, see Lockhart, *Spanish Peru*, esp. pp. 91, 94-95.

46. *SMF*, p. 321; ADA, Hernández, 24 May 1560, Juan de Vera, August 1571, Ufelde, 26 October 1595; AMA, leg. 6 (3 January 1583); BNP, ms. A512 (1557).

47. ADA, Muñoz, 1 February 1557; *SMF*, pp. 177-178; BNP, ms. A512 (1557).

48. *SMF*, pp. 94, 100, 170-171, 211, 251.

49. ANP, Compañía, Títulos, leg. 3 (1628-1652); BNP, ms. Z1264 (1562); ADA, Hernández, 16 August 1570, Aguilar, 24 August 1575, 10 March 1584, 10 July 1584, 9 September 1584, 5 March 1603, Hernando Ortiz, 6 July 1589, Diego Ortiz, 9 July 1594, Muñoz, 22 March 1600, Ufelde, 7 January 1616, 12 December 1616; AMA, leg. 6 (7 January 1571).

50. ADA, Juan de Vera, 1 December 1571, 8 December 1571; AMA, leg. 6 (7

January 1571).

51. *SMF*, pp. 169, 409; ADA, Hernández, 26 February 1570; ANP, Títulos, leg. 25, cuad. 663 (1612).

52. *SMF*, pp. 256-257; ADA, Hernández, 7 August 1549, 1 May 1556, 21 May 1556, 15 July 1570, Aguilar, 8 July 1575, 30 January 1584, 4 April 1584, 3 August 1591, Diego Ortiz, 28 July 1595; ANP, Compañía, Títulos, leg. 3 (1628-1652).

53. ADA, Aguilar, 7 October 1574; *SMF*, pp. 65-66, 69-75, 270-271, 340.

54. *SMF*, pp. 302-305.

55. Ibid., pp. 222-224, 340.

56. J. H. Parry, *The Spanish Seaborne Empire*, History of Human Society Series (New York: Knopf, 1969), chap. 10; *SMG*, pp. 70-75.

57. ANP, Compañía, Censos, leg. 1 (1567-1636), Compañía, Títulos, leg. 3 (1628-1652); ADA, Aguilar, 11 March 1575, 8 July 1575, 29 December 1575, 19 April 1605; AGI, Lima, leg. 464; *SMF*, p. 339.

58. AGI, Contaduría, leg. 1822.

59. *SMF*, p. 429; *SMG*, p. 57; ADA, Aguilar, 3 February 1584; AMA, leg. 1 (25 September 1590).

60. *SMF*, pp. 124, 280, 335, 339; *SMG*, pp. 57, 63-64; Lohmann Villena, *Americanos*, p. 2:88; ADA, Aguilar, 3 February 1584, 3 January 1605.

61. *SMG*, pp. 63-66; *BDA*, 3:361-362; ADA, Aguilar, 21 June 1596.

62. *SMF*, pp. 226, 429; *SMA*, p. 43; ADA, Aguilar, 3 February 1584, Hernando Ortiz, 15 July 1589; AMA, leg. 6 (14 May 1611); ANP, Compañía, Títulos, leg. 3 (1628-1652).

63. *SMG*, p. 66; *SMF*, pp. 273-274, 289-290.

64. ADA, Hernández, 11 January 1558, Juan de Vera, 1 August 1571, Aguilar, 7 July 1575; Ladislao Cabrera Valdés, ed., *Documentos primitivos del Cabildo* (Arequipa: Caritg y Rivera, 1924), pp. 78, 103; *BDA*, 3:358-359; *SMF*, pp. 8-11; *SMG*, pp. 55-56.

65. *SMF*, pp. 88-89, 338-339; ANP, Juicios de Residencia, leg. 1, cuad. 2 (1580); ADA, Aguilar, 18 April 1584, 22 April 1584, 31 July 1591, 1 September 1603, Diego Ortiz, 8 January 1594, 12 January 1594, 26 November 1594.

66. The Bueno family, for example, became linked to the de la Torres by their marriages into the Cárdenas family (*SMF*, pp. 41, 344).

67. *SMA*, pp. 33-55.

68. Examples are discussed later, especially in chap. 7.

69. ADA, Hernández, 16 August 1570, 13 August 1575, Aguilar, 3 February 1584.

70. *SMA*, pp. 38, 43-44, 52.

71. *SMF*, pp. 123-124; *SMA*, p. 49; ADA, Aguilar, 7 March 1584, 20 March 1584, 16 August 1591; AMA, leg. 1 (25 September 1590); ANP, Compañía, Censos, leg. 1 (1567-1636).

72. *SMA*, pp. 49, 55-56; *SMF*, pp. 424-425.

73. See assessments in Appendix B.

74. ADA, Aguilar, 17 January 1584, Tejada, 6 July 1612.

75. AMA, leg. 6 (4 December 1578); ADA, Aguilar, 18 January 1584, 29 January 1584, Hernández, 28 January 1570.

76. ADA, Aguilar, 19 June 1605, Tejada, 6 July 1612.

77. ADA, Aguilar, 17 January 1584, 18 January 1584.

78. *SMF*, pp. 60, 94, 100, 170-171; ADA, Tejada, 7 January 1616.

79. *SMF*, pp. 100-102, 256, 341, 428; ADA, Aguilar, 24 March 1584.

80. "Peruvian Encomenderos in 1630: Elite Circulation and Consolidation," *HAHR* 57 (November 1977):633-659; Lockhart, *Spanish Peru*, and idem, *Cajamarca*, pp. 17-42.

81. Leon G. Campbell, "A Colonial Establishment: Creole Domination of the Audiencia of Lima during the Eighteenth Century," *HAHR* 52 (February 1972):1-20; Jacques Barbier, "Elites and Cadres in Bourbon Chile," *HAHR* 52 (August 1972):416-435.

82. "Government and Elite in Late Colonial Mexico," *HAHR* 53 (August 1973):389-414; idem, *Miners and Merchants in Bourbon Mexico, 1763-1810*, Cambridge Latin American Studies, no. 10 (Cambridge: At the University Press, 1971), esp. part 1, chap. 5.

83. Mörner, *Race Mixture*; also see Lyle N. McAlister, "Social Structure and Social Change in New Spain," *HAHR* 43 (August 1963):349-370.

Chapter 5. The Wine Economy

1. Francisco Xavier Echeverría y Morales, "Memoria de la Santa Iglesia de Arequipa," in *BMHA*, 4:25-32, 35-39; ADA, Ufelde, 30 August 1595, Aguilar, 20 January 1596; AMA, leg. 1 (7 May 1661, 11 December 1587, 26 September 1583), leg. 6 (4 December 1578, 26 November 1599), leg. 7 (28 August 1566).

2. ADA, Hernando Ortiz, 12 January 1594, Ufelde, 30 August 1595, 14 September 1595, 5 October 1595, 22 October 1595, 26 October 1595, Muñoz, 20 November 1596. On the mule industry, see ADA, Muñoz, 13 April 1562, 14 March 1600, Aguilar, 18 May 1584; BNP, ms. B1351 (1600), ms. B415 (1603).

3. For examples of mortgages, see ADA, Aguilar, 11 March 1589, 16 June 1603, Laguna, 28 April 1595, Ufelde, 3 February 1595, 14 September 1595, 1 May 1596, 11 November 1596, Juan de Vera, 5 December 1609. Also see AMA, leg. 1 (7 May 1661), leg. 3 (18 February 1581), leg. 4 (24 April 1635), leg. 5 (27 April 1627); ANP, Compañia, Censos, leg. 2 (1636-1670).

4. AGI, Lima, leg. 116; ADA, Hernández, 16 January 1552, Muñoz, 17 July 1561, 22 November 1561, Aguilar, 17 January 1584, 22 April 1584, 9 May 1584, 12 August 1591, 19 September 1591, 18 November 1596.

5. ADA, Muñoz, 11 January 1592, 24 January 1622, 8 June 1622, Hernando Ortiz, 15 July 1589, Ufelde, 14 June 1610, 19 January 1616, 28 June 1616, 25 October 1616.

6. ADA, Aguilar, 28 June 1596, 8 November 1596, Hernández, 17 May 1560, Muñoz, 2 July 1561.

7. Gwendolin B. Cobb, "Supply and Transportation for the Potosí Mines, 1545-1640," *HAHR* 29 (1949):24-45; Antonio Raimondi, *El Perú*, 6 vols. in 5

(Lima: Imprenta del Estado, Gil, & Sanmartí, 1874-1913), pp. 2:141-142; Roberto Levillier, ed., *Gobernantes del Perú: Cartas y papeles. Siglo XVI. Documentos del Archivo de Indias*, 14 vols., Colección de Publicaciones Históricas de la Biblioteca del Congreso Argentino (Madrid: Sucesores de Rivadeneyra and Imprenta de Juan Pueyo, 1921-1926), pp. 3:542-619; Reginaldo de Lizárraga, *Descripción breve de toda la tierra del Perú, Tucumán, Río de la Plata y Chile*, Biblioteca de Autores Españoles, no. 216 (Madrid: Atlas, 1968), pp. 47-48; Pedro Cieza de León, "La crónica del Perú," in *Crónicas de la conquista del Perú*, ed. Julio Le Riverend Brusone, pp. 45-46 (Mexico City: Nueva España, n.d.); Boleslao Lewin, ed., *Descripción del virreinato del Perú: Crónica inédita de comienzos del siglo XVII*, Colección de Textos y Documentos series B, no. 1 (Rosario: Instituto de Investigaciones Históricas, 1958), pp. 104-105; Luis Urzúa Urzúa, *Arica, puerta nueva: Historia y folklore*, 2d ed. (Santiago de Chile: Editorial Andrés Bello, 1964), p. 21.

8. ADA, Aguilar, 17 January 1584, 18 January 1584, 27 January 1584, 1 February 1584, 7 March 1584, 10 March 1584, 20 March 1584, Hernando Ortiz, 15 July 1589, Muñoz, 2 January 1592, 10 January 1592.

9. Antonio Vázquez de Espinosa, *Compendio y descripción de las Indias Occidentales*, Biblioteca de Autores Españoles, no. 231 (Madrid: Atlas, 1969), pp. 337, 341; ADA, Corregimiento (Civil), 1590-1599.

10. For an example of the differences in wine prices over the course of a year, see ADA, Aguilar, 17 January 1584, 27 January 1584, 30 January 1584, 1 February 1584, 12 February 1584, 7 March 1584, 10 March 1584, 20 March 1584, 14 April 1584, 25 May 1584, 10 June 1584, 28 July 1584, 17 September 1584, 19 September 1584.

11. ADA, Juan de Vera, 1 August 1571, Aguilar, 26 November 1596, Ufelde, 28 June 1616, Muñoz, 24 January 1622.

12. ADA, Aguilar, 10 March 1584, 9 May 1584, 30 July 1591, 13 August 1591, 8 January 1596, 29 August 1596, Ufelde, 15 November 1596, 7 April 1616, Gordejuela, 18 August 1636, Diego de Silva, 1 September 1644.

13. ADA, Hernández, 16 January 1552, Aguilar, 9 May 1584, 30 July 1584.

14. ADA, Hernández, 7 April 1570, Juan de Vera, 1 August 1571, Aguilar, 30 July 1584, 16 August 1591, 19 September 1591, Ufelde, 24 October 1595, 28 June 1616.

15. BNP, ms. A377 (1594), ms. A459 (1597), ms. A245 (1599).

16. See chap. 6.

17. See table N.4.

18. ADA, Hernández, 8 June 1570, Aguilar, 4 January 1596, Gordejuela, 20 February 1636; José de Acosta, *Obras*, Biblioteca de Autores Españoles, no. 73 (Madrid: Atlas, 1954), pp. 298-299; AMA, leg. 6 (9 September 1595); ANP, Compañía, Títulos, leg. 2 (1606-1628), Juicios de Residencia, leg. 5, cuad. 9 (1584), Tribunal de Cuentas, Real Hacienda, Composiciones, Tierras y Indígenas, leg. 5, cuad. 23 (1644), cuad. 24 (1644); AGI, Justicia, leg. 1186, leg. 1190.

19. Eduardo L. Ugarte y Ugarte, ed., "Memoria y cuentas de Da. Juana Muñiz, vecina de Arequipa, sobre sus nietos hijos de Miguel Cornejo, 1570-1571" (unpublished, Arequipa, n.d.); ADA, Hernández, 9 August 1549, 11 March 1552, 14 August 1552, 7 June 1553, 16 November 1553, 3 January 1554, 27 May 1570, 3 June 1570.

Table N.4
Annual Compensation for Indian Workers on *Heredades*, 1568-1657

Notary	Date	Compensation Noted
Gaspar Hernández	18 March 1568	8 pesos[a], food, drink
Gaspar Hernández	26 April 1568	A land plot
Diego de Aguilar	23 June 1575	4 ps., 1 piece of clothing, food, religious instruction, land, and every other week off
Diego de Aguilar	29 December 1575	10 ps., 2 pieces of clothing, food, medical care, and religious instruction
García Muñoz	9 February 1595	12 ps., 2 pieces of clothing, food, medical care, and religious instruction
García Muñoz	18 July 1595	25 ps., 2 pieces of clothing, food, 2 land plots, and weekends off
Diego de Aguilar	22 January 1596	20 ps., 2 pieces of clothing, one-half fanega of maize per month, medical care, religious instruction
García Muñoz	10 March 1600	24 ps., 2 pieces of clothing, food, medical care, religious instruction
García Muñoz	25 September 1610	14 ps., 2 pieces of clothing, 6 baskets of maize, and trousers of fine cloth
García Muñoz	12 February 1622	40 ps., 2 pieces of clothing, 6 baskets of maize and wheat before harvest, and a land plot
García Muñoz	29 April 1622	60 ps., 2 pieces of clothing, and food
Diego de Silva	29 October 1644	12 ps., 2 pieces of clothing, 2 reales per month for meat
Antonio de Silva	22 September 1657	40 ps., 6 fanegas of wheat, 3 ps. to buy salt and clothing

[a] All are pesos of eight reales.

20. ADA, Aguilar, 3 February 1584, 22 April 1584, 18 May 1584, 31 August 1584, 19 April 1605, Ufelde, 5 October 1595; ANP, Compañía, Censos, leg. 1 (1567-1636); Vázquez de Espinosa, *Compendio*, p. 338; Acosta, *Obras*, pp. 298-299.

21. ADA, Aguilar 7 February 1573, 15 February 1596, 9 March 1596, 6 May 1596, 21 June 1596, 6 September 1596, 10 February 1603, 17 March 1603, 15 June 1605, Herrera, 10 October 1575, Muñoz, 30 January 1560, 9 May 1561, 7 July 1561, 31 December 1561, 2 May 1622, 1 July 1622.

22. BNP, ms. B415 (1603); AGI, Lima, leg. 32, leg. 571.

23. ANP, Títulos, leg. 1, cuad. 24 (1595); ADA, Ufelde, 5 October 1595, 27 November 1595, 22 August 1616, 29 August 1616.

24. See table N.5.

25. Vázquez de Espinosa, *Compendio,* pp. 335-348; Juan Antonio Montenegro y Ubaldi, "Noticia de la ciudad de Santa Catalina de Guadalcázar de Moquegua," *Revista Histórica* 1 (1906):70-109, 255-268, 321-336.

26. Rubén Vargas Ugarte, *Historia del Perú: Virreinato (1551-1600)* (Lima: A. Baiocco, 1949), pp. 132-134; Vázquez de Espinosa, *Compendio*, pp. 325-334; Lewin, *Descripción*, pp. 105-111; Robert G. Keith, *Conquest and Agrarian Change: The Emergence of the Hacienda System on the Peruvian Coast*, Harvard Historical Studies, no. 93 (Cambridge, Mass.: Harvard University Press, 1976), esp. 79.

27. AGI, Contaduría, legs. 1699-1735. These only document legal trade. Contraband from both the Ica-Pisco-Nazca and Arequipa areas to Lima was substantial (AGI, Lima, leg. 95, leg. 99, leg. 572). With access to Lima by land as well as by sea, the more northern areas probably had an advantage over Arequipa in illegal trade.

Table N.5
Indian and Black Slave Labor

Wages Paid Indians on an *Heredad*		Leasing Cost of Slaves for an *Heredad*	
1592		1632	
8 Indians—12 days' work	40 ps.	7 slaves—200 days' work (each cost one-half ps. per day)	700 ps.
Indians—staked vines	20 ps.		
4 Indians—for general work	20 ps.	Food for above (each received one-half fanega of maize per month)	462 ps.
Indians—for transport	20 ps.		
6 Indians—for weeding	30 ps	Clothing for above	70 ps.
Indians—for harvest	50 ps.	4 slaves—78 days' work at harvest (each cost one-half ps. per day)	156 ps.
Indians—cleaned ditches and staked vines	20 ps.		
15 Indians—12 days' work (cleaned *heredad*)	75 ps.	Maize for above (each received 1.5 fanegas)	66 ps.
Indians—cleaned the vineyard and staked vines	30 ps.	Meat for temporary and yearly slave laborers	50 ps.
		Fish for all slave laborers	30 ps.
		Cheese for all slave laborers	24 ps.

Sources: ADA, Corregimiento (Civil), 1590-1599; ANP, Títulos, leg. 1, cuad. 24 (1595).

28. AGI, Lima, leg. 33.

29. Woodrow Borah, *Early Colonial Trade and Navigation between Mexico and Peru*, Ibero-Americana Series, no. 38 (Berkeley & Los Angeles: University of California Press, 1954, pp. 112-113.

30. Lizárraga, *Descripción*, p. 49; AGI, Justicia, leg. 498C.

31. AGI, Lima, leg. 32.

32. AGI, Lima, leg. 33.

33. AGI, Lima, leg. 34, leg. 571; ANP, Títulos, leg. 3, cuad. 73 (1634).

34. AGI, Lima, leg. 33.

35. AGI, Lima, leg. 32, leg. 570.

36. Vargas Ugarte, *Historia (1551-1600)*, pp. 373-381; AGI, Lima, leg. 116, leg. 570.

37. Víctor M. Barriga, ed., *Los terremotos en Arequipa, 1582-1868* (Arequipa: La Colmena, 1951), pp. 55-184, 187-236; AGI, Patronato, leg. 191, doc. 23, Lima, leg. 35, leg. 94, leg. 95, leg. 111; AMA, leg. 5 (27 April 1627).

38. AGI, Lima, leg. 35, leg. 95, leg. 570.

39. Barriga, *Terremotos*, pp. 28, 32-42, 84-87, 90-91, 156, 163, 203, 206-213; AGI, Lima, leg. 95, leg. 570; BNP, ms. B571 (1619). The volcanic ash also helped in the recovery, since it improved yields (AGI, Lima, leg. 35).

40. Barriga, *Terremotos*, pp. 142-144, 216-218; AMA, leg. 5 (27 April 1627); ADA, Tejada, 1 September 1612.

41. AGI, Lima, leg. 1, leg. 34, leg. 94, Patronato, leg. 191, doc. 23; Barriga, *Terremotos*, p. 214.

42. AGI, Lima, leg. 94, leg. 95, leg. 111; Echeverría y Morales, "Memoria," pp. 36-38; Barriga, *Terremotos*, pp. 223-226; ADA, Muñoz, 3 November 1622.

43. ADA, Muñoz, 20 June 1600, 15 November 1600, Tejada, 21 April 1616, 25 June 1616, 12 December 1616.

44. See below for examples of sales within families (ADA, Tejada, 8 July 1615, 16 January 1616).

45. The families that retained their estates from 1583 to at least the 1620s were Salazar, Martínez de Ribera, Porres, Valderrama, Almonte, Orihuela, Pérez de Vargas, Peralta, Castro Tristán, Valencia, Zegarra, and de Tapia. Each of the following families that had owned *heredades* in 1583 still had a portion of their original estate during the early 1620s: Quirós Vozmediano, Herrera, Picado, Baltasar de Torres, Cristóbal de Torres, Luis Cornejo, and Diego Cornejo. (In the case of the Picado, Luis Cornejo, and Quirós Vozmediano families, portions of their estates that they no longer held had been given to the church.) The *heredades* of Leonor Méndez and the Navarro family had been sold before 1600. ANP, Compañía, Títulos, leg. 3 (1628-1652), Compañía, Censos, leg. 2 (1636-1670), Títulos, leg. 5, cuad. 150 (1662); BNP, ms. B428 (1645), ms. B1529 (1619); AMA, leg. 1 (6 March 1625), leg. 4 (24 April 1635), leg. 5 (17 April 1623), leg. 7 (11 April 1623, 15 July 1658); AGI, Contaduría, leg. 1822; ADA, Diego Ortiz, 12 January 1594, Aguilar, 18 November 1603, Ufelde, 7 January 1616, Tejada, 24 July 1612, 21 April 1616, 9 May 1616, Francisco de Vera, 18 January 1622, February 1622, 6

April 1622, Muñoz, 29 November 1595, 17 November 1600, 5 January 1622, 14 January 1622, 18 January 1622, 21 March 1622, 16 July 1622, 12 October 1622, 3 November 1622, Gordejuela, 2 September 1636, Diego de Silva, 12 May 1644.

46. ANP, Títulos, leg. 9, cuad. 265 (1623).

47. Lizárraga, *Descripción*, p. 48.

48. AMA, leg. 1 (6 March 1625), leg. 5 (16 January 1631, 17 April 1623, 23 August 1643); ADA, Ufelde, 25 June 1616.

49. AGI, Contaduría, legs. 1724-1732, Justicia, leg. 568B; Lewin, *Descripción*, pp. 67, 75, 82-83, 111; Nicholas P. Cushner, *Lords of the Land: Sugar, Wine, and Jesuit Estates of Coastal Peru, 1600-1767* (Albany: State University of New York Press, 1980), esp. chaps. 5 and 7.

50. Borah, *Early Colonial Trade*; AGI, Lima, leg. 571. No mention of the ban is made in AMuA, LAS, libros 10, 11.

51. Vázquez de Espinosa, *Compendio*, pp. 328, 337.

52. Local prices had been unusually high for a decade after 1604, because of the low supply of wine after the major earthquakes.

53. AGI, Lima, leg. 312.

54. Prices averaged 550 pesos (of 8 reales) from 1616 to 1653. A very low price for a male slave was 350 pesos; an unusually high price was 750 pesos. See ADA, Tejada, 27 February 1616, 2 April 1616, Ufelde, 23 March 1616, 27 April 1616, Francisco de Vera, 31 January 1622, Muñoz, 1 February 1622, 17 February 1622, 2 May 1622, 28 May 1622, 27 March 1630, Gordejuela, 16 May 1631, 10 September 1631, 2 January 1636, 22 January 1636, 9 February 1636, 23 February 1636, 17 October 1636, 19 December 1636, Diego de Silva, 13 February 1644, 23 February 1644, 20 April 1644, 27 April 1644, 16 October 1644, 12 August 1653, 26 September 1653, 9 October 1653, Laguna, 17 January 1653, 29 May 1653, 1 October 1653.

55. ADA, Muñoz, 29 March 1595, Ufelde, October 1595.

56. ADA, Muñoz, 22 January 1562, Hernández, 3 February 1570,18 February 1570, Juan de Vera, 21 June 1571; AGI, Justicia, leg. 568A, leg. 965, Lima, leg. 312.

57. AGI, Lima, leg. 99, Indiferente General, leg. 429, leg. 2690.

58. AGI, Lima, leg. 99.

59. AGI, Lima, leg. 52, leg. 572, Contaduría, legs. 1723-1745; Fred Bronner, "La Unión de Armas en el Perú: Aspectos políticos-legales," *Anuario de Estudios Americanos* 24 (1967):1133-1176.

60. See chap. 7.

61. A viceregal report on monastic holdings, dated 1 April 1612, noted that neither the three houses of the Franciscans, the Recolección de San Francisco, nor the Dominicans possessed rural property. The Order of San Agustín was credited with a small alfalfa *chácara*, and the Jesuits with farms and an *estancia* for large and small livestock. The Mercedarians owned vineyards and other farms (AGI, Lima, leg. 275). The report is inaccurate, because the Dominicans possessed at least one *chácara*, and the Convent of Santa Catalina de Sena, several estates (ADA, Aguilar, 5 March 1603, 6 December 1603). Whatever the case, the Crown's warning and

those of others that the church was appropriating too much land was misplaced in Arequipa's case (AGI, Lima, leg. 312, leg. 570, Indiferente General, leg. 428; Lewin, *Descripción*, p. 105).

62. Table N.6 lists some properties of Arequipa's Mercedarians. Unfortunately, the records of Arequipa's Franciscans, Dominicans, and nuns of Santa Catalina are not open to the public. A limited idea of their holdings can be gained from AGI, Lima, leg. 111, leg. 275.

Table N.6
Mercedarian Rural Holdings and Income

Date Held By	Property	Income
1. 1566	Arequipa Valley, *chácara*	
2. 1571	Arequipa Valley, small *chácara*	
3. 1597	Arequipa Valley, near Paucarpata, *chácara*	Rented in late 1590s for 60 ps/year
4. 1600	Arequipa Valley, near Socabaya, *chácara*	60 ps/year
5. 1611	Across Chili River from city of Arequipa, *chácara*	Rented in early 1600s for 50 ps/year
6. 1612	Mortgages and rural properties (?)	Income estimated at 2,000 ps/year
7. 1625	Near city of Arequipa, *chácara* (possibly no. 1 or 2, above)	
8. 1629	East of Cailloma, *estancia* Santa Bárbara de Moro	Rented in 1620s for 2,200 ps/year; in 1660s for 3,300 ps/year
9. 1656	Moquegua Valley, vineyard	Rented for 330 ps/year

Sources: AMA, leg. 2 (20 October 1625), leg. 3 (23 September 1667), leg. 6 (12 February 1571, 19 December 1597, 12 May 1600, 6 April 1611, 21 April 1656, 27 July 1656), leg. 7 (28 August 1566); AGI, Lima, leg. 275; BNP, ms. B1720 (1612).

Note: I could only ascertain that Mercedarians had land by date shown, as documents do not give the date when land was actually acquired.

63. AGI, Contaduría, leg. 1785; ADA, Aguilar, 5 February 1573, Hernández, 4 February 1552, 13 November 1553, 17 April 1556, 12 May 1556, 11 November 1570, Muñoz, 5 November 1561, Diego Ortiz, 8 January 1594; AMA, leg. 1 (16 August 1578), leg. 4 (15 September 1585); ANP, Títulos, leg. 4, cuad. 67 (1618), leg. 6, cuad. 155 (1600), cuad. 171 (1643); BNP, ms. A391 (1594); *BMHA*, 4:30.

64. AMA, leg. 1 (1625); ANP, Temporalidades, Expedientes sobre Titulos, Matarani y Lluta, Compañia, Censos, leg. 1 (1567-1636), Títulos, leg. 1, cuad. 4 (1557), cuad. 24 (1595), leg. 2, cuad. 65 (1625), cuad. 66 (1628).

65. ADA, Muñoz, 29 November 1595; ANP, Compañia, Títulos, leg. 1 (1539-1605).

66. ADA, Tejada, 4 June 1615; ANP, Compañía, Títulos, leg. 2 (1606-1628).

67. ANP, Real Hacienda, Arequipa (1646-1698).

68. BNP, ms. B1351 (1600); ANP, Juicios de Residencia, leg. 18, cuad. 46 (1600), leg. 31, cuad. 54, cuad. 55 (1610).

69. ANP, Compañía, Títulos, leg. 3 (1628-1652).

70. ANP, Compañía, Censos, leg. 1 (1567-1636), Real Hacienda, Arequipa (1646-1698), Títulos, leg. 5, cuad. 141 (1638), cuad. 150 (1660). The Convent of Santa Catalina de Sena's annual yield from mortgages topped 10,000 pesos during the 1600s (AGI, Lima, leg. 111).

71. The size comparison of holdings is based on assessments in an early 1660s survey of estates in the Vítor Valley (see Appendix C). The survey was done by the staff of the archbishop of Arequipa to raise money to pay for each year's salary for a priest in the valley.

72. For Cárdenas holdings, see ANP, Temporalidades, Expedientes sobre Títulos, San Javier de Vítor, Compañía, Títulos, leg. 3 (1628-1652), Tribunal de Cuentas, Real Hacienda, Composiciones, Tierras y Indígenas, leg. 5, cuad 13 (1644); BNP, ms. B428 (1645); ADA, Gordejuela, 2 September 1636, Antonio de Silva, 6 October 1657, Diez, 30 July 1674.

73. The Salazar family, the Peraltas, Benavideses, and Bedoya Mogrovejos each had as much land as the Mercedarians. On the last two, see note 79, this chapter, and note 29, chap. 7. For some of the Peralta properties, see ADA, Antonio de Silva, 4 June 1657; AMA, leg. 5 (24 January 1643, 23 August 1643); ANP, Compañía, Títulos, leg. 4 (1652-1675). Those of the Salazar family can be found in ADA, Gordejuela, 31 October 1636, Diego de Silva, 3 June 1644, 30 August 1644, 23 October 1654, Laguna, 19 February 1685, 23 March 1685; ANP, Compañía, Títulos, leg. 3 (1628-1652).

74. For examples of the costs involved in building an *acequia*, see ANP, Aguas, leg. 1, cuad. 3.3.1.3 (1613-1618), cuad. 3.3.1.8 (1632), cuad. 3.3.1.11 (1639), Compañía, Títulos, leg. 3 (1628-1652), Títulos, leg. 3, cuad. 73 (1634). On land retention and the high price of developed farms in the Arequipa Valley, see chap. 6.

75. Those lent money who had relatives in the order or who had a close affiliation were Diego de Cáceres (and family), Francisco de Vergara, Sebastián de Monteagudo, Diego de Carvajal, Alvaro Fernández, Francisco de Almonte, and the Tapia family. Those with possible or more remote ties were Diego Martínez de Ribera, two members of the Mejía family, Martín Sánchez Rendón, Juan de Salazar, Juan Ruiz de León, Don Fernando de Ribera. For loans, see AMA, leg. 1 (10 December 1590, 16 August 1578, 25 September 1590, 11 December 1587, 20 September 1591, 6 March 1625, 2 April 1584, 5 June 1610), leg. 2 (20 October 1625), leg. 3 (18 February 1581), leg. 4 (15 September 1585, 24 April 1635), leg. 5 (29 October 1597, 16 January 1631, 15 December 1598, 23 August 1643), leg. 6 (20 April 1627, 21 February 1590). On relatives and affiliation to convent, see AMA, leg. 1 (27 April 1584, 12 December 1587), leg. 7 (28 August 1566); *SMF*, pp. 58-59, 124, 216, 274, 287, 412, 434; Echeverría y Morales, "Memoria," p. 27.

76. AMA, leg. 1 (7 May 1661); *SMF*, p. 32.

77. ADA, Aguilar, 18 November 1603, Antonio de Silva, 29 June 1657, Tejada, 13 March 1616; AMA, leg. 4 (18 April 1603).

78. AGI, Lima, leg., 11; BNP, ms. B478 (1633).

79. ADA, Muñoz, 29 November 1595, 10 March 1600, Tejada, 1 September 1612, Ufelde, 12 December 1616, Gordejuela, 1 February 1631, Diego de Silva, 1 May 1644, 12 May 1644, 19 July 1644, 6 September 1644, Laguna, 25 August 1648, 26 October 1648, Antonio de Silva, 22 September 1657, 6 October 1657; AMA, leg. 1 (25 September 1590); ANP, Real Hacienda, Arequipa (1646-1698), Compañia, Censos, leg. 1 (1567-1636).

80. For children of *heredados*, see *SMC*, pp. 146-151; *SMF*, pp. 88-91, 94, 124, 255-256, 290, 335; *SMG*, p. 90; *SMA*, pp. 38, 40, 80, 83; ADA, Muñoz, 12 January 1598, 29 September 1600, 12 October 1622, Tejada, 10 July 1612, 9 May 1615, Ufelde, 7 January 1616, 25 June 1616; ANP, Títulos, leg. 9, cuad. 265 (1623), Compañia, Títulos, leg. 3 (1628-1652).

81. For example, see Ugarte y Ugarte, "Memoria y cuentas"; and ADA, Hernández, 16 August 1570.

82. ADA, Diego Ortiz, 18 May 1594, 2 August 1594, Ufelde, 14 September 1595, 5 October 1595, 15 October 1595, 23 October 1595. Children could not become economically independent because of high land prices. A *chácara* sold for 450 to 500 pesos; a large, developed coastal estate commanded 18,000 to 19,000 pesos; a small *heredad* brought 1,500 pesos; and an olive grove on the coastal hills fetched 3,000 pesos. I discuss land prices in the Arequipa Valley in chap. 6.

83. AMA, leg. 3 (10 January 1665); ADA, Aguilar, 9 January 1598, 12 May 1603.

84. ADA, Ufelde, 14 September 1595, Muñoz, 22 March 1600, 29 September 1600, Aguilar, 12 May 1603, Tejada, 16 July 1615.

85. ADA, Ufelde, 30 August 1595, Aguilar, 20 January 1596, 26 April 1596, 14 April 1603, 16 June 1603, Muñoz, 22 March 1600; *SMF*, pp. 257, 337, 378; also see examples in AMA, legs. 1, 6, 7.

86. ADA, Aguilar, 17 October 1573, 5 May 1584, 18 May 1584, Ufelde, 23 October 1595, Diego Ortiz, 9 May 1594, 18 June 1594, 2 August 1594, Tejada, 12 December 1616, Muñoz, 21 March 1622; ANP, Compañia, Censos, leg. 1 (1567-1636).

87. ADA, Ufelde, October 1594, Aguilar, 14 April 1603, 19 April 1605, 19 June 1605, Tejada, 10 July 1612, Muñoz, 12 October 1622.

88. ADA, Aguilar, 5 May 1584, 16 June 1603, Tejada, 1 September 1612, Ufelde, 12 December 1616, Muñoz, 12 April 1622.

89. ADA, Aguilar, 18 November 1603, Ufelde, 22 August 1616, 25 October 1616, 19 November 1616, 12 December 1616, Francisco de Vera, 17 January 1622, April 1622; AMA, leg. 4 (18 April 1603).

90. ADA, Corregimiento (Civil), 1590-1599.

91. ADA, Aguilar, 18 November 1603, Tejada, 13 March 1616; AMA, leg. 1 (7 May 1661), leg. 4 (24 April 1635); ANP, Compañia, Títulos, leg. 1 (1539-1605).

92. AMA, leg. 5 (27 April 1627); ANP, Títulos, leg. 5, cuad. 150 (1662), Compañia, Títulos, leg. 3 (1628-1652). As might be assumed, lenders were reluctant

to reduce mortgages and thus, many who bought property had to accept the entire debt; see, for examples, AMA, leg. 4 (24 April 1635), leg. 8 (11 April 1623).

93. ADA, Aguilar, 19 June 1605, Tejada, 10 July 1612, Ufelde, 9 May 1615, Gordejuela, 15 March 1631, Diego de Silva, 13 February 1644, 14 January 1653.

94. ADA, Diego de Silva, 17 June 1654, 6 October 1657; ANP, Compañia, Títulos, leg. 1 (1539-1605).

95. ADA, Ufelde, 31 December 1595, Francisco de Vera, 9 February 1622.

96. ADA, Ufelde, 14 September 1595, 5 October 1595, Tejada, 16 January 1616, Francisco de Vera, 21 June 1622, Diego de Silva, 20 June 1654; ANP, Compañía, Títulos, leg. 1 (1539-1605), Títulos, leg. 1, cuad. 24 (1595); AMA, leg. 1 (7 April 1623, 7 May 1661), leg. 5 (17 April 1623); *SMF*, p. 425; AGI, Justicia, leg. 1187, leg. 1189.

97. ADA, Ufelde, 12 December 1616, Diego de Silva, 22 March 1644, 25 September 1644; ANP, Compañia, Títulos, leg. 3 (1628-1652); AGI, Justicia, leg. 1189, leg. 1190.

98. ADA, Diego Ortiz, 9 August 1594, Tejada, 1 September 1612, 16 March 1615, 8 July 1615, Diego de Silva, 17 June 1654, 23 October 1654; AMA, leg. 1 (6 March 1625), leg. 6 (17 November 1620), leg. 7 (15 July 1658); ANP, Compañia, Títulos, leg. 1 (1539-1605).

99. ADA, Gordejuela, 1 February 1631, Antonio de Silva, 6 October 1657, 12 December 1657, Diego de Silva, 1 May 1644, 12 May 1644, 4 September 1644; ANP, Compañía, Títulos, leg. 3 (1628-1652), Títulos, leg. 5, cuad. 12 (1643).

100. *SMC*, pp. 147-151; ADA, Aguilar, 12 January 1598.

101. ANP, Títulos, leg. 9, cuad. 265 (1623); *SMF*, pp. 125-126; AMA, leg. 4 (24 April 1635).

102. ADA, Diego de Silva, 18 September 1653, 24 September 1653, 18 February 1654, Antonio de Silva, 4 June 1657; ANP, Compañía, Títulos, leg. 2 (1606-1628), leg. 3 (1628-1652), Títulos, leg. 5, cuad. 150 (1662); BNP, ms. B1687 (1673); AMA, leg. 5 (17 April 1623).

103. David A. Brading and Harry E. Cross, "Colonial Silver Mining: Mexico and Peru," *HAHR* 52 (November 1972):545-579; Peter J. Bakewell, "Registered Silver Production in the Potosí District, 1550-1735"; and idem, "Technological Change in Potosí: The Silver Boom of the 1570s," in *Jahrbuch für Geschichte von Staat, Wirtschaft und Gesellshaft Lateinamerikas*, 30 vols. (Cologne: Böhlau Verlag, 1964-1979), pp. 12:67-103, and 14:57-77, respectively; Maria Encarnación Rodríguez Vicente, "Los caudales remitidos desde el Perú a España por cuenta de la Real Hacienda. Series estadísticas (1651-1739)," *Anuario de Estudios Americanos* 21 (1964):1-24.

104. Peter J. Bakewell, *Silver Mining and Society in Colonial Mexico, Zacatecas 1546-1700*, Cambridge Latin American Studies, no. 15 (Cambridge: At the University Press, 1971); Frederick P. Bowser, *The African Slave in Colonial Peru 1524-1650* (Stanford, Cal.: Stanford University Press, 1974), esp. chap. 3.

105. Cushner, *Lords of the Land*, pp. 125-134, 164-171; Keith, *Conquest*, pp. 80-129. On Central America, see Murdo J. MacLeod, *Spanish Central America: A*

Socioeconomic History, 1520-1720 (Berkeley & Los Angeles: University of California Press, 1973), parts 2 and 3. For other regions, see, for example, Peter Marzahl, *Town in the Empire: Government, Politics, and Society in Seventeenth-Century Popayán*, Latin American Monographs, no. 45 (Austin, Tex.: Institute of Latin American Studies, 1978); Manuel Burga, *De la encomienda a la hacienda capitalista: El valle del Jequetepeque del siglo XVI al XX*, Estudios de la sociedad rural, no. 4 (Lima: Instituto de Estudios Peruanos, 1976); and Marta Espejo-Ponce Hunt, "The Process of the Development of Yucatan, 1600-1700," and John C. Super, "The Agricultural Near North: Querétaro in the Seventeenth Century," in *Provinces of Early Mexico: Variants of Spanish American Regional Evolution*, ed. Ida Altman and James Lockhart, pp. 32-62, and 230-251, respectively (Los Angeles: UCLA Latin American Center Publications, 1976).

Chapter 6. Colonial Expansion into the Indian Southwest

1. Reginaldo de Lizárraga, *Descripción breve de toda la tierra del Perú, Tucumán, Río de la Plata y Chile*, Biblioteca de Autores Españoles, no. 216 (Madrid: Atlas, 1968), pp. 46-50; Antonio Vázquez de Espinosa, *Compendio y descripción de las Indias Occidentales*, Biblioteca de Autores Españoles, no. 231 (Madrid: Atlas, 1969), pp. 334-350; Boleslao Lewin, ed., *Descripción del virreinato del Perú: Crónica inédita de comienzos del siglo XVII*, Colección de Textos y Documentos, series B, no. 1 (Rosario: Instituto de Investigaciones Históricas, 1958), pp. 92, 104-105; José de Acosta, *Obras*, Biblioteca de Autores Españoles, no. 73 (Madrid: Atlas, 1954), pp. 298-301.

2. Luis Urzúa Urzúa, *Arica, puerta nueva: Historia y folklore*, 2d ed. (Santiago de Chile: Editorial Andrés Bello, 1964), pp. 21, 45; AGI, Lima, leg. 116.

3. Rómulo Cúneo-Vidal, "El cacicazgo de Tacna," *Revista Histórica* 6 (1919):309-310, 316; Noble David Cook, "The Indian Population of Peru, 1570-1620" (Ph.D. diss., University of Texas at Austin, 1973), pp. 353-354; and compare *BDA*, 2:84-86, with AGI, Contaduría, leg. 1786, leg. 1822, Lima, leg. 464.

4. ANP, Juicios de Residencia, leg. 1, cuad. 2 (1580); ADA, Aguilar, 5 January 1575.

5. MNH, Visita de la Villa de Camaná, 1592.

6. Ibid. Here and throughout the chapter measures are given in acres; in the originals measures were given in *fanegadas*. See table 1 for conversions (BNP, ms. A561 [1585]; ANP, Tribunal de Cuentas, Real Hacienda, Composiciones, Tierras y Indígenas, leg. 5, cuad. 22 [1644]).

7. Cúneo-Vidal, "Cacicazgo," pp. 314-318.

8. AGI, Lima, leg. 135, leg. 199, leg. 200, Justicia, leg. 480; ANP, Juicios de Residencia, leg. 5, cuad. 9 (1584); "Relación de la provincia de los Collaguas para la discrepción de las Indias que su magestad manda hacer," in *Relaciones geográficas de Indias-Perú*, ed. Marcos Jiménez de la Espada, 3 vols., Biblioteca de Autores Españoles, nos. 183-185 (Madrid: Atlas, 1965), p. 1:332.

9. ANP, Juicios de Residencia, leg. 10, cuad. 25 (1593), leg. 17, cuad. 46 (1600), leg. 21, cuads. 53-55 (1610); BNP, ms. A54 (1591), ms. B1351 (1600), ms. B1109 (1601).

10. ANP, Juicios de Residencia, leg. 17, cuad. 46 (1600), leg. 21, cuad. 55 (1610).

11. Alejandro Málaga Medina, "Los Collaguas en la historia de Arequipa en el siglo XVI," in *Collaguas I*, ed. Franklin Pease G. Y., pp. 97-110 (Lima: P. L. Villanueva for Pontificia Universidad Católica del Perú, 1977); "Relación de la provincia de los Collaguas," p. 329.

12. ANP, Tierras de Comunidades, leg. 10, cuad. 86 (1792).

13. ANP, Juicios de Residencia, leg. 17, cuad. 46 (1600), leg. 21, cuad. 53 (1610), Derecho Indígena y Encomiendas, leg. 6, cuad. 121 (1648); "Visita de Yanquecollaguas (Urinsaya) (1519)," in Pease, *Collaguas I*, pp. 191-406.

14. ANP, Juicios de Residencia, leg. 21, cuad. 55 (1610), Derecho Indígena y Encomiendas, leg. 20, cuad. 494 (1790).

15. ANP, Juicios de Residencia, leg. 17, cuad. 46 (1600); "Visita de Yanquecollaguas," pp. 192-238.

16. ANP, Juicios de Residencia, leg. 4, cuad. 8 (1583-1598), leg. 5, cuad. 9 (1584), leg. 9, cuad. 22 (1591), leg. 33, cuad. 93 (1646).

17. ANP, Juicios de Residencia, leg. 9, cuad. 22 (1591), leg. 33, cuad. 93 (1646); AGI, Lima, leg. 309, Indiferente General, leg. 1660.

18. "Relación de la provincia de los Collaguas," p. 331; ANP, Juicios de Residencia, leg. 9, cuad. 22 (1591), Derecho Indígena y Encomiendas, leg. 6, cuad. 121 (1648); Cook, "The Indian Population," p. 366; "Visita de Yanquecollaguas," pp. 264-292.

19. "Visita de Yanquecollaguas," pp. 192-260. For Indian population trends, see chap. 3, note 35.

20. ANP, Juicios de Residencia, leg. 9, cuad. 22 (1591).

21. BNP, ms. A377 (1594), ms. A459 (1597), ms. A313 (1598), ms. A245 (1599); ANP, Juicios de Residencia, leg. 10, cuad. 25 (1593); AMuA, LAS, libro 7 (23 August 1591).

22. An exception was Francisco de Castellanos, who bought land from a *corregidor* of Condesuyos. The sale was denied by the royal government and his money returned (AGI, Contaduría, leg. 1703).

23. ADA, Tejada, 24 July 1612, 5 April 1615, 21 July 1615, Ufelde, 9 April 1616, 22 April 1616, 2 May 1616.

24. AMuA, LAS, libro 9 (13 March 1602), libro 11 (10 October 1612, 11 December 1615).

25. See chaps. 1 and 2; AMuA, LAS, libro 7 (13 August 1590).

26. AMA, leg. 6 (25 September 1599); ADA, Hernández, 10 May 1570, 20 May 1570, 15 July 1570, 18 August 1570, Diego Ortiz, 18 May 1594, 2 August 1594, Muñoz, 4 June 1622.

27. BNP, ms. A171 (1555), ms. A595 (1559), ms. Z1264 (1562); AMA, leg. 6 (26 November 1586); ADA, Aguilar, 19 September 1591.

28. AMA, leg. 1 (22 February 1583), leg. 4 (17 April 1595); ADA, Tejada, 23 October 1614, Muñoz, 17 June 1622.

29. ADA, Hernández, March 1568, 26 April 1568, May 1568, 4 June 1568, Juan

de Vera, 28 February 1571, Aguilar, 23 June 1575, 4 July 1575, Herrera, 14 October 1575.

30. Alejandro Málaga Medina, *Visita general del Perú por el Virrey D. Francisco de Toledo, 1570-1575* (Arequipa: El Sol, 1974), pp. 13-14; idem, "Las reducciones en el Perú (1532-1600)," *Historia y Cultura* 8 (1974):141-172; Eduardo L. Ugarte y Ugarte, ed., "Ordenanzas reales hechas para Arequipa y sus provincias por el señor dn. Francisco de Toledo en 2 de noviembre de 1575" (unpublished, Arequipa, n.d.); ADA, Tejada, 24 July 1612, 15 January 1616; AMuA, LAS, libro 6 (10 December 1586); ANP, Derecho Indígena y Encomiendas, leg. 23, cuad. 625 (1606).

31. ADA, Diego Ortiz, 20 June 1594; AGI, Lima, leg. 166; ANP, Tribunal de Cuentas, Real Hacienda, Composiciones, Tierras y Indigenas, leg. 5, cuad. 24 (1644).

32. ADA, Herrera, 15 October 1575, 16 November 1575.

33. ADA, Diego Ortiz, 3 February 1595; ANP, Títulos, leg. 25, cuad. 662 (1612); MNH, Visita de la Villa de Camaná, 1592.

34. The Indian *originario* population appears to have been halved between 1575 and 1600 (see AGI, Contaduría, leg. 1822).

35. AMuA, LAS, libro 6 (21 September 1589, 26 December 1589), libro 7 (30 June 1590, 13 August 1590, 17 September 1591, 26 February 1592, 17 February 1593, 13 March 1593), libro 8 (19 February 1594), 27 February 1594, libro 11 (21 March 1617).

36. AGI, Lima, leg. 116.

37. Several sources suggest that the non-Indian population barely grew between 1575 and 1600: AGI, Lima, leg. 111; Vázquez de Espinosa, *Compendio*, p. 338; Ralph A. Gakenheimer, "The Peruvian City of the Sixteenth Century," in *The Urban Explosion in Latin America: A Continent in Process of Modernization*, ed. Glenn H. Beyer, p. 47 (Ithaca, N.Y.: Cornell University Press, 1967).

38. AGI, Justicia, leg. 1186, leg, 1188, leg. 1190, Lima, leg. 309.

39. AMuA, LAS, libro 6 (10 December 1586), libro 8 (23 April 1597), libro 10 (15 February 1605), libro 12 (30 July 1627, 14 October 1628), libro 13 (31 October 1634), libro 14 (22 September 1642).

40. AMuA, LAS, libro 11 (1 August 1614, 31 December 1617); AMA, leg. 1 (24 April 1584).

41. AMuA, LAS, libro 10 (28 October 1604), libro 11 (18 February 1612, 1 June 1612, 11 March 1613), libro 12 (30 July 1627); ADA, Aguilar, 5 March 1603, 23 January 1604, 16 August 1604; AMA, leg. 6 (6 April 1611); Francisco Xavier Echeverría y Morales, "Memoria de la Santa Iglesia de Arequipa," in *BMHA*, 4:92.

42. AMuA, LAS, libro 12 (4 July 1625), libro 13 (8 July 1636).

43. AGI, Contaduría, legs. 1699-1704, 1822.

44. ADA, Aguilar, 31 July 1603, Tejada, 24 July 1612, 23 October 1614, 21 July 1615, 7 January 1616, 22 April 1616, 2 May 1616, 12 December 1616.

45. Eduardo L. Ugarte y Ugarte, ed., "Guasacache" (unpublished, Arequipa, n.d.); ADA, Diego Ortiz, 3 February 1595.

46. ADA, Aguilar, 5 March 1603, 12 May 1603, 9 August 1604, Ufelde, 2 May 1616, Tejada, 24 July 1612, 21 July 1615, Muñoz, 7 February 1622, 12 April 1622, Gordejuela, 14 May 1631, 10 September 1631, 22 February 1636, 10 March 1636, 31 December 1636.
47. ANP, Aguas, leg. 1, cuad. 3.3.1.3 (1613-1618), cuad. 3.3.1.8 (1632), cuad. 3.3.1.11 (1639), Compañia, Titulos, leg. 3 (1628-1652), Titulos, leg. 3, cuad. 73 (1634); *MP*, 1:328-331.
48. AMuA, LAS, libro 11 (12 January 1618).
49. AGI, Contaduria, leg. 1786, leg. 1822, Lima, leg. 116; ANP, Real Hacienda, Arequipa (1646-1698); ADA, Ufelde, 2 June 1610, Tejada, 9 May 1615, Francisco de Vera, 13 March 1622.
50. BNP, ms. B415 (1603), ms. B140 (1608); AGI, Lima, leg. 573; AMuA, LAS, libro 11 (31 October 1612, 7 August 1615, 11 December 1615), libro 12 (1 July 1623).
51. AGI, Lima, leg. 111, leg. 572; AMuA, LAS, libro 11 (22 May 1612, 26 July 1613, 11 April 1614, 8 June 1616), libro 12 (26 October 1625, 4 November 1625, 10 February 1626), libro 14 (6 May 1642, 5 June 1642), libro 15 (11 October 1655, 23 March 1656).
52. ANP, Derecho Indigena y Encomiendas, leg. 6, cuad. 1212 (1648), Juicios de Residencia, leg. 21, cuad. 53, cuad. 55 (1610); BNP, ms. B1109 (1601).
53. ANP, Juicios de Residencia, leg. 17, cuad. 46 (1600); AMuA, libro 12 (21 October 1622); AGI, Lima, leg. 95, leg. 571, leg. 573.
54. ANP, Derecho Indigena y Encomiendas, leg. 4, cuad. 67 (1618), leg. 23, cuad. 63 (1620); BNP, ms. B415 (1603), ms. B857 (1646); ADA, Tejada, 15 April 1615, Diego de Silva, 13 November 1653.
55. AGI, Lima, leg. 34, leg. 309, leg. 571; AMA, leg. 4 (7 November 1657), leg. 6 (5 November 1575); ANP, Real Hacienda, Arequipa (1646-1698); ADA, Ufelde, 9 April 1616.
56. AMuA, LAS, libro 12 (March 1626, 4 October 1626).
57. AGI, Contaduria, leg. 1730, leg. 1734, Indiferente General, leg. 1660; ADA, Diego de Silva, 12 May 1644.
58. ANP, Tribunal de Cuentas, Real Hacienda, Composiciones, Tierras y Indigenas, leg. 5, cuad. 24 (1644); AGI, Indiferente General, leg. 429, leg. 1660, Lima, leg. 166, leg. 573.
59. AGI, Indiferente General, leg. 1660, Lima, leg. 53, leg. 166, leg. 572, leg. 573.
60. ANP, Real Hacienda, Arequipa (1646-1698), Titulos, leg. 3, cuad. 75 (1651), Tribunal de Cuentas, Real Hacienda, Composiciones, Tierras y Indigenas, leg. 5, cuad. 25 (1654-1659); BNP, ms. B857 (1646).
61. ANP, Titulos, leg. 3, cuad. 75 (1651), Tribunal de Cuentas, Real Hacienda, Composiciones, Tierras y Indigenas, leg. 5, cuad. 25 (1654-1659); AMA, leg. 4 (7 November 1657).
62. AGI, Contaduria, leg. 1747, leg. 1754A, Justicia, leg. 568B, Indiferente General, leg. 1660, Lima, leg. 573; ANP, Real Hacienda, Arequipa (1646-1698),

Compañía, Títulos, leg. 3 (1628-1652), Títulos, leg. 3, cuad. 75 (1651).

63. AGI, Indiferente General, leg. 1660; ADA, Diego de Silva, 14 April 1644, 15 April 1644, 29 April 1644, 14 May 1644, 27 May 1644, 29 May 1644.

64. AGI, Contaduría, leg. 1730, leg. 1732; ADA, Diego de Silva, 15 April 1644, 20 April 1644, 27 October 1644; ANP, Real Hacienda, Arequipa (1646-1698).

65. ADA, Gordejuela, 23 April 1636, 1 August 1636, 19 August 1636, Diego de Silva, 8 April 1644, 26 April 1644, 11 July 1644, 27 July 1644, Laguna, 13 March 1648, 22 March 1648, 4 September 1648, Antonio de Silva, 26 December 1656, 10 July 1657, 22 September 1657, 8 October 1657, 13 October 1657.

66. ADA, Díez, 10 February 1663, 21 April 1664, 5 November 1664, 24 June 1665, 23 November 1673, Laguna, 20 April 1675, 6 May 1675, 9 May 1685, 10 November 1685; ANP, Aguas, leg. 3, cuad. 3.3.58 (1743).

67. Cúneo-Vidal, "Cacicazgo," pp. 309-316; *BDA*, 1:40-41; AGI, Contaduría, leg. 1776, Lima, leg. 309; Cook, "The Indian Population," p. 354.

68. *SMF*, pp. 56, 343; ADA, Hernández, 6 February 1570.

69. *SMF*, pp. 56-57, 425.

70. Vázquez de Espinosa, *Compendio*, pp. 344-345; *SMF*, pp. 125-126, 226, 284, 352.

71. AGI, Lima, leg. 116; Urzúa Urzúa, *Arica*, pp. 45, 84-103; *SMF*, pp. 72-73.

72. AGI, Justicia, leg. 568A.

73. ANP, Tribunal de Cuentas, Real Hacienda, Composiciones, Tierras y Indígenas, leg. 5, cuad. 9 (1643); AGI, Lima, leg. 100, Justicia, leg. 568A, leg. 568B; BNP, ms. B857 (1646).

74. See previous chapter.

75. ANP, Ministerio de Hacienda, leg. 1, cuad. 1 (1620); AGI, Indiferente General, leg. 1660.

76. Salvador Rodríguez Amézquita, *Monografía de la Villa de Pampacolca* (Arequipa: Miranda, 1971), pp. 50-51.

77. ANP, Títulos, leg. 3, cuad. 87 (1646); AGI, Contaduría, leg. 1731.

78. AGI, Indiferente General, leg. 1660.

79. Ibid.; ANP, Compañía, Censos, leg. 1 (1567-1636), Títulos, leg. 3, cuad. 87 (1646).

80. AGI, Lima, leg. 116, leg. 200, Indiferente General, leg. 1660, Justicia, leg. 1189, leg. 1190, Contaduría, leg. 1822; ADA, Tejada, 15 May 1614, Diego de Silva, 5 January 1644, 11 June 1644; ANP, Compañía, Títulos, leg. 1 (1539-1605), Títulos, leg. 1, cuad. 14 (1583); AMA, leg. 6 (13 May 1626); *SMF*, pp. 239, 341.

81. ANP, Derecho Indígena y Encomiendas, leg. 6, cuad. 121 (1648). For similar concern by *curacas*, see ANP, Compañía, Censos, leg. 1 (1567-1636).

82. Charles Gibson, *The Aztecs under Spanish Rule: A History of the Indians of the Valley of Mexico, 1519-1810* (Stanford, Cal.: Stanford University Press, 1964), chap. 10, esp. p. 277.

83. William B. Taylor, *Landlord and Peasant in Colonial Oaxaca* (Stanford, Cal.: Stanford University Press,, 1972), pp. 113-121.

84. François Chevalier, *Land and Society in Colonial Mexico: The Great*

Hacienda, trans. Alvin Eustis, ed. Lesley Byrd Simpson (Berkeley & Los Angeles: University of California Press, 1966), chap. 8; Murdo J. MacLeod, *Spanish Central America: A Socioeconomic History, 1520-1720* (Berkeley & Los Angeles: University of California Press, 1973), pp. 222-224; Manuel Burga, *De la encomienda a la hacienda capitalista: El valle del Jequetepeque del siglo XVI al XX*, Estudios de la sociedad rural, no. 4 (Lima: Instituto de Estudios Peruanos, 1976), pp. 96-102; Taylor, *Colonial Oaxaca,* pp. 6-7, 61, 102. Magnus Mörner, *Historia social latinoamericana (Nuevos enfoques),* Colección Manoa of the Universidad Católica Andrés Bello (Caracas: Arte, 1979), pp. 129-136, suggests that the importance of the land reviews carried out after 1641 should not be generalized.

85. Taylor, *Colonial Oaxaca*, pp. 195-202; Robert G. Keith, *Conquest and Agrarian Change: The Emergence of the Hacienda System on the Peruvian Coast*, Harvard Historical Studies, no. 93 (Cambridge, Mass.: Harvard University Press, 1976), chaps. 4 and 5. For an early eighteenth-century example of modest and dispersed holdings, see David A. Brading, *Haciendas and Ranchos in the Mexican Bajío: León 1700-1860*, Cambridge Latin American Studies, no. 32 (Cambridge: At the University Press, 1978), pp. 61-63.

Chapter 7. Land and Society in Seventeenth-Century Arequipa

1. Eduardo L. Ugarte y Ugarte, ed., "Memoria y cuentas de Da. Juana Muñiz, vecina de Arequipa, sobre sus nietos hijos de Miguel Cornejo, 1570-1571" (unpublished, Arequipa, n.d.); ADA, Aguilar, 3 February 1584.

2. Ibid.; ADA, Hernández, 29 March 1570, 6 November 1570, Aguilar, 27 January 1584, 1 April 1584, 11 July 1584, 15 July 1584; *SMF*, p. 170.

3. *SMF*, pp. 61-76, 267-305.

4. See, for example, ibid., pp. 65-66.

5. *SMG*, pp. 42-43, 62-63; AMuA, LAS, libros 3-6.

6. *SMA*, pp. 43-61; AMuA, LAS, libros 3-6.

7. J. H. Parry, *The Sale of Public Office in the Spanish Indies under the Hapsburgs* (Berkeley & Los Angeles: University of California Press, 1953); ADA, Diego de Silva, 25 September 1644, Ufelde, 14 September 1595, 16 January 1616; Victor M. Barriga, ed., *Los terremotos en Arequipa, 1582-1868* (Arequipa: La Colmena, 1951), p. 88; AGI, Lima, leg. 111. As noted previously, later in life Félix de Herrera would become a "don."

8. Francisco Xavier Echeverría y Morales, "Memoria de la Santa Iglesia de Arequipa," in *BMHA*, 4:25-39; *SMF*, pp. 32, 132-136, 199-200, 339; AGI, Lima, leg. 95, leg. 111.

9. Barriga, *Terremotos*, pp. 24-26, 30, 35-36, 44-46, 51; Echeverría y Morales, "Memoria," pp. 21-23; AGI, Patronato, leg. 5, docs. 15, 26.

10. AMA, leg. 1 (26 September 1583, 11 December 1587, 5 June 1610).

11. ANP, Títulos, leg. 6, cuad. 155 (1600), leg. 3, cuad. 73 (1634), leg. 6, cuad. 171 (1643).

12. *SMF*, pp. 115, 340; Echeverría y Morales, "Memoria," pp. 35-36.

13. *SMF*, pp. 12, 28-29, 58-59, 74, 125, 301-304, 309, 337, 340; AGI, Lima, leg. 95; ADA, Aguilar, 5 May 1584. The five families were Peralta Cabeza de Vaca, Alvarez de Carmona, Pizarro, Salazar, and Almonte. Families without children in the church were Hernández de la Cuba, de León, Herrera, Cárdenas, and Ruiz de León. Information gained from ADA, assorted notaries, and *SMF*, pp. 65-71, 267-305 passim, 339-341.

14. AGI, Lima, leg. 94; ANP, Juicios de Residencia, leg. 5, cuad. 9 (1584), Títulos, leg. 1, cuad. 14 (1583), cuad. 24 (1595); ADA, Juan de Vera, 1 August 1571, Aguilar, 7 July 1575, 30 July 1591, 19 August 1591, 8 January 1596, Diego Ortiz, 18 May 1594, 18 June 1594, 18 May 1596, Muñoz, 15 November 1600; *SMF*, pp. 19-55.

15. The families were de la Torre, Cáceres y Solier, Peralta Cabeza de Vaca, Bueno, Alvarez de Carmona, Cornejo, and Ruiz de León (*SMF*, pp. 19, 41-52, 88-90, 210-216, 274-281, 340-347, 430-436).

16. Elinor C. Burkett, "Early Colonial Peru: The Urban Female Experience" (Ph.D. diss., University of Pittsburgh, 1975), esp. p. 143.

17. *SMF*, pp. 274-281; ADA, Muñoz, 22 March 1600, Aguilar, 14 April 1603, 16 June 1603.

18. John Preston Moore, *The Cabildo in Peru under the Hapsburgs: A Study in the Origins and Powers of the Town Council in the Viceroyalty of Peru, 1530-1700* (Durham, N.C.: Duke University Press, 1954), esp. chap. 17.

19. AGI, Justicia, leg. 1189.

20. ACA, Francisca de Cabrera, viuda de Juan de Siles de Casillas, sobre el trabajo de su esposo, 6 April 1672.

21. Moore, *Cabildo*, pp. 96, 267-268; AGI, Lima, leg. 111.

22. *SMA*, pp. 9-39, 105-131.

23. BNP, ms. B1687 (1673). For examples of the expanded use of "don" and "doña," see ADA, Diego de Silva, 13 February 1644, 17 February 1644, 26 February 1644, 26 April 1644, 28 April 1644, 12 May 1644, 14 May 1644, 18 May 1644, 1 June 1644, 9 July 1644, 2 October 1644.

24. *SMF*, pp. 290-292, 311; AGI, Justicia, leg. 965, Contaduría, leg. 1822.

25. *SMF*, pp. 126, 280-281.

26. Ibid., pp. 84-117; *SMC*, pp. 148-149.

27. ADA, Aguilar, 19 April 1605; ANP, Compañia, Censos, leg. 1 (1567-1636).

28. *SMA*, pp. 49, 70, 80-82, 88, 102-104, 108-109, 118, 126, 133-134, 140-141; *SMF*, pp. 22, 31, 33, 58, 119, 125-126, 181, 226, 231, 276; ANP, Compañía, Títulos, leg. 3 (1628-1652); ADA, Gordejuela, 10 March 1636; AMA, leg. 1 (7 May 1661); AGI, Contaduría, leg. 230, leg. 1822, Justicia, leg. 965.

29. *SMA*, pp. 88, 133; *SMF*, p. 288; ADA, Diego de Silva, 14 June 1644, 23 July 1644, 30 August 1644, 23 October 1654, Gordejuela, 18 August 1636, Díez, 14 March 1664; AMA, leg. 1 (7 May 1661); Guillermo Lohmann Villena, *Los americanos en las órdenes nobiliarias (1529-1900)*, 2 vols. (Madrid: Artes Gráficas, 1947), p. 2:281.

30. Naturally, a few exceptional individuals managed it still. See, for example,

ADA, Ufelde, 25 June 1616.

31. On the royal government's land auctions, see chap. 6.

32. Men like Don Diego de Benavides and Juan de Adriasola do not appear to have brought relatives, at least not in the numbers that earlier functionaries had. Yet, some officials still encouraged their relatives to emigrate; see, for example, *SMF*, p. 31. The change was one of degree.

33. *SMF*, p. 292. However, some dowries, such as that of Doña Juana Dávila Pizarro (30,000 pesos), could be impressive.

34. Ibid., pp. 42-43, 275, 434-436.

35. All offspring of the fourteen landowning families are not included after the first period. Instead, one descendant of each family was selected in the second and third periods, and the children's marriages tallied.

36. *SMF*, pp. 52, 119, 412.

37. Ibid., pp. 36, 94, 274-281; AGI, Lima, leg. 94; ADA, Muñoz, 12 April 1622.

38. AMA, leg. 1 (25 September 1590); *SMA*, pp. 55-56, 87; *SMG*, p. 57; ANP, Compañía, Títulos, leg. 1 (1539-1605), Compañía, Censos, leg. 1 (1567-1636); ADA, Juan de Vera, February 1571, Ufelde, 23 August 1616.

39. ANP, Compañía, Títulos, leg. 3 (1628-1652); BNP, ms. B1529 (1619); ADA, Aguilar, 10 March 1584, Ufelde, 26 October 1595, Muñoz, 29 March 1596, Aguilar, 9 January 1598, 17 March 1603; *SMC*, pp. 148-150; *SMG*, p. 90; Lohmann Villena, *Americanos*, p. 2:124.

40. *SMF*, pp. 333-334; ADA, Diego Ortiz, 20 June 1594, Francisco de Vera, 4 June 1622; ANP, Archivo de Temporalidades, Expedientes sobre Títulos de Propiedad, Chiquita, Arequipa.

41. *SMF*, pp. 30-33, 41, 44-45, 48-49, 51-52, 119-120, 226, 230-231, 280-281, 288-293, 312, 335, 344, 416-419, 424-426, 443-434, 436, 443-444; *SMA*, pp. 73-74, 78, 82, 88, 96-97, 99-100, 106, 108-109, 113-116, 118-120, 124-128, 130, 133-145; *SMC*, pp. 72-73, 146-151; ADA, Gordejuela, 2 September 1636, Diego de Silva, 12 May 1644, 8 November 1644, 9 July 1653, 12 November 1653, 14 January 1654, 18 February 1654, Antonio de Silva, 12 July 1657, 6 October 1657, Laguna, 13 January 1638, 25 August 1648, 1 February 1675, Diez, 2 December 1666, 16 September 1673; ANP, Real Hacienda, Arequipa (1646-1698), Compañía, Censos, leg. 2 (1636-1670), Compañía, Títulos, leg. 3 (1628-1652), Títulos, leg. 4, cuad. 96 (1665), leg. 5, cuads. 12, 13 (1644); AMA, leg. 1 (6 March 1625), leg. 4 (24 April 1635), leg. 6 (12 May 1656).

42. *SMF*, pp. 89, 120-121, 344; *SMA*, pp. 89, 107, 120.

43. Countless examples could be cited; see *SMA*, index.

44. Lohmann Villena, *Americanos*, pp. 2:103-104, 124-125. For other examples of persons in this select group, see ibid., pp. 1:235, 2:87-88, 211-212. A few born in Arequipa, descendants of government officials who resided temporarily in the city, can be found in ibid., pp. 2:82-83, 199-200.

45. Ibid., 2:23-24; *SMF*, pp. 42-43, 279.

46. AMA, leg. 6 (3 January 1583).

47. ADA, Muñoz, 17 November 1600, Tejada, 6 July 1612; AMA, leg. 1 (7 May

1661).

48. AMA, leg. 5 (27 April 1627).

49. ADA, Aguilar, 15 October 1604; AMA, leg. 7 (11 April 1623). See also table 5.

50. *SMF*, pp. 170, 211; AMA, leg. 3 (20 September 1591), leg. 5 (27 April 1627); ADA, Francisco de Vera, 9 February 1622, Gordejuela, 31 March 1636, 31 December 1636.

51. ADA, Aguilar, 18 November 1603, 19 June 1605, Tejada, 10 July 1612, 22 August 1616, Ufelde, 25 June 1616, Muñoz, 7 February 1622, Gordejuela, 31 March 1636, Diego de Silva, 17 July 1644; *SMF*, pp. 169, 207; AMA, leg. 5 (27 April 1627); ANP, Compañia, Títulos, leg. 3 (1628-1652), Compañia, Censos, leg. 1 (1567-1636), Títulos, leg. 3, cuad. 74 (1651).

52. ANP, Títulos, leg. 3, cuad. 87 (1646).

53. See chap. 6; and John Frederick Wibel, "The Evolution of a Regional Community within Spanish Empire and Peruvian Nation: Arequipa, 1780-1845" (Ph.D. diss., Stanford University, 1975), chaps. 3 and 4, passim.

54. Salvador Rodríguez Amézquita, *Monografía de la Villa de Pampacolca* (Arequipa: Miranda, 1971), esp. pp. 29-49.

55. *SMA*, p. 95; Reginaldo de Lizárraga, *Descripción breve de toda la tierra del Perú, Tucumán, Río de la Plata y Chile*, Biblioteca de Autores Españoles, no. 216 (Madrid: Atlas, 1968), p. 48.

56. For a major source on which some rely for their characterization of landed elites, see François Chevalier, *Land and Society in Colonial Mexico: The Great Hacienda*, trans. Alvin Eustis, ed. Lesley Byrd Simpson (Berkeley & Los Angeles: University of California Press, 1966). Conditions similar to those that prevailed in Arequipa can be found described in various essays of Ida Altman and James Lockhart, eds. *Provinces of Early Mexico: Variants of Spanish American Regional Evolution* (Los Angeles: UCLA Latin American Center, 1976).

57. Several historians have suggested that landholding was quite unstable in colonial America: William B. Taylor, *Landlord and Peasant in Colonial Oaxaca* (Stanford, Cal.: Stanford University Press, 1972), pp. 158-163; Nicholas P. Cushner, *Lords of the Land: Sugar, Wine, and Jesuit Estates of Coastal Peru, 1600-1767* (Albany: State University of New York Press, 1980), chap. 2, esp. p. 51. David A. Brading discussed a similar pattern during the eighteenth century in Mexico: see *Haciendas and Ranchos in the Mexican Bajío: León, 1700-1860* (Cambridge: At the University Press, 1978), chap. 6 and table 32.

Conclusion

1. The classic treatments of the first interpretation are François Chevalier, *Land and Society in Colonial Mexico: The Great Hacienda*, trans. Alvin Eustis, ed. Lesley Byrd Simpson (Berkeley & Los Angeles: University of California Press, 1966); and Woodrow Borah, *New Spain's Century of Depression*, Ibero-Americana Series, no. 35 (Berkeley & Los Angeles: University of California Press, 1951). For some statements and use of the newer interpretation, see Lockhart's introduction in

Ida Altman and James Lockhart, eds., *Provinces of Early Mexico: Variants of Spanish American Regional Evolution* (Los Angeles: UCLA Latin American Center, 1976); Herman W. Konrad, *A Jesuit Hacienda in Colonial Mexico: Santa Lucía, 1576-1767* (Stanford, Cal.: Stanford University Press, 1980); Eric Van Young, *Hacienda and Market in Eighteenth-Century Mexico: The Rural Economy of the Guadalajara Region, 1675-1820* (Berkeley & Los Angeles: University of California Press, 1981); Enrique Florescano, *Precios del maíz y crisis agrícolas en México (1708-1810)*, (Mexico City: El Colegio de México, 1969).

2. Murdo J. MacLeod, *Spanish Central America: A Socioeconomic History, 1520-1720* (Berkeley & Los Angeles: University of California Press, 1973), Magnus Mörner, *Perfil de la sociedad rural del Cuzco a fines de la colonia* (Lima: Universidad del Pacífico, 1978), chap. 5.

3. Charles Gibson, *The Aztecs under Spanish Rule: A History of the Indians of the Valley of Mexico, 1519-1810* (Stanford, Cal.: Stanford University Press, 1964).

4. Mario Góngora, *Encomenderos y estancieros: Estudios acerca de la constitución social aristocrática de Chile después de la conquista, 1580-1660* (Santiago de Chile: Editorial Universitaria, 1970).

5. Manuel Belaúnde Guinassi, *La encomienda en el Perú* (Lima: Mercurio Peruano, 1945); Virgilio Roel, *Historia social y económica de la colonia* (Lima: Gráfica Labor, 1970).

6. An exception is the work of Mario Góngora: see especially his *Encomenderos*. Details on mid-colonial people can be found in Peter Marzahl, *Town in the Empire: Government, Politics, and Society in Seventeenth-Century Popayán*, Latin American Monographs, no. 45 (Austin, Tex.: Institute of Latin American Studies, 1978).

7. John Frederick Wibel, "The Evolution of a Regional Community within Spanish Empire and Peruvian Nation: Arequipa, 1780-1845" (Ph.D. diss., Stanford University, 1975).

8. James Lockhart has established this point for the early colonial period. See *Spanish Peru, 1532-1560: A Colonial Society* (Madison: University of Wisconsin Press, 1968), and *The Men of Cajamarca: A Social and Biographical Study of the First Conquerors of Peru*, Latin American Monographs, no. 27 (Austin: University of Texas Press for the Institute of Latin American Studies, 1972).

9. Konrad, *Santa Lucía*; Nicholas P. Cushner, *Lords of the Land: Sugar, Wine, and Jesuit Estates of Coastal Peru, 1600-1767* (Albany: State University of New York Press, 1980). Also see William B. Taylor, *Landlord and Peasant in Colonial Oaxaca* (Stanford, Cal.: Stanford University Press, 1972), chap. 5; Manuel Burga, *De la encomienda a la hacienda capitalista: El valle del Jequetepeque del siglo XVI al XX*, Estudios de la sociedad rural, no. 4 (Lima: Instituto de Estudios Peruanos, 1976), pp. 115-122.

10. Wibel, "Arequipa, 1780-1845," chap. 3.

11. Lockhart, *Spanish Peru*, pp. 41-48, Fred Bronner, "Peruvian Encomenderos in 1630: Elite Circulation and Consolidation," *HAHR* 57 (November 1977):esp.

pp. 641-642; Marzahl, *Town in the Empire*, pp. 38-40.

12. David A. Brading, *Miners and Merchants in Bourbon Mexico, 1763-1810*, Cambridge Latin American Studies, no. 10 (Cambridge: At the University Press, 1971); Doris Ladd, *The Mexican Nobility at Independence, 1780-1826*, Latin American Monographs, no. 40 (Austin, Tex.: Institute of Latin American Studies, 1976); Jacques A. Barbier, "Elites and Cadres in Bourbon Chile," *HAHR* 52 (August 1972):416-435; Wibel, "Arequipa, 1780-1845," pp. 86-91, 94-95.

13. Lockhart, *Cajamarca*, pp. 44-59; Bronner, "Encomenderos."

14. Magnus Mörner, *Historia social latinoamericana (Nuevos enfoques)*, Colección Manoa of the Universidad Católica Andrés Bello (Caracas: Arte, 1979), pp. 49-51.

Glossary

Acequia: Irrigation canal or ditch
Alcabala: Excise tax
Alcalde: Judge
Alférez real: Royal standard-bearer
Almojarifazgo: Import and export duty
Almud: Unit of measure; one-twelfth of a fanega
Arroba: Unit of measure; eight liters
Audiencia: Royal high court and governing council

Botija: Earthen jugs, standardized at eight liters

Cabildo: Municipal council
Castas: Castes; persons of mixed racial ancestry
Chácara: (Small) farm
Corregidor: District officer
Curaca: Indian official or chieftain

Diezmo: Ten percent assessment in kind; tithe

Encomendero: Holder of an encomienda
Encomienda: Grant of Indians (rights to tribute and labor varied)
Estancia: Denoted site for livestock-raising in Arequipa
Estanciero: Owner of an estancia

Fanega: Unit of measure; 1.5 bushels
Fanegada: Unit of agricultural land: 3.90 acres in Arequipa; 7.19 in Lima

Hacienda: Common name for large, landed estate
Hanansaya: Branch of an ethnic group in a moiety-like arrangement
Heredad: Rural estate in Arequipa

Heredado: Owner of an heredad in Arequipa
Hidalgo: Minor nobleman
Hurinsaya: Branch of an ethnic group in a moiety-like arrangement

Maravedí: Monetary unit: 450 equaled a pure gold peso; 272 equaled a common gold peso
Mayorazgo: Entailed property
Mayordomo: Steward; heredad manager
Mestizo, mestiza: Person of white and Indian ancestry

Originario: Indian native of a region

Peso: Monetary unit; of eight reales unless otherwise noted

Real: Monetary unit; normally eight to a common silver peso
Regidor: Councilor

Sierra: Highlands

Tinaja: Large earthen container holding 400 liters

Villa: Town, with certain privileges by charter

Yanacona: Preconquest servile group; later, an Indian worker unattached to a native community

Index